D1287663

IRONWORKS

A History of Grumman's Fighting Aeroplanes

Fla. museum remembers 1st moving U.S. carrier landing

PENSACOLA, Fla. (AP) — Eighty years ago Saturday, Navy Lt. Cmdr. Godfrey Chevalier made the first landing aboard a moving U.S. Navy ship, the experimental aircraft carrier USS Langley as it steamed in Chesapeake Bay near Norfolk, Va.

A hook attached to the belly of his Aeromarine 39B snared arresting wires strung across the flight deck. "Pies" and "fiddle bridges," used to prop up the wires, went flying in every direction.

The flimsy biplane then nosed over, damaging its propeller. The landing Oct. 26, 1922, was not pretty, but it was historic. The National Museum of Naval Aviation is marking the event with special tours focusing on exhibits associated with the Langley and early carrier aircraft.

"This was the beginning of carrier aviation," said Dick Griffith, 75, a former Civil Air Patrol pilot and volunteer tour guide at the museum on Pensacola Naval Air Station.

Others had landed aboard ships before. An American civilian, Eugene Ely, did it in 1911 by setting down on a 120-foot platform aboard the battleship USS Pennsylvania while anchored in San Francisco Bay.

The British then begin landing planes aboard moving ships in 1917, but Chevalier was the first U.S. pilot to accomplish that feat.

Unlimited
nights and week

plus

900 anytime min

$39⁹

Night and Weekend Mi
start earlier at 8pm

FREE Features

Telos

FREE

and annoyed with the situation. The chosen few to whom he's confided his vacation plans say I'm crazy for allowing things to escalate this far. I'm beginning to agree.

My husband recently had a heart attack and takes numerous medications. I have stuck by his side all these years while he was in and out of the hospital with vari-

IRONWORKS

A History of Grumman's Fighting Aeroplanes

TERRY C. TREADWELL

Motorbooks International
Publishers & Wholesalers ®

To Wendy

This USA edition published in 1990 by Motorbooks International
Publishers & Wholesalers, PO Box 2, 729 Prospect Avenue,
Osceola, WI 54020, USA

Copyright © Terry C Treadwell, 1990

First published by Airlife Publishing Ltd., Shrewsbury, England,
1990

All rights reserved. With the exception of quoting brief passages
for the purposes of review no part of this publication may be
reproduced without prior written permission from the publisher.

Motorbooks International is a certified trademark, registered with
the United States Patent Office.

Printed and bound in Singapore by Kyodo Printing Co
(Singapore) Pte Ltd.

The information in this book is true and complete to the best of
our knowledge. All recommendations are made without any
guarantee on the part of the author or publisher, who also disclaim
any liability incurred in connection with the use of this data or
specific details.

We recognize that some words, model names and designations,
for example, mentioned herein are the property of the trademark
holder. We use them for identification purposes only. This is not
an official publication.

Library of Congress Cataloging-in-Publication Data
ISBN 0 87938 488 3

Motorbooks International books are also available at discounts in
bulk quantity for industrial or sales-promotional use. For details
write to Special Sales Manager at the Publisher's address.

Contents

Acknowledgements

I would like to thank the following people for their help in making the writing of this book as enjoyable and interesting as it was.

Ralph Clark, one has heard all the platitudes before with regard to the help people have been given in the past, but in this case they are all true. Without Ralph's help there is no way that this book would have been finished, or as accurate, or as interesting or, or . . . I would go on and write another book just on him. It was Ralph who read and corrected the FF-1, F3F, F4F, F6F, F7F, F8F, F9F and F11F sections. He also became a good friend, and guided me throughout the three years it has taken to complete this book.

Lois Lovisolo, Grumman's historian, who in my opinion has one of the finest aviation company archives in the world. She supplied me with nearly all the photographs in the book and with reams of information, pointed me in the right direction when I wanted to get sections checked, and still found time out of her frantic schedule to read and check the 'Company' section. I enjoyed the 'Hero' Lois!

The A-6 draft was read by designer Larry Mead, whose contributions were invaluable, as well as being fascinating.

Designer Bob Kress read the F-14 Tomcat draft and put me right on a number of points, and gave me a new insight to this fabulous aircraft.

Joe Lippert, designer of the Ag-Cat and a member of the WF-1 design team, read the Ag-Cat draft and the 3 'T' draft with great care. He also allowed me to interview him and use the information on the tapes in this book.

The Space section of the book was read by a number of people who passed it amongst themselves; it came back with a number of corrections and a great deal of additional information.

Bob Mikesh of the NASM, and Matthew Rodin of the Sea Islands Shuttle Company, read the amphibian section with great care, and besides correcting the mistakes contributed a great deal of additional information.

Test pilot Bob Smyth and engineer Charlie Coppi of Gulfstreams, took time out from their extremely busy schedules to check through and alter the Gulfstream and F-14 drafts.

The Mohawk draft was checked by Ralph Clark and proved that it doesn't matter how much research you do, there is always something new to discover.

Admiral Thomas F. Connolly, US Navy, former DCNO, who double-checked the F-14 Tomcat section with great care and interest, because he was one of a number of people who were instrumental in its development. Tom Connolly also became a good friend and used his considerable experience to guide me in the right direction.

Admiral Charles Griffin, for allowing me to quote from his articles in the *Foundation* magazine, about early test flying of Grumman aircraft.

Tony Theobald for his help in researching the World War II aircraft, and John Batchelor for allowing me the freedom of his own archives.

Roy Grossnik and John Elliott, of the US Naval History Office, for their help in the more obscure photographs.

Graham Mottram and his staff at the Fleet Air Arm Museum at RNAS Yeovilton, for allowing me a free rein in their archives.

Photo Credits: Grumman Corporation, Fleet Air Arm Museum, Ralph Clark, Ted Wilbur, Chaz Bowyer.

Introduction

This book is about the aircraft of the Grumman Aircraft Corporation, which came to be known affectionately as the 'Grumman Ironworks' during the Second World War, when many Grumman aircraft were able to return to their aircraft carriers and land-bases badly damaged, by virtue of the aircrafts' strength and durability, and the skill of their pilots.

The company started life as one man's dream, and became one of the most respected aircraft manufacturers in the world. The span of success covered a period from building centreline floats for Vought seaplanes in the 1930s, to designing and building a spacecraft that took twelve men to another world and back.

It was during the Second World War in the Pacific that Grumman came into its own as an aircraft manufacturer, with the Wildcats, Hellcats and Avengers — the Japanese came to hate the name Grumman. The initial attack on Pearl Harbor knocked the American air defences for six, but gradually the ruggedness of the American aircraft and their pilots overwhelmed the Japanese, and Grumman aircraft played a major part in that victory. During the Korean and Vietnam wars, Grumman aircraft — Bearcats, Panthers and Cougars were in action again, and once more left their mark on the enemy and the world of aviation.

The space era brought new opportunities for Grumman. They built the OAO (Orbiting Astronomical Observatory), the Lunar Module that took man to the moon, the wings of the Space Shuttle Orbiter, and most recently, appointed one of the teams to work on the Space Station Programme Support contract.

The development of the A-6 Intruder, possibly today's most sophisticated aircraft, avionics-wise, and the F-14 Tomcat, one of the deadliest, keep Grumman in the forefront of aviation. Over the years Grumman have diversified from the field of aviation, making truck bodies, yachts, hydrofoils, and even a railway engine, their TLRV (Track Levitated Research Vehicle).

To try and write a complete history of Grumman would take volumes; each aircraft alone deserves a book, so I have tried to present what I feel is the most interesting and informative parts of the history, and hope you will derive as much pleasure from reading it as I did in researching and writing it.

Terry C. Treadwell

Grumman the company

When the banking firm of Hayden, Stone and Company bought the Loening Aircraft and Engineering Company in 1928, little did they know that they would be instrumental in creating one of the most famous aircraft manufacturers in the world. It was decided to merge the Loening Company with the Keystone Aircraft Company under the Curtiss-Wright conglomerate, and to close the plant in New York City and move to Bristol, Pennsylvania. The manager and chief engineer, Leroy Grumman, realized that his roots were too deep in Long Island, and he and several of his colleagues decided to create their own aircraft manufacturing company. The 1929 collapse of the stock market on Wall Street made things difficult, but after putting nearly everything he owned ($16,000), together with $30,000 invested by the Loening Brothers and $15,000 from five other colleagues, Roy Grumman started the Grumman Aircraft Engineering Corporation.

Leroy Randle Grumman was born on 4 January 1895 in Huntington, New York. His father, George Tyson Grumman, was a New England carriage builder, which is where Roy Grumman probably got his interest in building and designing machines. Roy was educated locally and at Cornell University, where he received a Bachelor of Science degree in Mechanical Engineering. He then went to work for the New York Telephone Company in their engineering department, and had just completed the company's engineering course when the United States entered the First World War. He joined the US Naval Reserve, and after initial training, became a Machinist's Mate 2nd Class. Because of his engineering background, the Navy decided to send him on a six-week course at Columbia University, to study the operation of the petrol engine.

At Columbia University he applied for aviation duty, and was accepted. He was sent to the Massachusetts Institute of Technology (MIT) for the ground school section of his flight training, and after completion of the course, went to Miami for elementary flying instruction. He was posted to Pensacola in July 1918 for advanced training, where he graduated in September and was designated Naval Aviator No. 1216, with the rank of Ensign. His natural flying ability was soon noticed and he remained at Pensacola as an advanced flying instructor on a bomber squadron. This soon became too mundane to the ever restless Grumman, and he applied for a four-month Aeronautical Engineering course at MIT, during which the First World War came to an end. On completion of the course, the Navy posted him to League Island Naval Yard on the Delaware River as a project engineer and test pilot. With the job came promotion to Lieutenant.

The Loening brothers, Albert and Grover, were building aircraft in Philadelphia at the time, and Roy Grumman's job as the Navy's project engineer was to oversee the building of the aircraft and then test fly them. Because of the reduction of the peacetime Navy, his rank was reduced to Ensign, and Grumman resigned his commission and accepted an offer the Loening brothers had made to join them as their test pilot. As the company progressed, so did Roy Grumman, first as factory manager, then as general manager with total responsibility for aircraft design. Under his dynamic leadership the company grew, building single-engined amphibians for the Navy and the Army. They also built a civilian version for wealthy businessmen, costing $30,000, of which a large number were sold. The company continued to prosper until 1928, when the corporate mergers started, and it was this that was to be the

Above: The 'B' float production line, Valley Stream, 1932.

primary reason for Grumman breaking away and forming his own company.

Among Loening's employees who joined Roy Grumman were Leon 'Jake' Swirbul, the production supervisor, who was later to become Roy Grumman's right-hand man, William T. Schwendler, project engineer and assistant general manager, and Ed Poor, Loening's book-keeper. The Grumman Aircraft Engineering Company came into being, and several months later, a second initial financing took place, boosting the funds to $86,750. Having finance was one thing, starting to manufacture aircraft was another. Rundown premises were found in Baldwin, Long Island, and the stockholders got down to the business of turning the building into an aircraft manufacturing plant.

Roy Grumman and Jake Swirbul made the perfect team: Grumman the innovator, Swirbul the decision-maker, and together with the team of natural talent they had collected around them, they got ready to take the aviation world by storm. By 18 January 1930, with a total staff of twenty-one, they had submitted a proposal to the Army Air Corps for a two-seat flying-boat. The proposal was not accepted, but the Grumman Company continued to exist repairing the flying-boats that had been built by the Loening Company.

Occasionally the odd job came along that gave them a handsome profit. One example was when they bought a wrecked aircraft from an insurance company for $450. It was at the bottom of a lake in Connecticut, with only its tail showing above the water, but after hauling it out, the aircraft was repaired and sold for a handsome profit of nearly $20,000.

After hearing that the US Navy were having problems with an amphibian float for its Vought Corsairs, Grumman submitted a design proposal for a new float. The float incorporated a very unusual design of retractable landing gear, and was lighter than the conventional floats, so the US Navy ordered two Model A floats costing $33,700. Because Grumman was an unknown company in the aviation manufacturing field, sceptics claimed that the floats would not stand up to the catapult loads that would be imposed upon them. To prove they would, Roy Grumman and Jake Swirbul had themselves catapulted twice from a ship in an aircraft equipped with one of their floats. The Navy ordered a further six floats costing $59,000 and later an additional fifteen of an improved design. So began one of the closest relationships between an aircraft manufacturer and a military service anywhere in the world, one that continues to this day.

making aluminium truck bodies, so that by the end of the year, Grumman showed a profit of $5,476 and had increased its staff to twenty-three.

The Navy took delivery of the fifteen Model B floats they had previously ordered, and even considered using the retractable landing gear on their day fighters, but the fighters were too slim to accommodate them. This gave Roy Grumman the idea of designing and building a fighter around his retractable undercarriage, the XFF-1. It was powered by a Wright R-1820E, nine-cylinder, 660 horsepower Cyclone engine, which gave the aircraft a top speed of 200 miles per hour. The two-seat cockpit was enclosed and the armament carried consisted of two fixed and one moveable .30 calibre machine gun. The XFF-1 could climb at 1,320 feet per minute to a service ceiling of 23,600 feet and had a range of 818 miles.

The Navy ordered a prototype XFF-1, with an option for a second. Critics thought that retractable landing gear on a high-speed fighter would slow the aircraft down and cause instability. They were wrong: the XFF-1s top speed was thirty miles per hour faster than any fighter the US Navy had at the time. But unfortunately there were a few problems involving the landing gear, which kept folding up, much to the frustration of Jake Swirbul and his team. Finally these faults were overcome, however, and the Navy were delighted with their first fighter with a retractable undercarriage.

The Navy placed an order for twenty-seven FF-1s at a cost of $641,250, and Grumman was able to increase its staff to forty-two. On 20 August 1932, the second XFF-1 was built, with a number of modifications. Primarily designed as a scouting aircraft and redesignated XSF-1, it was the forerunner of thirty-three such aircraft to be built. The engine was changed to a Wright R-1820-78 Cyclone, that developed 700 horsepower, and the wingspan was increased to 34 ft. 6 in. (upper) and 31 ft. 6 in. (lower), which ultimately increased the wing area to 310 square feet. One fixed gun and its ammunition were removed, enabling the space to be used for additional fuel. The top speed was increased to 206 miles per hour, but the service ceiling was reduced to 23,400 feet.

With the increase of orders and the need to take on more staff, the company needed larger premises. These were found at an unused US Naval Reserve hangar at Valley Stream, on an airfield called Curtiss Field. The first FF-1s were soon coming off the production line, and with the production contract came a resident Inspector of Naval Aircraft complete with staff, whose job was to oversee the manufacture and final acceptance of the aircraft, prior to delivery to the fleet.

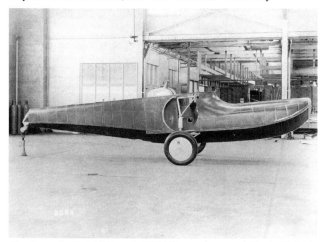

Based upon the Model A float, the XJF-1 float was longer and, like the Model A, had a retractable undercarriage.

By the end of 1930, the aviation industry was declining, but somehow Grumman managed to hang on, despite the stock market crash, which bankrupted many old-established aircraft manufacturers. To diversify, Grumman got involved in

An early production model preparing for a test flight from Valley Stream.

The first production model of the FF-1 in the livery VF-11.

In 1931, following the success of the Model A and B floats, Grumman decided to submit a design for an amphibious aircraft, designated the XJF-1 and powered by a Pratt and Whitney R-1830-62 fourteen-cylinder, twin Wasp engine. The first flight was on 4 May 1933, and by the time the last one had flown in 1945, over six hundred JF-1s, or Ducks as they were to become affectionately known, had been built. They were sold not only to the US Navy and US Coast Guard, but also to the Argentine Navy and the US Army.

A Columbia-built J2-F Duck, known as the G-20, in Argentinian livery.

The success of the FF-1 prompted the US Navy to ask Grumman if they would produce a single-seat fighter that would stay afloat in the unlikely event of the aircraft having to ditch. Grumman produced an aircraft with a fat, watertight fuselage and when they put it in the wind tunnel for testing, it achieved an indicated top speed twelve miles an hour faster than had been envisaged. Designated the XF2F-1, the Navy snapped it up and gave Grumman a contract for fifty-five, worth $996,200. The first XF2F-1 was delivered in December 1933 (and the last in 1935), and it had an even higher top speed (250 mph) than the wind tunnel tests had indicated.

Although business appeared to be booming, Grumman realized that the company could not survive on Navy contracts alone, so he decided to explore the commercial markets. Amphibians were Roy Grumman's forte, and in 1935 he began building luxury amphibians for the rich and famous. The aircraft in question was an eight-seater amphibian called the G-21, or Grey Goose, and was of a revolutionary design for this period. The high-winged monoplane was extremely successful, and over 345 were produced for the military, domestic and foreign markets, the last one being built in 1945. There are still some flying commercially in the Caribbean, and elsewhere. Among his clients were King Abdul-Aziz ibn-Saud of Saudi Arabia, Colonel Robert R. McCormick of the *Chicago Tribune* newspaper, and Lord Beaverbrook, the British newspaper magnate, who purchased two.

In the spring of 1935, the company produced another fighter for the Navy, the XF3F-1. It was a development of the F2F-1 and powered by the same engine, although it had a higher speed, a longer range and an increased service ceiling of 29,300 feet. The first flight took place on 20 March and was flown by contract test pilot Jimmy Collins. On 22 March the aircraft crashed during high-speed dive tests, and the pilot was killed; the news stunned Grumman, and the crash attracted much more publicity than normal, mainly because at the time Jimmy Collins was writing a series of articles on the life of the test pilot for the *New York Daily News*.

Two months later a replacement XF3F-1 was airborne, and again there were problems. This time the aircraft failed to recover from an induced spin, and crashed, but the pilot, Lee Gelbach, survived. Using parts from the crashed aircraft, Grumman engineers produced a third XF3F-1 in an unbelievable three weeks, and this time all went well. The Navy ordered fifty-four F3F-1s, the first to be delivered in January 1936. Later, some of the FF-1s were sent to the Naval Air Facility in Philadelphia, to have dual controls installed; they were redesignated FF-2s.

On 6 December 1936, Grumman produced a very unusual aircraft, the G-22 or Gulfhawk, which was built for Major Al Williams, Gulf Oil's exhibition pilot. The aircraft was to replace the special Curtiss that he had been using. The G-22 was ostensibly an F3F-2 with the wings of an F2F, the engine was a Wright R-1820-G, and it had been specially braced and rigged for aerobatics. It had an incredible rate of climb for an aircraft of that period, 3,000 feet per minute, and looked spectacular in a finish of orange fuselage with blue and white sunburst patterns on the wings and tail and chromium-plated struts. It attracted crowds wherever it went and served as a publicity aircraft, not only for Gulf Oil, but also for Grumman. The Gulfhawk is presently on display in the National Air and Space Museum.

Roy Grumman and the Grumman Company were now so well established, and producing so many aircraft, that they ran out of working capital. The board decided that this was the time to 'go public' and were in the process of floating the first public issue when the stock market crashed again. Fortunately a Wall Street broker by the name of Bernard 'Sell 'em Ben' Smith stepped in and underwrote the stock issue. In December 1937, 95,000 shares were offered to the public at $7 each, and by the following April, 500,000 shares were selling for $24 each.

Grumman continued to expand steadily and by May 1939 had delivered three series of the F3F to the US Navy, a total of 162 aircraft. Whilst the F3F had been upgrading, the company had been developing a new type of fighter, a monoplane designated the XF4F-2. Its first flight was in September 1937, and it was the forerunner of the Wildcat fighter. The XF4F-2 was the first of these fighters; there was no XF4F-1, which was to have been a biplane; Grumman decided on a monoplane design for the finished aircraft.

In 1937 the whole plant was moved to Bethpage, Long Island. In less than a couple of weeks the production lines were going flat-out again, only this time with much more room to manoeuvre. By the end of 1939 war had broken out in Europe, and Grumman were employing over 800 people, with a turnover of $4.5 million.

Roy Grumman realized the potential of his XF4F-2 fighter, and started tooling up for mass production. The US Navy was to place orders for several hundred of the carrier fighters, but the company still continued to produce the J2F, F3F and G-21 Goose amphibian for the Army and the Navy.

Orders started to come in from Europe for the F4F Wildcat, as it was now called. The French placed an order for eighty-one Wildcats but before they could take delivery, France was overrun. The Royal Navy, quick to spot a good aircraft, took over the contract in order to replace its ageing carrier biplanes. They renamed the F4F the G-36A Martlet, and took delivery of all the aircraft between July and October 1940.

Grumman's production lines had to be increased dramatically to keep pace with the demand and it was fast becoming one of the world's major aircraft manufacturers. An order for thirty F4F-3As came from Greece, to help repel an invasion attempt by the Italians, but before they could be delivered, the country was overrun by the Germans. The aircraft had reached Gibraltar where they were quickly appropriated by the British, who renamed them Martlet IIIs and put them

aboard their Mediterranean-based carriers. The Royal Navy even had the latest F4F variation, the F4F-4, before the US Navy or Marine Corps. This variation of the fighter was equipped with folding wings which enabled aircraft carriers to more than double their carrying capacity. The folding wing concept was not new to the aviation world; the main difference between the Grumman wing and the others was safety. Grumman designed the wings to lock automatically. The 'Stowing', as it was called, played a major part in the battle against U-Boats in the North Atlantic. 'U-Boat Alley' was fast becoming a graveyard for merchant convoys that sailed between the United States and Europe; land-based aircraft could give only limited protection to the convoys, thus leaving them at the mercy of the U-Boats for part of their journey. The problem was tackled by converting merchant ships into escort carriers, or Woolworth carriers as they were known.

Back at Bethpage the whole factory was on overtime. 148,000 sq. ft. had been added to the shop floor, and 3,000 sq. ft. added to the engineering section. There was still time to start up a test programme, however, and on 1 April 1940 an experimental twin-engined fighter, the XF5F-1, made its first flight. It was an interesting aircraft with an exceptional climb rate of 4,000 feet per minute. It was given the name Skyrocket, and was capable of 380 miles per hour. Right from the start, however, there were problems with the engine cooling, and although the cooling ducts were redesigned a number of times, a solution was never found. The test programme was delayed for modifications to be made, but these only seemed to add to the problems. Eventually fate took a hand and after a number of landing accidents, it was scrapped.

In August 1941 Jake Swirbul visited Britain to find out first hand how the Grumman aircraft in use by the Royal Navy were faring. He was looking to see if any improvements could be made to the aircraft, and this he did by talking to the men who flew them. This was a move that was to be followed by all the Grumman representatives, in future, and one that was to earn them tremendous respect with their customers.

The previous April, Grumman had won a contract for two experimental torpedo-bombers, and that December they were awarded a production contract for 286 TBF-1s or Avengers, as they came to be known. This aircraft was to become the US Navy's and the Royal Navy's primary tactical offensive weapon during World War II, but fortunately the second one was almost ready and the production line was well under way.

The number of Grumman employees had multiplied seven-fold by the end of 1941, and to celebrate the completion of a second plant, Grumman held an open house for all their employees and their families on Sunday 7 December. During the festivities, the company executives heard of the attack on Pearl Harbor. At first Americans were stunned, then angry. All they could think of was retaliation; the production lines moved into top gear.

The production of non-military aircraft ceased almost at once, and the whole factory went into production of warplanes. Grumman designers were hard at work creating new aircraft; one such aircraft, the F6F Hellcat, was already on the drawing boards. At the same time, some of the TBF Avengers, so named because of the attack on Pearl Harbor, were to be manufactured (as TBMs) at Trenton by the General Motors Corporation at their newly named Eastern Aircraft Division, production starting on 12 January 1942. Other divisions of General Motors became involved in production of Grumman aircraft, and at Linden, New Jersey, they started to build the FM version of the F4F; by 1945 they had produced 5,927. All these plants were called 'dispersals'; by the middle of 1942, there were eleven spread around Bethpage. Grumman organized the dispersal of production, following the British innovation of 'shadow factories' into such bizarre places as underground shooting galleries, wheelbarrow factories and even tents. A fleet of trucks transported finished sub-assemblies into Bethpage every day, delivering fresh work to the outworkers at the same time.

In the spring of 1942, the US Navy had its first ace. Lt. Edward (Butch) O'Hare, flying an F4F-3, intercepted a number of Japanese 'Betty' bombers about to attack the *USS Lexington*, and after a fierce battle which lasted only four minutes, he had shot down five and damaged a sixth. For this heroic exploit, he was awarded the Medal of Honour.

Whilst production was still going on at the various plants, research into ways of improving the existing fighters continued. The F4F-4B made its appearance in February, and was identical to the F4F-4A except for a Wright 1820 engine in the B, against the Pratt and Whitney 1830 in the A. The other difference was the addition of the Hamilton Standard hydromatic propeller in the B. The first to receive the F4F-4B were the British, who redesignated it the Martlet IV, and received 220 of them on lend-lease agreements. So determined were the British to get Grumman aircraft that they established a Royal Navy Fleet Air Arm unit at Roosevelt Field, where they accepted and tested all American aircraft destined for the Royal Navy. Even Winston Churchill extolled the virtues of the Martlet, with this note to the First Sea Lord:

First Sea Lord.

Even half a dozen Martlets would be an invaluable addition to the equipment of *Illustrious* and *Formidable*, and might easily teach enemy bombers at sea, lessons which would greatly add to the security of H.M. Ships in the Mediterranean.

I am very glad to hear about the Brewsters.

WSC
3.1.41

In the Pacific theatre, progress in the air against the Japanese was achieved mainly because of the rugged construction of the F4F - Wildcat, which was capable of absorbing the Japanese Zero's firepower. The light magnesium-metal constructed Zero literally came apart when hit by a direct blast from the Wildcat's six .50 calibre machine-guns.

March 1942 saw the last J2F-5 Duck completed; for the time being, the last biplane, although some twenty years later another biplane, the Ag-Cat, was to make its appearance. At the end of May, the Japanese launched a major invasion against the island of Midway and although greatly out-numbered, the Wildcats and Avengers held their own and beat off the attack. Of the six Avengers that entered the battle, only one returned to Midway and that was flown by Ensign Bert Earnest from VT-8. At the end of the battle, the Japanese had lost four aircraft carriers and the Americans one. The tide had turned and from that moment on, the Japanese were in retreat.

Back at Bethpage, the first of a new breed of fighter was being put through its paces, the XF6F-1 Hellcat. The Hellcat was far superior to the F4F: it was faster, had a longer range, could carry more weapons and was even able to carry a torpedo. A total of 12,275 were delivered to the US Navy, the Royal Navy, and the Royal New Zealand Navy. It is interesting to note that so good was the basic design of this aircraft, that only minor modifications and changes were necessary throughout the different models. Grumman suddenly found themselves in a unique situation; they were making aircraft (660 per month), faster than the Navies could use them. Production of the F4F was taken over by Eastern Aircraft Division of General Motors which meant releasing all the drawings, materials parts etc., and also giving access to all the Grumman plants and subcontractors. Eastern were not geared for the fast mass production of aircraft, so the volume was reduced dramatically. This enabled Grumman to concentrate on the manufacture of the F6F Hellcat, as well as the development of future aircraft.

Grumman continued to produce rugged no-nonsense aircraft. Vice-Admiral John S. McCain summed it up by saying, 'The name Grumman on a plane or a part, has the same meaning to the Navy that "Sterling" has on silver.' By the end of 1942, the number of employees on the payroll had gone up to 19,556, and a large proportion of these were women on the production lines and assembly lines, in the design departments and even as 'Plane Captains', who checked out the aircraft prior to their first flights. Grumman also employed three female production test pilots, Cecile 'Teddy' Kenyon, Barbara Kibbee Jayne, and Elizabeth Hooker. Their job was to carry out all the pre-delivery check flights. Although there were a number of production test pilots, there was only one fatal accident at Grumman during the war period, which happened to a Bobby McReynolds, who crashed on his approach to the field. This record highlights the quality of the aircraft that were built there.

October 1943 brought good news to the employees of Grumman, when the War Labour Board announced that the Grumman Incentive Bonus Plan had been approved. This meant that a percentage of normal salary could be paid to employees as a bonus for increased production. Such was the work rate at Grumman that the workers regularly received a bonus of between 25 per cent and 30 per cent. Grumman supplied nearly all the US Navy's carrier-based fighters from 1939 to 1942, and 98 per cent of the US Navy's torpedo-bombers were either made by Grumman or designed by them. In the battle of Guadalcanal, James V. Forrestal, the Secretary of the Navy said, 'In my opinion Grumman saved Guadalcanal.'

As the American advance in the Pacific continued, so did the production rate, and Grumman aircraft continued to wreak havoc on the Japanese. When the Japanese-held island of Truk was attacked by seventy-two F6F Hellcats and twelve TBF-1C Avengers, not one of these aircraft was lost, but eighty-five Japanese aircraft were either shot down or destroyed on the ground.

With the war progressing in the Allies' favour, Grumman realized that it would soon be over. With this in mind a small group of design engineers were detached from regular operational work to explore the field of post-war light aircraft production. They produced a small, two-seat, all metal, low-winged monoplane. It was designated G-63 and given the name of Kitten, because it vaguely resembled a smaller version of the Hellcat.

Also, with an eye towards the future, Grumman announced the commencement of the Grumman Scholarship plan. The scholarship would cover the cost of four years' study at an accredited engineering school for residents of Suffolk and Nassau counties. The plan was extremely successful and to date has provided some of the best engineers and executives in the company. It has become a permanent competition and because of the interest, has been expanded.

On the military production front, a revolutionary new aircraft made its appearance, the XF7F-1. The only resemblance to any of Grumman's previous fighters was the square-cut wing-tips. It was a single-seat fighter with tricycle undercarriage, powered by two Pratt and Whitney R-2800-22W two-speed engines. Two hundred and forty-eight were built, and the various mark numbers went from F7F-1 to F7F-4N.

The XF7F-1 opened up a completely new field of aviation for Grumman. Its firepower exceeded that of any previous fighter, and although primarily a fighter, it was capable of carrying a reasonable-sized bomb load over a long distance. Although the twin-engined F7F was fairly successful, the F8F Bearcat that followed reverted to being a single-engined, single-seat fighter. It was the fastest propeller-driven aircraft in the world at the time, being some three thousand pounds lighter than the F6F Hellcat, had a slower cruising speed, but was twice as manoeuvrable and could climb at the rate of one mile per minute! Grumman wanted to replace the Hellcat with the Bearcat, but the US Navy wanted Hellcat production to continue until after August 1945, when they could be assured of air superiority. Although they agreed that the Bearcat was superior to the Hellcat in all departments, the Hellcat had proved its capability in combat, and the Bearcat was an unknown quantity. Grumman agreed to the request and continued production of 300 per month until August, but said that after that date they would gradually phase the Hellcat out. All sorts of figures were worked out, but these were cancelled when the Japanese surrendered on 14 August 1945.

The war was over. Between February 1940 and August 1945, Grumman had built and delivered 17,573 aircraft to the US Navy, US Marine Corps and the Allies, the majority from the plants on Long Island. Of the total, 12,275 were Hellcats, 1,978 were Wildcats, 2,293 were Avengers, 248 were Tigercats, 151 were Bearcats — although no F7Fs or F8Fs saw action — and 628 were utility aircraft. General Motors Eastern Aircraft Division built 7,546 Avengers and 5,927 Wildcats, with the Columbia Aircraft Company building 300 J2F-6 Ducks.

With the cessation of hostilities, came a reduction in orders and Roy Grumman realized that he was going to have to cut the workforce drastically. He eventually announced over the public address system that all plants were to be closed down immediately and all personnel were to go home, taking their tools and personal effects with them. The heads of the various departments then got together and compiled a list of all the personnel they considered to be vital to the company. Of the 20,511 employees sent home, 5,411 were recalled by telegram. There were still contracts to be completed, but now the pressure was off and the numbers of aircraft somewhat reduced.

In addition to the building of military aircraft, Grumman decided to go back into the repair business, just as they had done when they first started. Over 500 of the G-21 and G-44 amphibians had been built and a large number had survived the war, so with war surplus stocks being sold off there was a great demand for overhaul work.

On 4 January 1946, Admiral Chester Nimitz announced that the Navy wanted a further 12,000 aircraft for the peacetime Navy. These would be used on a gradual replacement basis for the wartime aircraft that were currently being used. The news delighted everyone at Grumman, because they knew they could well get the lion's share of the contracts. Grumman resumed interest in the light aircraft market also, with the introduction of the new G-72 Kitten II. It was capable of carrying a pilot and two passengers and differed from its predecessor, the G-63, by having a tricycle undercarriage. After a great deal of time and effort, however, it was decided to abandon the project and only one aircraft was ever built.

A new amphibian made its appearance, the G-73 Mallard. It was the first aircraft to be placed on the commercial market since the end of the war. Designed to carry eight or ten passengers in real luxury, it had a thermostatically-controlled heating and ventilation system, amongst other unique systems that were incorporated in the aircraft.

The F6Fs were gradually being replaced by the F8F Bearcat, and the last of the modified F7Fs was delivered to the Navy on 6 November 1946. This was the F7F-4N version with the small radome that was deemed necessary for carrier operations.

Bethpage at this time was playing host to a DC-3 Flying Laboratory belonging to the Air Transport Association. The aircraft was being used to test experimental equipment for Ground Control Approach (GCA) and the Instrument Landing System (ILS) apparatus. This was the dawn of the missile age and in December 1946, Grumman initiated a missile programme of its own. A team of designers and engineers, under Oscar 'Pete' Erlandsen, carried out studies on the development of a medium range surface-to-surface missile for the Bureau of Aeronautics. Various missile types were studied, and the end result was Project Rigel, which

was a submarine-launched missile with a range of 500 miles. It was powered by Mark 2 ramjets and guided by a radio-navigation system. The project was to develop over the next ten years, committing Grumman to the missile programme, and ultimately the Space programme.

Aviation was still the byword at Grumman, however, and the XTB3F-1 was just one of the aircraft under development at the time. It was designed to be a successor to the TBF Avenger and had one major difference, an auxiliary jet engine mounted in the aft section of the fuselage. The engine, a Westinghouse 19XB-2B (J30-WE-20) was intended to be used as a booster, and developed 1,500 pounds of thrust. In addition to this, the new Grumman GR-1 auto-pilot was installed and the 'breakaway' wing tips used on the F8F Bearcat.

The project was never a success; the jet engine was run-up on the ground several times, but never used whilst airborne. The engine was later removed. The XTB3F-1 crashed and was destroyed during Navy tests, but two others, XTB3F-1S and XTB3F-2S, carried out tests with new anti-submarine tracking equipment aboard. They were to be the forerunners of the AF-2S Guardians. The large radome mounted beneath the fuselage housing the APS-20 radar, caused the aircraft to be named 'Fertile Myrtle'. The APS-20 radar was the same as that used in the TMB-3W Avenger. The F8F Bearcat and the G-44As were still the mainstay of the production lines at the end of 1946.

Production was stepped up for the F8F Bearcat, as news came that the Navy was mothballing the F6F Hellcat. The F8F-2 made its first appearance, and although almost the same as the F8F-1, it had a different engine, the Pratt and Whitney R-2800-30W, different armament and different tail surfaces.

Early in 1947, Grumman announced that the Rolls-Royce Nene engine was to power the XF9F-2, Grumman's first jet. The original design for the XF9F-1 was a two-seat, four-engined night fighter, but such were the problems that Grumman opted for a single-seat, single-engined day fighter. Pratt and Whitney came to an arrangement with Rolls-Royce to licence-manufacture the Nene engine in the United States. The engine was designated J42-P-6, and was the same as the original, except for a Bendix Fuel Control Unit. The US Navy liked the design of the XF9F-2, but asked for a second aircraft to be built, this one to have an Allison engine. The Navy wanted a back-up engine for the aircraft, in case Pratt and Whitney and the Rolls-Royce engine arrangement did not work out. The first flight of the XF9F-2 Panther was made in November, flown by test pilot Corky Meyer. The test flights showed great promise, but times were hard and contracts few and far between.

The successor to the Goose, the XJR2F-1 Albatross, also took to the air that year. It was originally called the Pelican and was primarily designed for air/sea rescue work, but also had the capability of being used as an ambulance, for photo-reconnaissance, and as a personnel transport. The flight testing went well and the US Navy expressed a great deal of interest in it, but unfortunately had no funding available to purchase it. So Grumman decided to offer the Albatross to the newly independent United States Air Force, which had expressed an interest in it. After flight testing the aircraft, the Air Force placed orders for a total of 300 SA-16As, as they designated it. This order was one of the very first placed for aircraft by the USAF. As more money became available to the Navy, they placed an order for eight and changed the designation to UF-1, and when the US Coast Guard purchased theirs, they were directed to change the designation to UF-1G. Eventually a total of 464 SA-16s were built, including a triphibian version that could land on water, land on snow, and was used by the USAF in the Arctic. The Albatross was certified in 1987 to carry twenty-eight passengers by the CAA and a number are presently in service in the Caribbean.

The F8F continued to be built, and the latest model, the

F8F-2P photo-reconnaissance version, was delivered to the Navy on 26 February 1948. Statistics for the US Navy's air war in the Pacific were released that May; they showed that Grumman aircraft had accounted for two out of every three Japanese aircraft shot down. The strengtrh of the F8F Bearcat was never made more apparent than when one of the test pilots, Tommy Leboutillier, made a forced landing after his engine had failed. He hit and demolished several trees, smashed into the side of a house and came to rest upside down. It was virtually impossible to identify what was left of the aircraft, but the only injuries sustained by the pilot were a smashed finger, a dislocated shoulder and a few bruises.

Awards started to come Roy Grumman's way in 1948, and in July he was awarded the Guggenheim Foundation Medal for 'Outstanding achievement in successfully advancing aircraft design for naval and peacetime use'. Also that month, Roy Grumman and Jake Swirbul were summoned to the White House to be presented with the Presidential Medal for Merit by President Harry S. Truman, in recognition of the company's wartime production record.

The new XF9F-2 made its first public appearance at the dedication of New York International Airport (now known as John F. Kennedy International Airport) on 1 August 1948, and the first production model XF9F-3 Panther, powered by the Allison J33-A-8 engine, made its first flight on 15 August. The first two F9F-2 Panthers were delivered to the Navy that December, both being fitted with wingtip tanks to increase their range. By the beginning of 1949, the production lines for the F9F Panther and the AF Guardians were fully operational, whilst in another section of the plant, G-73 Mallards continued to make their appearance.

The G-22 Gulfhawk was formally handed over to the Smithsonian Institute at a ceremony at Washington National Airport on 11 October. Gulf Oil's replacement for the aircraft was the G-58, a civilian version of the F8F Bearcat.

Anti-submarine warfare had become a priority with the US Navy, and production of the AF-2S and 2W was hastened. On 19 November 1948 the first production model AF-2 Guardians, as they were to be called, took to the air. One month later, the second of the 'hunter/killer' Guardians took to the air, the AF-2S.

The last of the propeller-driven fighters, the F8F Bearcat, left Bethpage for the Navy on 9 July 1949. Although too late to see any action in World War II, it was involved against the rebels in French Indo-China (Vietnam), in the hands of the French Navy. Meanwhile back at Bethpage, a second G-58A Bearcat was assembled from spare parts, and was used as a company aircraft by the head of the service department Roger Kahn. It looked resplendent in red with black trim. After eleven years of company service, it was presented to the Cornell Aeronautical Laboratories for experimental work, and was still flying in the late seventies. One innovation fitted to the F8F Bearcat that caused a great deal of controversy was the 'break-away' wingtips, designed to break off if the pilot exceeded the operating restrictions during violent manoeuvres. They were to cause some potentially very serious incidents. There were to be ten variations before they were removed permanently.

The United States Air Force took delivery of an SA-16A Albatross on 29 July 1950, the first of fifty-three, and within a few months it was involved in a rescue mission. The first of the AF-2Ss and AF-2Ws were delivered to the US Navy after completing their acceptance trials, the fastest completed BIS trials in USN history.

In 1950 the seemingly forgotten 'Police Action' in Korea by the United Nations suddenly erupted into a full-scale war, involving the United States and the other member countries. The production lines at Grumman were soon busy supplying the US Navy with aircraft. As the war progressed, reports from Korea indicated that the F9F-2 Panther was more than holding its own against the Russian-built MiGs of the North Koreans.

In July that year the Allison-powered F9F-4 Panther made its first flight, but it was to be a further two months before it went into production. Earlier in the year, the USAF's Third Rescue Squadron returned from service in Korea with its SA-16As, and related tales of incredible rescue operations off the coast of Korea saying that only the Albatross could have carried out the rescues; they could not speak highly enough of the Grumman aircraft and the people who had built them. Later that year a new variation of the SA-16A Albatross appeared, called the Triphibian. It was a standard SA-16A that had been modified to operate from snow and ice, and had skis fitted. Of the 150 built, ten were sold to the Royal Canadian Air Force and the rest to the USAF.

20 September 1951 saw the appearance of the F9F-6 Cougar. This was a swept-wing version of the Panther, without the wingtip tanks. Additional fuel was carried in the wings, making this one of the first 'wet-wing' jet aircraft in the world. A group of executives representing the top aviation companies in Great Britain made a flying visit to Bethpage in October to see Grumman's set-up. Jake Swirbul took them on a tour of the plants, happy to pay back the hospitality the British had shown him when he had visited them during World War II. The British were impressed with the production lines, and more importantly by the very good relationship between management and the shop floor.

By early 1952 the production lines were busy producing F9F-6 Cougars, and the Navy prepared to take delivery of them. The Korean War put increased pressure on Grumman for aircraft delivery, so the company had to resort to old wartime ways of production, farming out work to other companies. For example, the Plymouth Division of the Chrysler Corporation in Evansville, Indiana built fuselages for the SA-16A Albatross, and the Twin Coach Company of Buffalo, New York built wings for the AF Guardian.

The XF10F-1 was a completely new design and had a number of previously untried features, the main one being the revolutionary variable sweep wing that could be adjusted in flight by the pilot. The XF10F-1 also had a most unusual, high T-shaped tail, which controlled the longitudinal stability of the aircraft during flight. It was powered by a Westinghouse J40-WE-8 axial flow engine that created 11,600 pounds of thrust and was capable of pushing the aircraft along at 722 miles per hour. The whole programme was beset with problems, the main one being that the aircraft was grossly underpowered, and after a year of flight testing the project was dropped. A great deal of the information gathered was to prove invaluable to the F-111 programme, however, which was to appear some ten years later.

A new variation of the AF Guardian, the AF-3S, made its appearance on 27 October 1952 and was the first to be equipped with the MAD (Magnetic Anomaly Detector). Just over one month later the first one was delivered to the Navy. Two days after the first delivery was made, the successor to the AF Guardian made its first flight. This was the XS2F-1. It was known at the time as a 'single package' concept, designed to take over both the roles carried out by the two earlier types, the AF-2S and the AF-2W, and it was to prove more efficient and more economical. Two XS2F-1s were built, one for extensive tests by the Navy, and the other was retained by Grumman for experiemental electronic equipment tests. So impressed were the Navy by the original proposals, that they placed a production order even before the experimental models had flown.

Variations of the F9F Cougar continued to come off the production line, and in January 1953 the first F9F-6 photo-reconnaissance version flew, an elongated nose housing various cameras and equipment. The aircraft also incorporated the first powered 'flying tail', which controlled the longitudinal stability in high-speed flight, with a manual system for low-speed flight. The increased production produced a need for expansion, but unfortunately there was no more room at Bethpage. The increase in staff over the years, had meant an increase in housing development and the facilities that go with it, and increased expansion of the plant would have ultimately meant an increase in noise over the built-up areas. The problem was solved when the Navy acquired more than 7,100 acres of land at Calverton, some fifty miles to the east of Bethpage. It was known officially as the United States Naval Air Facility Calverton, and was leased to Grumman for the manufacture and flight testing of aircraft. The agreement showed the measure of the relationship enjoyed by Grumman and the Navy. The plant became operational in October 1954 and proved to be an invaluable addition to the Grumman Company.

On 11 April 1953 the last of the AF Guardians was delivered to the Navy, production of the S2F-1 Tracker was well under way, and the first of the F9F-7s were also coming off the production lines. Of the 160 ordered, only 110 were to be F9F-7s, the remainder were delivered as F9F-6s, all within fourteen months of the start of production.

July 1953 saw the end of the Korean War; Grumman's contribution had been outstanding. Of the 826 US Navy and Marine aircraft that had been in action, 733 were of Grumman manufacture. The American Institute of Management bestowed upon Grumman the honour of being one of the best managed companies in the country, something the employees had known all the time.

The first aircraft carrier with both a steam catapult and an angled deck, the *USS Antietam*, was commissioned in 1953 and the aircraft chosen for testing were Cougars. Both the catapult and the angled deck had been a British innovation.

Although the jet aircraft was now well established in the world of aviation, in Indo-China the F8Fs and the old Hellcats of the French Navy were still making their presence felt against the Vietnamese rebels.

The S2F Tracker became so successful that de Havilland Aircraft of Canada asked Grumman for permission to manufacture it under licence. This was granted, and 100 were built with the designation CS2F-1. The S2F-1 Tracker was chosen for the catapult trials of the new C-11 steam catapult aboard the carrier *USS Hancock* in June. In July the updated version of the S2F-1, the S2F-2, made its appearance. There were some very noticeable differences between them, the S2F-2 having a much larger bomb bay and a wider horizontal tail. Between July 1954 and November 1955, sixty S2F-2s were built.

A completely new design of aircraft appeared in July. Although designated the F9F-9, it bore no resemblance to the F9F Panther or Cougar. It was later redesignated the F11F-1 and the layout of the fuselage was designed on the new 'area rule' concept. The idea was to reduce considerably the drag on the aircraft, with a fuselage design that resembled the famous 'Coke-bottle' shape.

The TF-1 Trader, which appeared in January 1955, was not exactly a new aircraft, just a variation of the S2F-1 Tracker, the main difference being a deeper fuselage, which provided more space for cargo and passengers. It was in fact the first purpose-built COD (Carrier On-board Delivery) aircraft that the Navy acquired. They had adapted TBFs and TBMs for a similar purpose during World War II, but these had been restricted to carrying a few passengers and the mail. The TF-1 was to turn out to be an extraordinary aircraft, with an exceptional maintenance record. Between 1955 and 1958 eighty-six were built, and thirty years later almost fifty were still in commission.

The Navy's Blue Angels aerobatics team returned to Bethpage to take delivery of their new aircraft, the F9F-8 Cougar. It was a proud moment for Grumman because, since their conception the Blue Angels had flown only Grumman aircraft.

Another version of the F9F, the F9F-8P made its maiden flight in August 1955. This version was the unarmed photographic model. It could photograph a continuous ten-mile-wide strip of land for five hours, and also had in-flight refuelling capabilities. The paint scheme was changed at this time on all Navy aircraft; out went the overall glossy, dark sea-blue and in came a non-specular light gull-grey on the upper surfaces and gloss white on the under surfaces.

Early 1956 brought a new version of the Albatross, the SA-16B. It was developed for the US Air Force and had to satisfy certain special requirements, the main ones being an increased performance and a larger payload capacity. The majority of the SA-16Bs were in fact updated SA-16As that had had an additional sixteen feet added to the main wing; very few purpose-built SA-16Bs ever appeared.

The Super Tiger, or F11F-1F, made its initial flight on 22 May 1956 from Edwards Air Force Base. Two were built, having both started life as F11F-1s, but their airframes had been taken off the production line and modified to take the new General Electric J79-GE-7 engine. The aircraft was an immediate success and proceeded to break records nearly every time it flew. But despite all the success, even though the Blue Angels changed their F9F-8s for the F11F-1Fs and extolled its virtues, the contracts never came.

The last version of the Cougar, the F9F-8T Cougar Trainer made its appearance in July. Equipped with a tandem seating arrangement and an in-flight refuelling capability, the airframe was similar to that of the F9F-8. It could be used purely as a trainer, or with a minimum amount of effort, could be turned into a combat-ready fighter. Three hundred and ninety nine were built, and they were the backbone of the US Navy jet training programme for years.

Grumman decided to widen its interests in the boating field. Already the manufacturer of aluminium canoes, it assigned a number of engineers and researchers to investigate the development of hydrofoils. The results that came back from the researchers convinced them that this was a worthwhile field in which to invest, and in August 1956 Grumman obtained a fifty per cent interest in a company called Dynamic Developments, who were heavily involved in the research and development of hydrofoils.

Grumman hit the news again in September when F11F test pilot Tom Attridge shot himself down whilst on a gunnery test run. It appeared that he had fired the guns whilst the aircraft was on a straight and level course, then seconds later the engine flamed out and the pilot was unable to restart the engine. As he headed for home, he realized that he was unable to maintain height, so he put the aircraft down in some scrub land. The aircraft caught fire, but Attridge managed to get out with only minor injuries. It was later discovered that some of the bullets fired had been defective and had slowed down in the air, with the result that the F11F caught up with them and ingested them through the air intakes of the engine. This caused the engine to malfunction and the flame-out that followed.

In Florida, it was discovered that some old F6F Hellcats were being refurbished to be used as air taxis. Four seats were to be installed in the fuselage and a door built into the starboard side. Although it is known that the conversion work was started, there is no record of them being used.

The TF-1 Trader was becoming a huge success, and at the end of 1956 the Navy awarded Grumman a contract worth $24 million for additional TF-1s. The Navy decided to use some of the Traders as flying test-beds for experimental electronic equipment, so Grumman produced four Traders, designated TF-1Qs. These bristled with aerials and their fuselages were crammed with equipment. The prototypes of much of the electronic equipment used today in AEW aircraft were initially tested in the TF-1Qs.

A brand new aircraft made its debut in May 1957, the Ag-Cat. The idea of venturing into the agricultural market was the brainchild of Joe Lippert of Engineering Preliminary Design, and it was he who approached Roy Grumman with the idea. The crop-spraying market was getting ever bigger, and the only aircraft being used at the time were either converted light aircraft or government war-surplus trainers.

There were many problems associated with these types of converted aircraft, most of them proving fatal.

Perhaps the most striking feature of the Grumman Ag-Cat was that it was a biplane. This arrangement ensured a high safety factor and increased controlability at low speeds. Grumman assigned a number of engineers to the project, but left the manufacturing to the Schweizer Aircraft Company with whom they had agreed a production contract, while marketing it themselves.

In April 1957, the Blue Angels changed their F9F-8s for F11F-1s, despite heavy competition from other aircraft manufacturers. None of the other company's aircraft could match the stringent aerobatic conditions demanded by the team.

In June a second new aircraft appeared on the drawing boards, after Grumman had won a competition for a new observation aircraft. They were awarded a contract to design and build a twin-engined, two-seat light observation aircraft for the Army, Navy and Marines. It was designated the AO-1 for the Army, and OF-1 for the Navy and the Marines.

The same year also brought the first commercial passenger aircraft since the Mallard, the Gulfstream. Designed to carry twelve passengers, it was powered by two Rolls-Royce Dart turboprop engines, and was aimed at the corporate executive market.

The British Martin-Baker company formed the start of what was to become a close relationship with Grumman that September. Martin-Baker were, and still are, the foremost manufacturers of aircraft ejection seats in the world and had been selected by Grumman to build and fit the ejector seat for the F9F Cougar, which subsequently became standard equipment for most of Grumman's aircraft. What sold Grumman on the Martin-Baker seats was the fact that they were zero-90 seats, which meant that as long as the aircraft speed was in excess of 90 knots, the pilot could eject out of the aircraft even at ground level, and parachute to relative safety. In August, Flying Officer Sidney Hughes of the RAF had demonstrated the zero-90 capability of the ejection seat by safely ejecting himself from the back seat of an F9F-8T at US Naval Air Facility Patuxent River. It was the first time such an experiment had been carried out in the United States, and was witnessed by several hundred members of the armed forces and aircraft manufacturers.

January 1958 was the start of an exciting year for the company: not only did it have four different production models, the F9F-8T, F11F-1, S2F-1 and TF-1, in the process of being delivered to the Navy, but the latest aircraft, the WF-2 Tracer, was ready for its first flight. In addition to this, the Gulfstream and the Ag-Cat were under production. The other Grumman divisions were also enjoying a bumper period. The Metal Boat Division was having one of its best periods ever, and the Aerobilt Bodies Division was building more truck bodies, containers and shipping containers than ever before.

In 1957 Grumman and eight other aircraft manufacturers had submitted bids to build a subsonic attack aircraft for the Navy, and in January Grumman were awarded the contract. The aircraft was designated the A2F-1, or A-6 as it was to become known later, and was to become one of the most valuable aircraft in the US Navy's inventory for many years. Even today, the basic airframe is still of the same design and construction. With the contract for the A2F-1 came the need to recognize the great importance of avionics. The setting up of an avionics group at Bethpage was the key that opened the door to an entirely new age of aviation for Grumman, the electronic age.

The first of the new breed of aircraft, the WF-2 Tracer, or 'Willy Fudd' as it became affectionately known, took to the air on 1 March 1958. The basic airframe was that of the S2F and its role was to provide airborne early warning to the fleet in the event of a threatened attack. It carried a variety of avionics, including APS-82 Radar and TACAN (Tactical Air

and Navigation), the radar being housed in a 20 ft. × 30 ft. radome mounted on top of the fuselage. The first production WF-2 was flown on 4 April, only four weeks after the prototype had flown.

News came back to Grumman that someone had found a use for the old TBFs, TBMs and Tigercats. A forest fire-fighting company on the West Coast was using them as water-bombers against forest fires that were inaccessible to normal fire-fighting teams. The aircraft carried a 750 kilogram rubber weather balloon in the bombbay filled with water and borate. When the pilot opened the bombbay doors, the balloon burst and sent the contents cascading on to the fire below.

The first of the Gulfstreams, the G-159, took to the air on 14 August 1958 with test pilots Fred Rowley and Carl Alber at the controls. The Gulfstream was designed to carry between ten and thirteen passengers plus baggage, the design also providing for nineteen- and twenty-four-seat passenger versions. A tremendous amount of safety research went into the development of the Gulfstream, including submerging the fuselage in a water tank and subjecting it to pressures that were equivalent to fifty years of flying time. That August, the Department of Defense placed an order for thirty-five AO-1 Mohawks, giving Grumman only the third contract they had ever had with the Army, the first being for the OA-9 in 1938, the second for the XP-50 in 1941.

Grumman continued to expand, not only in volume, but in equipment and facilities. In September they had an IBM 704 data processing system installed and with it, a large round radome on top of Plant 5. The radome was affectionately called the Golfball at first, that was until the Grumman logo was painted on it, then it became, and still is a landmark for the Grumman plant. The range of Grumman aircraft was increasing by the year, and thought was being given to how big the company would eventually grow.

In December 1958 Grumman announced that they were to build a replacement for the WF-2/E-1B Tracer, called the W2F-1 Hawkeye. The Hawkeye would be the largest carrier-borne aircraft in the US Navy, with an eighty-foot wingspan, and would carry some of the most sophisticated AEW equipment in the world. Another string was added to the Grumman bow, when the Grumman/Bendix team were awarded a Navy contract to build the Eagle missile.

With increased interest in the space programme, Grumman formed an alliance with two other aircraft companies, Republic and Fairchild. Together they formed the 'Long Island Space Team' and explored various projects connected with the space tracking station being assembled by Grumman at their Plant 5. Later in the year Grumman were awarded a contract by NASA to study the recovery of astronauts after a space mission. This was highlighted by a visit to Bethpage by Werner von Braun, the German rocket pioneer and Chief Engineer for NASA.

The export market picked up with the delivery of five Albatrosses, designated UF-2s, to the German Navy, which left Grumman complete with their insignia of a black German cross and anchor. Italy, Japan and the Netherlands also took delivery of S2F-1s at the beginning of 1959. Another contract came the company's way with the award of a design and development contract from the Maritime Administration for a jet-powered hydrofoil. Grumman were chosen because of their extensive research and studies in the field of hydrofoils.

On 13 April, the YAO-1 Mohawk took to the air, with test pilot Ralph Donnel at the controls. The tail of the Mohawk had been changed — originally it had been designed in a 'T' configuration, but subsequent tests proved that a three-finned and rudder tail, mounted on a horizontal stabiliser above the fuselage, gave the aircraft greater single-engined controlability and stability. It had dual controls for the two-man crew, and was equipped with the latest Martin-Baker ejector seats. It was classified as a STOL (Short Take-Off and Landing) aircraft because of its low stalling speed of only 55 miles per hour. The first production Ag-Cat came off the line in May and was promptly put to work, not by a farmer, but by Grumman themselves. They subjected the aircraft to a nine-hour spraying session spread over one week, at their Peconic plant. The original intention was to use mechanical spreaders to enrich the soil there, but it was decided to use the Ag-Cat instead, and the job was completed in less than half the time.

The Gulfstream was issued with its first FAA certificate at the beginning of the year, only seven months after the first flight; the issuing of the final certificate in May announced that the Gulfstream was ready for the commercial market. One month later, the first one was delivered to the Sinclair Refining Company.

In early 1960 the last F9F-8T Cougar left the Peconic facility for Norfolk, Virginia. Over twelve years had passed since the first XF9F-2 Panther had taken to the air, but as one jet aircraft passed into history, another was born to take its place. This was the A2F-1 Intruder, or A-6 as it was known. The A-6 was to become one of the most influential of all naval aircraft. Production models were to be equipped with some of the most up-to-date electronic equipment available, including DIANE (Digital Integrated Attack Navigation system). It had an all-weather capability and a computer system that could deliver a weapon load on target, in zero visibility and extremely adverse weather conditions.

Another Gulfstream was sold, this time to the National Distillers Company, and one month later it flew across the Atlantic on one of its first business trips. The first Ag-Cat to be sold abroad flew to Uruguay, some 9,000 miles away, for delivery to a sugar company.

On 28 June, Grumman suffered a tragic loss when the President of the Company, Leon 'Jake' Swirbul died. It would be fair to say that every employee at Grumman not only lost a great company president, but also a good friend. The Board of Directors appointed Clint Towl to take his place, whilst Bill Schwendler was made Chairman of the Executive Committee and Lew Evans, vice president.

The Royal Canadian Air Force took delivery of the first of the Albatross SA-16B Triphibians on 21 July 1960, redesignating them CSR-110s. This really was a remarkable aircraft, able to operate from ice, snow, mud, land and water. The hull skis were removable, as were the floats, and all ten aircraft ordered were delivered within four months. One of the most exciting AEW aircraft, the W2F-1 Hawkeye, took to the air on 21 October. The aircraft was a flying computer and communications centre, and together with other Hawkeyes, would be able to throw a security ring around any task force. In October, Grumman received one of the most exciting contracts in their history. NASA had selected them to design, build and test an advanced earth-orbiting satellite, the OAO (Orbiting Astronomical Observatory). This was to put Grumman in the forefront of space technology.

Back down on earth, the Army's latest version of the Mohawk, the OV-1B, was coming off the production line. This model differed from the earlier one, being equipped with SLAR (Sideways Looking Airborne Radar). The antenna was housed in a long rectangular container below the fuselage that extended from just forward of the trailing edge of the wing, to roughly two feet forward of the aircraft's nose. The antenna could 'paint' a beautiful radar picture 75 kilometres into enemy territory, without over-flying it.

At the beginning of December 1960, the Navy awarded Grumman a contract worth $70 million for the production of the A2F-1 Intruder.

In the spring of 1961, the space section facility developed a hypersonic shock tunnel, designed to create air speeds above Mach 20. The facility was later enlarged by 140 feet, so that it could be used in conjunction with probes into interplanetary travel conditions. This, combined with a plasma physics laboratory and a hyper-acoustic tank, was to be used later as part of the test facility for the OAO programme. Other technological developments included the largest anechoic chamber in the country, which was added to the new

electronics centre at Calverton. It had 65,000 square feet of floor space and contained a 2,000 ft AEW antenna test range, plus a 300 ft antenna and model test range.

What was to be one of the most controversial decisions of the decade was made when Secretary of Defense McNamarra 'suggested' to the aircraft industry that they got together and designed a bi-service fighter/bomber. The Navy made it obvious from the start that in their opinion it would not be acceptable, and were only placated when they found out that Grumman were to be the chief sub-contractor to General Dynamics. It was decided that there were to be two versions, the F-111A and the F-111B, the A for the United States Air Force and the B for the US Navy. The F-111A was to serve the USAF well, but the B, as the Navy predicted, was of virtually no use at all, mainly because of its weight of 35 tons when readied for a mission. Grumman anticipating that there might be a cancellation of the programme in a few years, embarked on one of its own — the F-14A. The F-111B programme tended to momentarily direct attention away from the other Grumman projects being built at the time, like the Lunar Module, but at the end of March 1969 the Bureau of Aeronautics awarded the company a $38 million contract for the W2F-1 Hawkeye. Also at that time, the first of the UF-2 Albatrosses destined for the Japanese Self-Defence Force was flown, and at the beginning of May the first one of the six ordered, was delivered.

Later that month, an ASW version of the Albatross appeared and it made its first flight the same month. This aircraft became very popular with foreign air forces, and under the Military Assistance Defence Programme, Norway, Peru, Spain, Chile, Pakistan, Thailand and Indonesia placed orders for the aircraft.

Grumman ventured further into the space programme that June when they were awarded another contract by NASA, this time for cannisters for the Echo II Communications Satellite Project. The cannisters were to carry a large inflatable balloon into orbit, and were contained within an adaptor assembly, which in turn was fitted on top of the launch vehicle. The idea was to launch the rocket into orbit around the earth, the cannister would then detach itself from the adaptor by means of an explosive charge and open up and release the balloon, which then inflated. The balloon was to be used extremely successfully as a communications signal reflector, a forerunner of the communications satellites.

On the aviation side, an A2F-1 made a non-stop flight across the USA, coast-to-coast in December, a total of 2,583 miles, on internal fuel only. Later that month, the Navy awarded Grumman a further contract worth $67,900,000 for additional W2F-1 Hawkeyes. A $29 million contract from the Navy heralded the start of 1962. It was for S2F-3s and provided a much needed boost to the company. At the end of January, the Echo II project was successfully launched and placed in orbit. The Grumman cannister worked perfectly.

The last of the WF-2 Tracers left the factory in September, and the way was made clear to accommodate a new $86 million order for the A2F Intruder.

Development of the A2F Intruder brought with it a number of problems, the main one being that these sophisticated aircraft required highly complex day-to-day maintenance. This meant that the complicated electronic systems had to be of the highest quality and reliability. The early Intruders were built and tested without encountering any great problems with the aircraft itself, but there were serious failings in the reliability of certain components in the weapons system. Solid state electronics had not arrived at this time and the whole weapons system had a mean time between failures of about one hour, hardly satisfactory for a three- to four-hour mission aircraft. The carrier environment further exacerbated the problem. The constant hammering down on to the steel deck of a carrier, and the constantly changing environment, played havoc with the electronic systems. Grumman decided that the equipment needed to be upgraded for ease of maintenance, and immediately started to develop support test equipment that would locate all the problem areas as and when they arose. It was a tremendously successful project and one that eased the burden of maintenance for future and even more complex electronic aircraft.

Also in 1962, perhaps the most controversial aircraft ever to be built in the United States arrived, the F-111, or TFX as it was originally known. It was designed and built by General Dynamics, with Grumman as the prime sub-contractor building the landing gear, the horizontal tail section and the aft fuselage. One of the unique innovations built into the F-111, was the escape system. Instead of ejector seats for the crew, the whole cockpit area was ejected as one unit. It was a remarkable aircraft, for the Air Force that is, but for the Navy it was to be a complete failure. The reasons for this are explained in greater detail in the F-14 chapter of the book.

A very important contract for Grumman at this time was that awarded by NASA, to build the Lunar Excursion Module for the Apollo missions. This turned out to be one of the most successful projects in the history of the manned space programme.

Activity increased on the A-6 programme, formerly the A-2F, as the EA-6A, followed by the EA-6B, made their appearance. As with all the variants of the A-6, they used the same basic airframe. Ten A-6As or 'Dogships' as they were known, were set aside to be used as test-beds.

The Eagle missile was cancelled at the end of 1962 after three years of research and testing and only one firing, but it had served a useful purpose and many of its features were used later on the Phoenix missile programme.

The Gulfstream I was beginning to make an impression on the executive aircraft market, albeit very slowly, and Grumman engineers and designers began to explore the possibilities of a twin-jet Gulfstream II. Another passenger aircraft made its appearance in 1962, the C-2A Greyhound. This aircraft was not for the civilian market, but was a replacement for the C-1A Trader used by the Navy for logistic air support. Basically, it was a COD aircraft capable of carrying 28 passengers and five tons of cargo, with a range of 1,900 miles. During the Vietnam conflict, the Greyhound was to carry out daily deliveries of virtually anything between the fleet and land bases.

Grumman's involvement in the space programme dominated the 1960s, virtually overshadowing everything else, especially after the first moon landing. But the other projects did not grind to a halt; the OV-1 Mohawk continued to be upgraded, and research began on the development of high-tech metals like titanium, and composites such as boron fibre.

In 1966, the Grumman Aircraft Company were stunned by the announcement that Roy Grumman was resigning as chairman of the board. He was 71 and had been suffering from a chronic eye ailment for many years, but even so his going was quite a shock to everyone at Grumman, because it heralded the end of an era. Although his retirement ostensibly meant the end of his active participation in the company, he still retained the title of honorary chairman, and his seat on the board of directors.

The first flight of the Gulfstream II took place on 2 October 1966 and before the first deliveries began at the beginning of 1967, some sixty aircraft had been ordered. All through the sixties, Grumman aircraft were being updated, and in 1968 the third generation Hawkeye, designated the E2C, appeared. It was the result of a $100 million contract from the US Navy and made the 'eyes of the fleet' even more sharp-sighted.

The wrangling over the F-111B was finally over in 1968 and the project laid to rest. The US Navy then asked for designs and proposals from the aerospace industry for a new fighter, one that would take them into the 1990s. The Grumman design was selected, and so one of the most exciting aircraft ever to fly was born — the F-14 Tomcat.

Grumman was still investing heavily in new technology. In two years they spent $41 million on computer-controlled

milling machinery; they invested in an electron-beam welder; a hypersonic wind-tunnel; a carbon-dioxide laser cutting tool for titanium; a jouls capacitor bank that could push out 30 billion watts for six millionths of a second, which was used for plasma research and to help study radiation during space flights, and a three million-volt van de Graaff accelerator.

Two years after Roy Grumman's retirement, a major restructuring took place: Grumman Aircraft Engineering Company became the Grumman Corporation and all the other subsidiaries were formed into four major divisions, Grumman Aerospace, Grumman Allied, Grumman International and Grumman Data Systems. In the following year these were joined by a fifth subsidiary, Grumman Ecosystems Corporation.

The underwater explorer Jacques Picard, son of August Picard, the famous Swiss physicist and underwater explorer, brought his 130-ton research submarine, the *Benjamin Franklyn*, to Grumman's marine facility at West Palm Beach, in May 1968. During the early 1960s, when Grumman started to enter the field of underwater research, they had formed an alliance with Jacques Picard. In exchange for his expertise in the field, Grumman helped him with his Gulf Stream Drift Project. The project was started on 14 July 1969 and was completed thirty days later. During this time, the submersible travelled submerged from Florida to Nova Scotia, a distance of 1,500 miles, and obtained the most enormous amount of scientific data, most of which is still being evaluated. The project never received the acclaim it deserved, because the mission coincided with the first manned landing on the moon, which for obvious reasons completely overshadowed their remarkable performance.

By the end of the 1960s, Grumman's employee count had reached 33,000. This was unusually high and had come about through an additional 12,000 personnel being employed on the Lunar Excursion Module programme. The 1970s started on a high note with the Lunar Module (the word Excursion had been dropped because it was thought flippant) completing its final mission to the moon, and establishing a 100 per cent reliability and safety record.

In 1972, the company faced the threat of bankruptcy. The situation had come about after inflation had sent the production costs of the F-14 soaring out of control. The company had accepted the contract from the US Navy at a fixed price. At the time of signing, in 1969, the US inflation rate had averaged 3.4 per cent for the previous ten years, but unfortunately for Grumman it appeared to soar immediately afterwards, and Grumman were affected by this. The F-14 is built of 24 per cent titanium, and it was this that was the major problem, because its price increased by over 40 per cent within two years of the signing. After a great deal of wrangling, Grumman persuaded the Navy to renegotiate the contract, although, even so, it cost the company a quarter of a billion dollars. It was nearly three years before the F-14 became a viable.

Because Congress was worried about the cost of the F-14, they suggested to the US Navy that they reduce the number of aircraft ordered, and this forced Grumman to look around for other customers. One such customer was the Shah of Iran, who after seeing the aircraft demonstrated at the Paris Air Show, ordered thirty, intending to purchase a further 50 F-15s later. When he saw the cost of supporting two different types of aircraft, he cancelled the F-15 order and increased his order for F-14s by fifty, much to the chagrin of the USAF. Encouraged by this export order, Grumman introduced the Iranians to one of their subsidiary companies that had developed a low temperature, low pressure shipping container, called the Dormavac. This could enable meat to be transported from Australia to Iran without freezing. The first shipment was a disaster, and then, because of the Iranian revolution, everything folded, with a loss to Grumman of $45.6 million.

There followed two further ill-judged diversions into other

forms of industry; one was Ecosystems which was to turn waste products and garbage into electricity. This unfortunately turned in a loss of $50 million. Grumman's most expensive venture to date, the Flexible Bus, also lost money. From day one the project, acquired from Rohr Industries, never worked properly, and Grumman seemed forever to be repairing them. To date the cost has reached $250 million.

The second of the OAOs (Orbiting Astronomical Observatory) was 'switched off' in 1972, after four years of continuous operation during which it had passed back an incredible amount of information. During its life span the OAO had observed a supernova in a galaxy 20 million light years away from Earth. The third OAO was launched the following year, but failed to reach orbit and was burnt up as it re-entered the Earth's atmosphere. The fourth and final OAO was launched successfully in August 1972, and transmitted a great deal of information back before it too was switched off in 1976.

Amongst Grumman's commercial ventures away from aerospace was one remarkable project, the TLRV (Tracked Levitated Research Vehicle), which created a great deal of interest. Together with the Department of Transportation, Grumman attempted to apply its aerospace technology to the construction of a high speed inter-city transportation system. Powered by three JT-15D Air Supply engines, the TLRV was designed to travel on a thin cushion of air at speeds of up to 150 mph. The LIM (Linear Induction Motor) model was designed to be capable of speeds of up to 300 mph. Tests are still going on, but at present there are no plans to put the vehicle into production.

In the aviation field, Grumman were looking at a revolutionary new idea for an aircraft, called the 'Nutcracker'. Designed as a VSTOL (Vertical Short Take-Off and Landing) aircraft, the Nutcracker had a fuselage that hinged half-way along its length, enabling the rear half to articulate downwards to an angle of ninety degrees. Based on the OV-1 Mohawk and powered by two General Electric TF-34 engines fixed to the rear part of the fuselage, the aircraft was designed to go into a hovering attitude, similar to that of the British Aerospace/McDonnel Douglas AV-8B Harrier, while the nose section engaged a ship-mounted dual-jointed crane with a stabilized head. The aircraft could then be swung aboard, refuelled, re-armed and, by reversing the landing procedure, launched. Once the fuselage was returned to its normal configuration, the aircraft could assume horizontal flight and carry out its mission.

A model of the Grumman 'Nutcracker' VSTOL aircraft.

As with all revolutionary aircraft, there were problems. One concerned the effect of loss of power from one of the two engines whilst in the hover, but according to the designer, Bob Kress, there would be mechanical cross-shafting of the fans between engines which would activate in the event of an engine failure.

At the beginning of 1971, the first EA-6B Prowler had made its appearance with the US Navy, and by the end of the 1970s two further versions had appeared, one of which was the A-6E. The end of the 1970s also marked the end of the company's commercial aircraft business, which was sold to American Jet Industries for around $40 million. The Gulfstream division was sold with the proviso that Grumman complete the development of the Gulfstream III. The company was sold again six years later for $680 million.

As a result of the problems which had dogged the company in recent years, morale was beginning to show signs for concern. This was not helped by the announcement of a takeover bid for the company by a Texan conglomerate with the name of LTV (Ling-Temco-Vought). To block LTV's bid, the executors of the Grumman pension fund and employees' investment plan started to use the money to buy large quantities of Grumman stock. Unfortunately, although this thwarted the takeover bid, it laid the top executives of Grumman open to Federal charges of using the pension money illegally. Over three-quarters of the pension plan's participants signed petitions supporting the Chairman, John Bierwirth, and his executives, even though their shares had lost ground on the stock market. This fall in the price of the shares did not last long, and by the end of the year they were back on an even keel. The way everyone rallied around in the crisis emphasized the close-knit community that made up Grumman. Faced with this kind of opposition, LTV's executive withdrew from the fray. With these problems behind them, Grumman went back to the business of making aircraft.

The Argentine invasion of the Falkland Islands in the spring of 1982, and the subsequent sinking of the British destroyer *HMS Sheffield*, brought home to the US military the need for an early warning capability. The Secretary of the US Navy, John Lehman, said, 'If the British Navy had had the E2C Hawkeye as a surveillance aircraft, the Argentine jet that fired the missile would not have got anywhere near the ship before interceptors dealt with him.' Grumman is continuing to update the E2C Hawkeye and one of the latest innovations is 'conformed radar', radar antennas embedded in the aircraft's fuselage, in the leading edges of the wings and in the trailing edges, to decrease weight and drag. Ten E2C Hawkeyes were delivered in 1982, six to the US Navy and four to the Japanese Air Self-Defence Force. Later, in September, Egypt ordered four of the aircraft, the first to be delivered in 1985. Because of the EF-111's role in the strike against Libya, interest in the aircraft has increased and Grumman and TRW (Thompson-Ramo-Woolridge) are constantly updating the navigation and communications systems.

An additional thirty-nine C-2A Greyhounds were ordered at the beginning of 1982 for the US Navy under a $678 million contract. This was a unique contract because the last C-2A was built in 1968, and it was only the foresight of Grumman engineers in keeping the original tooling in storage that enabled these aircraft to be built at a realistic price.

Grumman still continues to overhaul and modify the various Grumman aircraft used by the military. Although the last OV-1 Mohawk was delivered to the Army in 1967, the aircraft is continually being upgraded. In 1988 the OV-1D was delivered to them for test and evaluation.

The whole of Grumman was stunned by the news that Leroy Grumman had died after a long illness, on 4 October 1984. He was 87. Even though he had not been active in the running of the company for many years, his death left an emptiness in everybody who had known him. Dick Hutton, former senior vice-president of Engineering, summed up Roy Grumman, when he said, 'Mr Grumman had a great rapport with the Navy. He was open, honest and possessed a strong desire to do the right thing for the customer. This in turn rubbed off on others at the company. He never wanted to be in the forefront; he tried to avoid publicity. He was quiet and reserved; he was a good listener and easy to talk to. He was a great engineer, respected by many and now missed by many.'

Because of the increased acceptance of the use of graphite-epoxy composites, and Grumman's acknowledged expertise in the field, the Israelis asked the company to make the wings and tail section for their new strike fighter, the Lavi. Grumman engineers created a new graphite-epoxy formula, called 'intermediate modulus graphite fibre'. The first flight of the Lavi, with the new wings and tail sections, was in 1986 and was an unqualified success.

One of the most exciting projects for years began in the mid-eighties. This was the Bell/Boeing Tilt Rotor, or V-22 Osprey. The Osprey is revolutionary in its construction, inasmuch as its airframe is built almost entirely of advanced composites. Grumman's job is to build the large, complex twin-tail section. At the time of writing, the V-22 Osprey has not flown, but no problems are envisaged and the future for the aircraft, according to the manufacturers, looks good.

It is a sad thought, when one thinks of the great aircraft built by Grumman in the past, to realize that it is quite possible that the F-14D and the EA-6B will be the last Grumman-designed aircraft. Grumman are now amongst the top electronic designers and manufacturers in the world of aviation: more than half of their current backlog of work is for electronics, including space programmes, surveillance, missiles and communications systems. One of the largest contracts ever received by Grumman from the US Air Force, for $657 million, is for the Joint STARS (Surveillance Target Attack Radar System). This will provide real-time battlefield surveillance, enabling Air Force commanders to locate and track enemy armour and troop movements far behind enemy lines. Although Joint STARS is an airborne facility, an Army version is currently under production by Motorola, which will be able to link up with the Grumman-built one.

Presently under test and evaluation is a robotic system called the 'Ranger'. A four-wheeled vehicle on a diamond-shaped chassis, with one wheel on each side and one front and back, the Ranger is three feet high and capable of carrying anti-tank missiles, modern infantry weapons and a TV scanning sight. Weighing 380 pounds and capable of speeds up to 10 mph, the Ranger can be controlled by a single soldier from a portable control console the size of a suitcase. Also mounted on the Ranger is a video camera, and by using the screen on the console as a gunsight, the operator can launch missile attacks against various targets. The capabilities of this vehicle are endless and it will become a tremendous asset to the infantry.

A third STA (Shuttle Training Aircraft) was ordered from Grumman by NASA in 1983, and the same year Grumman joined forces with Lockheed in taking over the control of the launch and recovery operations from the Kennedy Space Centre and the Vandenburg Launch Complex. In charge of this was the former astronaut Fred Haise, whose experience as a Lunar Module pilot on Apollo 13, and later as a Shuttle Orbiter Test Pilot, gave Grumman the expertise needed.

In 1984 the Grumman/DARPA (Defence Advanced Research Projects Agency) X-29 was displayed. Unusually, it had forward-sweeping wings, situated at the front of the fuselage. It was not the first aircraft to have had forward-sweeping wings, however; that distinction belongs to the Junkers 287 built during the Second World War. The X-29 is described in more detail later in the book.

The highly publicized and controversial SDI (Strategic Defence Initiative), or Star Wars programme, as it has become more commonly known, includes the Boost Surveillance and Tracking System developed by Grumman. This enables the system to track missiles during the 'boost' phase of their launch, the point immediately after launch, and to guide defence missiles to destroy them.

Although Grumman has kept a low profile with regard to the space programme since the Apollo 17 mission, the company has always kept its finger on the pulse of NASA's progress. It was to Grumman that NASA turned when they were choosing the teams that were to build the Space Tug, or Orbiting Manoeuvring Vehicle. With Rockwell and Boeing as the prime contractors, Grumman are building the pilot's console, the propulsion modules, automatic testing equipment and mechanical ground support equipment.

In August 1986, Grumman released details of a shipborne VTOL RPV (Vertical Take-Off and Landing Remotely Piloted Vehicle) that could provide ships with a defence surveillance capability. Powered by a Rolls-Royce XJ99 lift-engine with 900 pounds of thrust, and a Garrett F109 lift/cruise-engine of 1,300 pounds thrust, the RPV will be capable of cruising at 210 knots for 14 hours at an altitude of 27,000 to 37,000 feet, whilst carrying a payload of 1,500 pounds. Although the US Navy and the Royal Navy have shown interest in it, Grumman only plan to fly a one-seventh scale radio-controlled model at present.

The first flight of the F-14A+, or Super Tomcat, took place in September 1987. Powered by two General Electric F110-GE-400 turbofan engines producing 28,000 pounds of thrust, the aircraft went supersonic, reaching Mach 1.2, on the first flight. The F110 engines will be fitted in the F-14D, due to be delivered to the US Navy in 1990.

Grumman's continued involvement with the space programme was made plain when it was announced that they had been awarded a contract to support the design and development of a space station. The contract, which is to run for more than ten years, will be worth around $1 billion to the company. Grumman's role will be to assist NASA in the management of the four companies that have been selected to design and build the space station. They will also develop the test equipment for the verification of the assembly and integration of the components.

From a very humble beginning, Grumman has expanded virtually out of all recognition, and in doing so, has become one of the major aerospace corporations in the world today. Without doubt, Grumman will also be one of tomorrow's.

FF-1 and F2F-1

The US Navy's association with Grumman as an aircraft manufacturer started on 29 December 1931, when they accepted delivery of the XFF-1. Earlier that year, however, Grumman had supplied the US Navy with a float that had a retractable undercarriage, for converting the Navy's Vought seaplanes into amphibians.

The XFF-1 was a two-seat fighter capable of a maximum speed of 195 mph, had a service ceiling of 23,600 feet which was reached at a climb rate of 1,320 feet per minute, and had a range of 818 miles. Its armament consisted of two fixed .30 calibre machine guns and one .30 calibre moveable weapon. The XFF-1 was the first US Navy aircraft that had a retractable undercarriage capable of operating from an aircraft carrier. It was 20 mph faster than any other aircraft of the day, and had the luxury of a fully-enclosed cockpit. The engine was initially a Wright R-1820E generating 575 horsepower, but this was later replaced by a 750 horsepower Wright R-1820F, which boosted the speed to 201 mph. A US Navy team of test pilots, led by a Lt. Oftsie, gave the XFF-1 a thorough evaluation and were more than pleased with the little, barrel-shaped fighter. The barrel shape was to become synonomous with Grumman during the war years.

There were some initial problems with the undercarriage during the trials — it collapsed on a number of occasions, much to the embarrassment of Grumman. It was said that after one such incident, Jake Swirbul roared at the ground crew to get the undercarriage fixed. They apparently did it so

well, that when the Navy later flew the aircraft to St. Louis, it would not come down at all! Despite this initial setback, the Navy ordered twenty seven FF-1s at a cost of $641,250.

Grumman built a second experimental aircraft, designated the XSF-1. It was very similar to the XFF-1 and was designed primarily as a scouting model. The engine was a 700 horsepower Wright R-1820-78 Cyclone (later changed to a Wright R-1820-84), and the fuel capacity increased by 45 gallons. The Navy placed an order for thirty-three SF-1s. As with the FF-1s, these were to be assigned to a squadron aboard the *USS Lexington*. Both the FF-1 and the SF-1 were biplanes, and although the trend at the time was for monoplanes, there were none that could seriously compete aboard an aircraft carrier.

It was just prior to the delivery of the first production FF-1, and the start of production on the SF-1, that the whole Grumman company moved from Valley Stream to Farmingdale. The production model FF-1 had some slight modifications that made it differ from the XFF-1; the wing area was increased, a more powerful engine, the R-1820-78, was installed and provision was made for a .50 calibre machine gun. Top speed rose to 201 mph, and speeds in excess of 285 mph were achieved in dives, but the service ceiling and the range dropped to 22,400 feet and 732 miles respectively. It is interesting to note that during the dives, pull-outs of over 5 g

Above: A centre of gravity test on the XFF-1 at Valley Stream, New York.

were recorded, which emphasized the sturdiness of the aircraft's construction.

The first production FF-1s went to VF-5B (Fighting Five) Squadron aboard the *USS Lexington*. The SF-1s went to VS-3B (Scouting Three) Squadron. Thirty-three SF-1s were built, all except two being distributed amongst various squadrons as scout aircraft. One of the two was redesignated XSF-2 and fitted with a 650 horsepower Pratt and Whitney R-1535-72 engine, and a Hamilton Standard two-bladed controlled pitch propeller. The other, redesignated XSBF-1, was adapted to carry a 500 lb. bomb slung from a frame on the engine mount. Later, in 1933, a few FF-1s were assigned to the *USS Saratoga* and *USS Ranger* in a utility role. The operational life of the FF-1 was short, its role being taken over by the XF2F-1, a new single-seat fighter. The FF-1s were sent to the Naval Air Factory in Philadelphia for conversion to dual-control aircraft, and then assigned to Naval Reserve squadrons, finally being struck off the register in 1942.

The XSBF-1 at Valley Stream.

This was not the end of this remarkable little fighter aircraft's story though. In 1937, the Canadian Car and Foundry Company, Can-Car, the largest manufacturer of railway equipment in Canada, expanded its interests to include aircraft production. Representatives of the Turkish Government had expressed an interest in the FF-1, even though it was virtually obsolete as far as Grumman was concerned. Rather than lose the goodwill of the Turks, Grumman granted the manufacturing licence of the FF-1 to the Canadian company. The Turks immediately ordered forty of the aircraft. With the licence to manufacture, Grumman sent the GG-1 aircraft. This aircraft was a mixture of an FF-1 and an SF-1, powered by a Wright R-1820F-52 engine generating 775 horsepower at 5,800 feet and 890 horsepower at sea level. The GG-1 was originally used as a demonstrator by Grumman, but was sent to Can-Car as the prototype for the G-23 (the Canadian version of the FF-1). There was, as it turned out, a rather sinister side to this transaction. The Spanish Civil War had been raging in Europe for about a year. Although the United States had put an embargo on the supply of war materials to the two warring factions, the Turkish authorities were acting as buyers on behalf of the Spanish Republican Government. What should have aroused suspicion was the fact that the aircraft were routed via Le Havre and Barcelona, before reaching their supposed destination of Istanbul. The first three fuselages were built by Grumman and delivered to the Can-Car plant, whilst the wings and tail surfaces were built by the Brewster Aircraft Company. The assembly and production was supervised by a Miss Elsie MacGill, who managed to complete the order within one year. Powered by an 800 horsepower Wright R-1820F-52 Cyclone engine, the GE-23, as it was designated, had a maximum speed of 216 mph. On arrival in Barcelona, the aircraft were given serial numbers AD-001 to AD-040, and were immediately assigned to the Republican Air Arm for reconnaissance and strafing missions, which they carried

The GE-23, built by Can-Car. This was one of the first Canadian-built FF-1s.

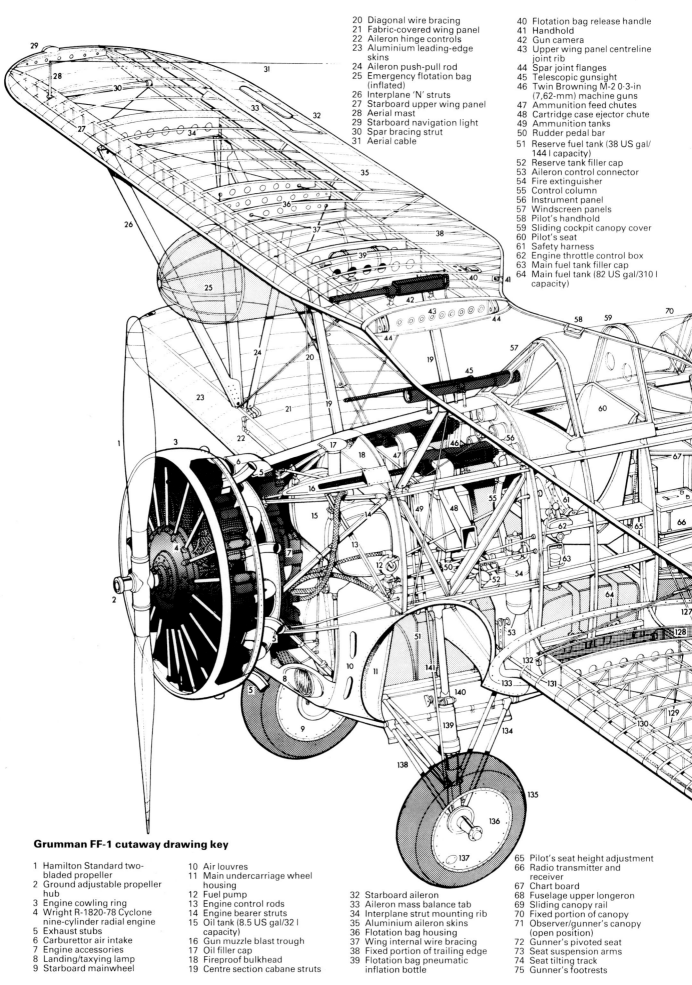

20 Diagonal wire bracing
21 Fabric-covered wing panel
22 Aileron hinge controls
23 Aluminium leading-edge skins
24 Aileron push-pull rod
25 Emergency flotation bag (inflated)
26 Interplane 'N' struts
27 Starboard upper wing panel
28 Aerial mast
29 Starboard navigation light
30 Spar bracing strut
31 Aerial cable

40 Flotation bag release handle
41 Handhold
42 Gun camera
43 Upper wing panel centreline joint rib
44 Spar joint flanges
45 Telescopic gunsight
46 Twin Browning M-2 0·3-in (7,62-mm) machine guns
47 Ammunition feed chutes
48 Cartridge case ejector chute
49 Ammunition tanks
50 Rudder pedal bar
51 Reserve fuel tank (38 US gal/ 144 l capacity)
52 Reserve tank filler cap
53 Aileron control connector
54 Fire extinguisher
55 Control column
56 Instrument panel
57 Windscreen panels
58 Pilot's handhold
59 Sliding cockpit canopy cover
60 Pilot's seat
61 Safety harness
62 Engine throttle control box
63 Main fuel tank filler cap
64 Main fuel tank (82 US gal/310 l capacity)

Grumman FF-1 cutaway drawing key

1 Hamilton Standard two-bladed propeller
2 Ground adjustable propeller hub
3 Engine cowling ring
4 Wright R-1820-78 Cyclone nine-cylinder radial engine
5 Exhaust stubs
6 Carburettor air intake
7 Engine accessories
8 Landing/taxying lamp
9 Starboard mainwheel

10 Air louvres
11 Main undercarriage wheel housing
12 Fuel pump
13 Engine control rods
14 Engine bearer struts
15 Oil tank (8.5 US gal/32 l capacity)
16 Gun muzzle blast trough
17 Oil filler cap
18 Fireproof bulkhead
19 Centre section cabane struts

32 Starboard aileron
33 Aileron mass balance tab
34 Interplane strut mounting rib
35 Aluminium aileron skins
36 Flotation bag housing
37 Wing internal wire bracing
38 Fixed portion of trailing edge
39 Flotation bag pneumatic inflation bottle

65 Pilot's seat height adjustment
66 Radio transmitter and receiver
67 Chart board
68 Fuselage upper longeron
69 Sliding canopy rail
70 Fixed portion of canopy
71 Observer/gunner's canopy (open position)
72 Gunner's pivoted seat
73 Seat suspension arms
74 Seat tilting track
75 Gunner's footrests

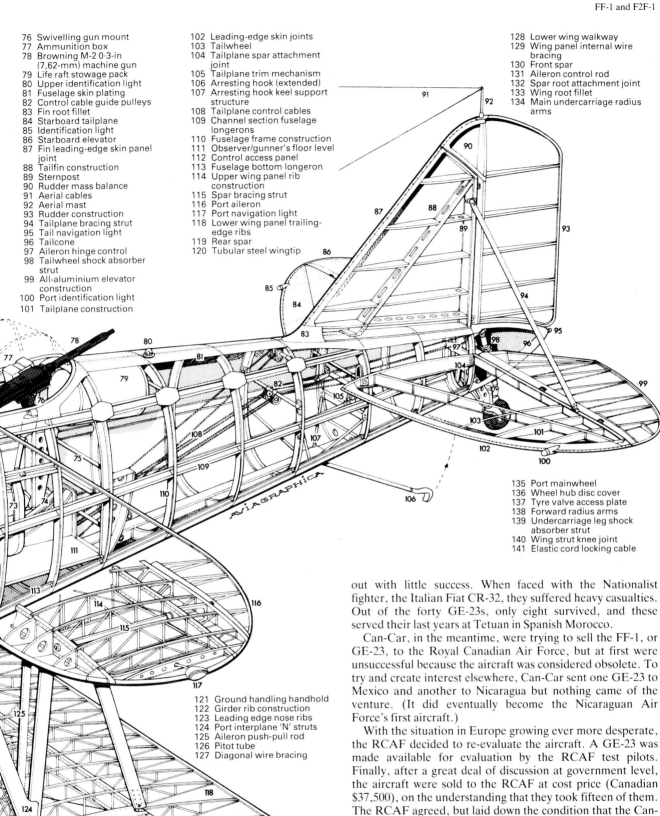

76 Swivelling gun mount
77 Ammunition box
78 Browning M-2 0·3-in (7,62-mm) machine gun
79 Life raft stowage pack
80 Upper identification light
81 Fuselage skin plating
82 Control cable guide pulleys
83 Fin root fillet
84 Starboard tailplane
85 Identification light
86 Starboard elevator
87 Fin leading-edge skin panel joint
88 Tailfin construction
89 Sternpost
90 Rudder mass balance
91 Aerial cables
92 Aerial mast
93 Rudder construction
94 Tailplane bracing strut
95 Tail navigation light
96 Tailcone
97 Aileron hinge control
98 Tailwheel shock absorber strut
99 All-aluminium elevator construction
100 Port identification light
101 Tailplane construction

102 Leading-edge skin joints
103 Tailwheel
104 Tailplane spar attachment joint
105 Tailplane trim mechanism
106 Arresting hook (extended)
107 Arresting hook keel support structure
108 Tailplane control cables
109 Channel section fuselage longerons
110 Fuselage frame construction
111 Observer/gunner's floor level
112 Control access panel
113 Fuselage bottom longeron
114 Upper wing panel rib construction
115 Spar bracing strut
116 Port aileron
117 Port navigation light
118 Lower wing panel trailing-edge ribs
119 Rear spar
120 Tubular steel wingtip

121 Ground handling handhold
122 Girder rib construction
123 Leading edge nose ribs
124 Port interplane 'N' struts
125 Aileron push-pull rod
126 Pitot tube
127 Diagonal wire bracing

128 Lower wing walkway
129 Wing panel internal wire bracing
130 Front spar
131 Aileron control rod
132 Spar root attachment joint
133 Wing root fillet
134 Main undercarriage radius arms

135 Port mainwheel
136 Wheel hub disc cover
137 Tyre valve access plate
138 Forward radius arms
139 Undercarriage leg shock absorber strut
140 Wing strut knee joint
141 Elastic cord locking cable

out with little success. When faced with the Nationalist fighter, the Italian Fiat CR-32, they suffered heavy casualties. Out of the forty GE-23s, only eight survived, and these served their last years at Tetuan in Spanish Morocco.

Can-Car, in the meantime, were trying to sell the FF-1, or GE-23, to the Royal Canadian Air Force, but at first were unsuccessful because the aircraft was considered obsolete. To try and create interest elsewhere, Can-Car sent one GE-23 to Mexico and another to Nicaragua but nothing came of the venture. (It did eventually become the Nicaraguan Air Force's first aircraft.)

With the situation in Europe growing ever more desperate, the RCAF decided to re-evaluate the aircraft. A GE-23 was made available for evaluation by the RCAF test pilots. Finally, after a great deal of discussion at government level, the aircraft were sold to the RCAF at cost price (Canadian $37,500), on the understanding that they took fifteen of them. The RCAF agreed, but laid down the condition that the Can-Car books would be kept open for government auditors to ensure that Can-Car would not make a profit out of the deal.

Having got the GE-23s, the RCAF had to decide what role the aircraft could play. In December 1940, the GE-23s, or Goblins as they had been named, were assigned to A flight of No 118 Squadron, based at Dartmouth, Nova Scotia, to be used obstensibly for coastal patrol work. In fact at one time they were Canada's only fighter force on the East coast. Just over a year later, the Goblins were replaced by Curtiss P-40E Kittyhawks. Ten Goblins were scrapped and the remaining five were transferred to No 123 Squadron, with a view to converting them for target towing. The idea proved to be impracticable, so they too were scrapped.

Above left: G-23s of the RCAF practising formation flying.

Below left: This FF-1 is a rebuilt version of a Canadian Car Foundry FF-1. The heraldic badge on the fuselage is that of VF-513, 'The Red Rippers'.

In 1961, an agricultural pilot by the name of J. R. Sirmons, was spraying a plantation in Chinandega, Nicaragua, when he spotted the remains of a GE-23 Goblin on the Zolotan Airfield, the aircraft graveyard of the Nicaraguan Air Force. After examining it, he discovered that it was restorable, and after lengthy negotiations, he bought it from the Air Force and set about the task. With the help of his wife, some friends, and three years of hard work, the GE-23 took to the air as if she had never been away. Arrangements were made to fly her back the 2,100 miles to the United States. The trip took three days, with a total of 15 hours and 40 minutes' actual flying time, bringing back to the United States the only FF-1 left in the world. After being completely re-restored by Grumman, and painted in the original colours of an aircraft of the US Navy in the 1930s, the aircraft is now on display at the Naval Air Museum at Pensacola, Florida.

On 2 November 1932, Grumman were awarded a contract for a single-seat fighter, the first to be built by the company. The XF2F-1, like the FF-2 and the SF-1, was barrel-shaped, but even more pronounced than its predecessors. This was largely due to the shape of the engine, a fourteen-cylinder, two-row Pratt and Whitney XR-1535-44 Twin Wasp Junior radial, which produced 625 horsepower at 8,400 feet. Covered by a smooth cowling, the engine turned a twin-bladed, Smith R-3 propeller of 8 ft. 6 in. diameter. The main fuel tank was mounted aft of the engine and contained 75 gallons, whilst the reserve tank was mounted forward of the main bulkhead and contained 35 gallons. Slightly smaller than the FF-1, the fuselage was of a semi-monocoque construction, with Z-shaped section formers and longerons, all covered in aluminium alloy. Only the upper surfaces of the staggered wing had ailerons; as with the moveable tail surfaces, these were fabric-covered metal frames. The fixed tail surfaces were covered with light alloy sheet. The undercarriage was retractable by means of a handcrank in the cockpit, which took 32 turns to complete the operation. When fully extended, a positive lock engaged, and if the throttle was closed without the undercarriage being down, an alarm buzzer sounded in the cockpit.

The armament carried by the XF2F-1 comprised two .30 Model 2 Browning machine guns, fixed in the upper forward fuselage, firing through the cowling and the propeller by means of synchronization. The pilot had a telescopic sight fixed to the top of the fuselage in front of the cockpit and protruding through the windscreen. Two Mk XLI bomb racks were fitted beneath the lower wing, capable of carrying two 116 lb. bombs.

By contemporary standards, the XF2F-1 turned in an outstanding performance. It was fast (maximum speed 229 mph) and extremely manoeuvrable. It had a climb rate of 3,080 feet per minute, and a service ceiling of 29,800 feet, but it also had an unforgiving nature. If stalled, the XF2F-1 had a tendency to go into a spin, but fortunately the stall warning and recovery characteristics were good. Of course, this only applied if the pilot had enough height, so special care had to be taken on take-off and landing. So good were the warnings, in fact, that the Navy decided that even a novice pilot would

The XF2F-1 on one of its first test flights. The pilot is possibly Jimmy Collins, who later died in a crash testing the XF3F-1.

have difficulty in entering an involuntary spin, and decided that it was an acceptable risk.

Before accepting final delivery, the Navy decided that they would like to run the aircraft through their own test and evaluation programme, using their own test pilots. This they did, taking six months to complete it, but they came up with a number of minor modifications they required before accepting the aircraft. They required the upper wing span to be extended by six inches to increase stability, the cockpit canopy to be enlarged, and a redesigned engine cowling, incorporating rocker-arm blisters, to improve the cooling.

Following these alterations, the Navy ordered fifty-five F2Fs at a total cost of $1 million, the largest single order for an aircraft at that time. The money came from the National Industrial Recovery Act of 1933, which had given the Navy $7 million to build up their aviation strength. The production model was to be fitted with the R-1535-72 version of the direct drive, single-stage, supercharged Twin Wasp Junior engine producing 650 horsepower. The first squadron to take delivery of 18 F2F-1s was VF-2B (Fighting Two), on 19 February 1935, on board the aircraft carrier *USS Lexington*. A few months later VF-3B took delivery on board the aircraft carrier *USS Saratoga*, followed closely by VF-5B, who replaced their obsolete FF-1s with nine F2F-1s from the San Diego Battle Force Pool. VF-2B operated the F2F-1 continuously from the carrier *USS Lexington* for more than five years, and when they finally replaced them, all 18 aircraft sported the much sought-after 'E for excellence' emblem. This was the first time in the history of US Naval Aviation that every aircraft on a squadron had been awarded the letter. VF-5B (originally VF-3B) continued to operate the F2F-1s until 1938, when they were replaced by F3F-2s. The F2Fs were then assigned to a new squadron, VF-7, for operation off the carrier *USS Wasp*, together with nine F2Fs from the carrier *USS Saratoga*'s VF-3 Squadron. Nine F2F-1s were loaned to VF-5B (Bombing Five) from the San Diego Battle Force Pool, to be used for bombing during the Panama manoeuvres. When the first US Marine squadrons were formed, one of them, VMF-2, was assigned three F2F-1s and six F3F-1s, but the F2Fs were replaced within six months by F3F-2s. With the arrival of the F3F, the writing was on the wall for the biplane, but it was to be another year before the monoplane eventually arrived on the scene.

Technical details FF-1 and F2F-1

FF-1

Wing span — upper	34 ft. 6 in.
Wing span — lower	31 ft. 6 in.
L.O.A.	24 ft. 6 in.
H.O.A.	11 ft. 1 in.
Weight empty	3,076 lb.
Weight loaded	4,655 lb.
Speed (max.)	201 mph.
Speed (cruising)	122 mph.
Range	732 miles.
Service ceiling	22,400 ft.
Rate of climb	1,150 ft. per min.
Armament	2 × .30 calibre M/G.
	1 × .30 calibre M/G (flexible)
	2 × 100 lb. bombs
Engine	Wright R-1820-F, 750 hp.

F2F-1

Wing span — upper	28 ft. 6 in.
Wing span — lower	26 ft.
L.O.A.	21 ft. 3 in.
H.O.A.	10 ft. 8 in.
Weight empty	2,622 lb.
Weight loaded	3,782 lb.
Speed (max.)	231 mph.
Speed (cruising)	140 mph.
Range	750 miles.
Service ceiling	27,000 ft.
Rate of climb	2,200 ft. per min.
Armament	2 × .30 calibre M/G (fixed)
	2 × 100 lb. bombs.

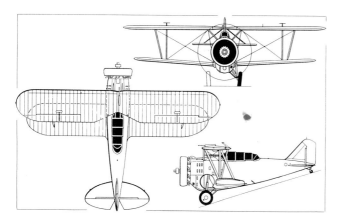

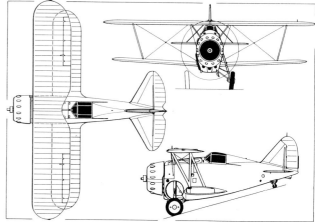

FF-1 model variations

XFF-1
The first aircraft to be built by Grumman. A biplane powered by a Wright R-1820-E, it was the first Navy fighter to have a retractable undercarriage, and the first to have an enclosed cockpit.

FF-1
Production model of the XFF-1. Engine changed to the Wright R-1820-F. Twenty-seven were built, all going to the US Navy.

FF-2
Twenty-two were built, all of them FF-1s. They were taken to the NAF (Naval Air Factory) and converted to dual-control aircraft and given the designation FF-2.

XSF-1
Basically the same design as the FF-1, but with an extended engine cowling. All the guns and ammunition were removed and larger fuel tanks installed, giving an increase of 45 gallons.

SF-1
Production model of the XSF-1. Powered by the Wright R-1820-78 engine, it was used as a scout aircraft. Thirty-three were built, but the last one became the XSF-2.

XSF-2
The same as the SF-1, but powered by the Pratt and Whitney R-1535-72 engine.

XSBF-1
This was a one-off version of a scout/bomber capable of carrying one 500 lb. or two 100 lb. bombs.

F2F-1 model variations

XF2F-1
The second of Grumman's fighters. It had a metal semi-monocoque fuselage and fabric-covered metal wings. The engine was a Pratt and Whitney XR-1535-44 Twin Wasp Junior.

F2F-1
Production model of the XF2F-1, armed with 0.3 inch Browning machine guns. Powered by Pratt and Whitney R-1535-44 engine.

F3F

With the F2F nearing the end of its operational life, a new, more powerful fighter was needed and Grumman received a contract for $78,850 to produce one. Designated XF3F-1 by the Bureau of Aeronautics and G-11 by Grumman, the new fighter retained the same engine as the F2F-1, but incorporated a number of design changes. The length of the fuselage was increased by 1 ft. 10 in., which improved the stability of the aircraft considerably, the wings were extended by 3 ft. 6 in., increasing the overall wing area by 31 square feet and the engine was given a longer chord.

The XF3F had a disastrous start. It took off on its maiden fligth on 20 March 1935 and completed three successful flights. On 22 March, the pilot, Jimmy Collins, who was a contract test pilot, was instructed to carry out a series of terminal velocity dives during the 6 flights scheduled. On the last dive, Collins took the XF3F-1 to 20,000 feet and dived with instructions to level off at 10,000 feet and subject the aircraft to its maximum design limitations of 9g on recovery. But the pull-out was too abrupt, according to observers, and it was estimated that the aircraft was subjected to something between 11g and 15g, way above the design limitations. The sudden pull-out ripped the engine from its mountings and tore the left wing off, with the result that the XF3F-1 plunged into the ground killing Collins instantly.

Within two months a second XF3F-1 was completed and readied for testing. Lee Gehlbach was to fly the tests. On 9 May, the second prototype took off on its maiden flight and completed its initial tests with no problems at all. The aircraft was then taken to NAS Anacostia for dive and spin tests. Lee Gehlbach completed the dive tests that had killed Jimmy Collins, and started to test the aircraft under spinning conditions. Gehlbach took the aircraft to 12,000 feet and put it into a spin to test the stability of the XF3F-1. After a few seconds of spin, Gehlbach was seen struggling with the controls. He was even seen standing upright in the cockpit, hoping that the wind pressure on his body would bring the aircraft out of the spin. But on reaching an altitude of 2,000 feet, with the earth rushing towards him at 200 feet per second, Gehlbach took to his parachute. Seconds later the XF3F-1 smashed into a tree, while Lee Gehlbach floated down to safety.

Within three weeks, Grumman had built a third XF3F using some of the salvaged parts from the second of the prototypes. This time the aircraft was fitted with an enlarged rudder and the initial testing began on 20 June 1935. Three weeks later, extremely rigorous Navy acceptance trials commenced. This time all went well, the XF3F completing all the tests faultlessly. Surprisingly, few modifications were requested, and the offical handing-over took place on

Above: Three F3F-1s of VF-4 Squadron on exercise.

1 August 1935. Three weeks later an order for a further fifty-four F3F-1s was placed.

These aircraft were to have the improved R-1535-84 Twin Wasp Junior engine generating 700 hp, with a Hamilton-Standard, 8 ft. 6 in. diameter bladed propeller that had a hydraulically-controlled pitch (the other prototypes had had the Lycoming-Smith mechanically-controlled pitch propellers).

The F3F-1 was armed with fixed machine-guns: one .30 Model 2 Browning mounted on the port upper side of the fuselage, with 500 rounds of ammunition, and a .50 Browning mounted on the starboard upper side of the fuselage, with 200 rounds of ammunition. A telescopic sight was installed on the upper part of the fuselage in front of the pilot, and protruding through the windscreen, and a gun camera was mounted on the upper wing. Provision was made for two 100 lb. bombs to be fitted beneath the lower wings.

The G-32A, also known as the 'Little Red Ship', was used as a demonstrator by Grumman.

Although the F3F-1 was much more manoeuvrable than any of its predecessors, doubt was still expressed about its spinning characteristics. The Navy forbade intentional spinning in the aircraft and restricted recovery to 8 g. Pilots soon found that flying the F3F was like driving a sports car, the controls were light to the touch and extremely responsive, in fact so responsive that if the pilot was not careful he could easily overstress the aircraft pulling it out of high-speed dives. Despite being heavier and larger than the F2F-1, it was possible to be airborne within 200 feet at a speed of 50 knots, and although having an inferior climb rate (1,900 feet per minute) it achieved the same speed of 230 mph at sea level.

The first squadron to receive the F3F, was VF-5B aboard the aircraft carrier *USS Ranger,* in June 1936. Whilst the squadron was familiarising itself with the F3F and practising bombing tactics, an identical accident to that which had

happened to the test pilot Jimmy Collins the previous year occurred. The pilot concerned, Ensign Milton Stephens, was practising bombing with miniature bombs, dropping them from a 70 per cent dive at an altitude of 2,000 feet and levelling out at 1,000 feet. These figures had to be strictly adhered to: if they were not, then the drop would be disqualified. The pull-out was at 1,000 feet, which, if the whole operational sequence was done properly, would result in a maximum of 5.5 g, well within the stress limits for the aircraft. Ensign Stephens calculated that if he released his bombs at an altitude of 1,400 feet and then levelled out with a snap pull-out at 1,000 feet, he would greatly increase his accuracy. On the occasion that he actually carried out this manoeuvre, his accelerometer read 16 g, which was more than twice the accepted limit. On the final day of the series of trials, Ensign Stephens was the last to go and after releasing the bombs, his aircraft literally came apart in the air as he pulled out of the dive, with the result that the aircraft was destroyed and the pilot killed. All the aircraft of VF-6B were grounded until they had been examined, but nothing was ever found and the result of the investigation was put down to pilot error. There were a few other stress related accidents during 1936 involving the F3F, with the result that the Bureau of Aeronautics carried out a static test on the aircraft to stress it to destruction. As a result of their findings the upper wing beam was strengthened together with the aileron bell-cranks, and the stress limit was raised to 9 g.

With these problems resolved, distribution of the F3F recommenced, including six to VMF-1 of the US Marine Corps. But the wind of change was sweeping through the aircraft industry and the Bureau of Aeronautics was already looking at the next generation of single-seat fighters; this precluded building any more biplanes.

On 2 March 1936, the US Navy asked Grumman to build another single-seat fighter around the Wright XR-1670 engine. The aircraft was designated XF4F-1 and had originally been designed as a biplane. Grumman decided that time was running out for the biplane, and redesigned it as a monoplane, with the designation XF4F-2. The F3F was still in production at this time and it was decided that the last production model would have the Wright Cyclone XR-1820-22 engine. This engine was installed in the XF3F-2 and was a nine-cylinder, two-speed, supercharged, air-cooled radial engine generating 850 hp, turning a three-bladed, Hamilton-Standard, constant pitch propeller of 9 ft diameter. The diameter of the Wright Cyclone engine, was some ten inches greater than that of the Twin Wasp Junior engine, which exaggerated the barrel shape of the aircraft even more. The XF3F-2 carried a total of 130 gallons of fuel, 83 gallons in the main tank and 47 gallons in the reserve, considerably more than the XF3F-1. The XF3F-2's performance was considerably better all round than

An F3F-1 of VF-4 Squadron.

The prototype of the XF3F-2.

An F3F-2 of VMF-2, US Marine Corps, after a wheels-up landing. Very little damage was sustained.

the XF3F-1 and so impressed the Navy that they placed the largest order to date with Grumman for eighty-one.

There were some initial problems prior to delivery to the various squadrons, including carburettor and oil cooling, but these were quickly resolved and on 1 December 1937, VF-6 took delivery of the first two F3F-2s aboard the *USS Enterprise*. The next six F3F-2s were delivered to the US Marine Corps squadron VMF-2, followed later by a further six. VMF-1 received a total of seventeen and VF-6 a further

An F3F-2 of VF-6 'Fighting Six' Squadron at Farmingdale, prior to delivery to the US Navy.

sixteen, which completed the complement for their squadrons; the remainder were kept as spares. One of the spares was redesignated XF3F-3 and sent for evaluation tests at Anacostia after minor changes to the cowling and undercarriage.

Grumman also built three civil versions of the F3F and the first, the G-22, licence number NR-1050, was completed in December 1936, which meant in fact that it was flying even before the production F3F-2. In reality it was not a true F3F — it was a hybrid. The fuselage was that of an F3F-2 with a Cyclone engine, and the wings were that of an F2F-1, but it had one unusual feature and that was an enlarged rudder. This aircraft was the Gulfhawk II and was the fastest of all Grumman's biplanes, with a top speed of 290 mph and a climb rate of 3,000 feet per minute. Powered by a Wright R-1820-G engine, it was lighter than the military version, and was specially rigged for aerobatics. Al Williams, Gulf's aviation manager, took the highly-polished aircraft on a European tour in 1938 and during the war years, General Hap Arnold ordered the aircraft to tour the Air Force's training bases, giving exhibitions in precision flying and aerobatics. To enable the aircraft to carry out inverted flying for up to thirty minutes, a second scavenger pump and five drain lines were installed.

In 1938, Gulf Oil had another Gulfhawk built, the G-32, licence number NC-1051, named appropriately Gulfhawk III and primarily used as a utility aircraft by Major Williams. It differed from the previous model inasmuch as the wings were standard F3F-2 wings, and a second cockpit was installed which, although having a continuous centre section of the canopy, had two rearward-sliding sections. The addition of split flaps on the trailing edges of the upper wing completed the overall differences. It was powered by a Wright GR-1820-G5 Cyclone engine generating 950 hp. In 1942, Gulf Oil gave the aircraft to the US Army to be used as a ferry pilot trainer.

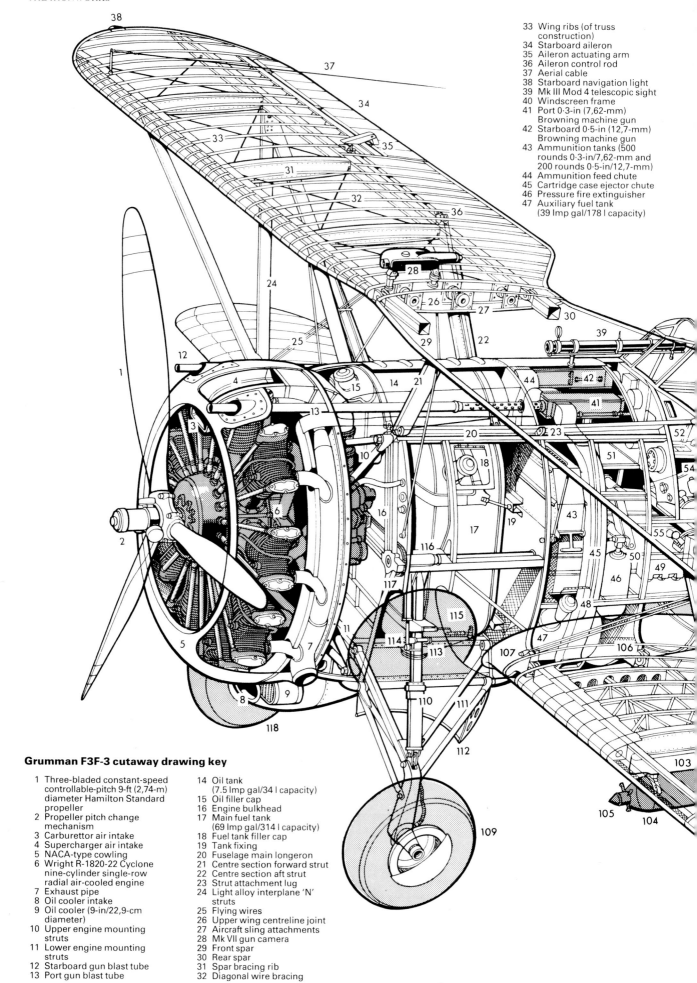

Grumman F3F-3 cutaway drawing key

1 Three-bladed constant-speed
   controllable-pitch 9-ft (2,74-m)
   diameter Hamilton Standard
   propeller
2 Propeller pitch change
   mechanism
3 Carburettor air intake
4 Supercharger air intake
5 NACA-type cowling
6 Wright R-1820-22 Cyclone
   nine-cylinder single-row
   radial air-cooled engine
7 Exhaust pipe
8 Oil cooler intake
9 Oil cooler (9-in/22,9-cm
   diameter)
10 Upper engine mounting
   struts
11 Lower engine mounting
   struts
12 Starboard gun blast tube
13 Port gun blast tube

14 Oil tank
   (7.5 Imp gal/34 l capacity)
15 Oil filler cap
16 Engine bulkhead
17 Main fuel tank
   (69 Imp gal/314 l capacity)
18 Fuel tank filler cap
19 Tank fixing
20 Fuselage main longeron
21 Centre section forward strut
22 Centre section aft strut
23 Strut attachment lug
24 Light alloy interplane 'N'
   struts
25 Flying wires
26 Upper wing centreline joint
27 Aircraft sling attachments
28 Mk VII gun camera
29 Front spar
30 Rear spar
31 Spar bracing rib
32 Diagonal wire bracing

33 Wing ribs (of truss
   construction)
34 Starboard aileron
35 Aileron actuating arm
36 Aileron control rod
37 Aerial cable
38 Starboard navigation light
39 Mk III Mod 4 telescopic sight
40 Windscreen frame
41 Port 0·3-in (7,62-mm)
   Browning machine gun
42 Starboard 0·5-in (12,7-mm)
   Browning machine gun
43 Ammunition tanks (500
   rounds 0·3-in/7,62-mm and
   200 rounds 0·5-in/12,7-mm)
44 Ammunition feed chute
45 Cartridge case ejector chute
46 Pressure fire extinguisher
47 Auxiliary fuel tank
   (39 Imp gal/178 l capacity)

48 Auxiliary tank filler
49 Very pistol cartridge holder
50 Rudder pedal
51 Chart board
52 Instrument panel
53 Pilot's seat
54 Throttle and propeller controls
55 Bomb release levers
56 Tailplane trim control
57 Access step
58 Cockpit floor structure
59 Adjustable seat support structure
60 Headrest
61 Aft-sliding canopy
62 Life raft
63 D/F loop
64 Junction box
65 Equipment bay access door
66 Dynamotor unit
67 Radio transmitter
68 Radio receiver
69 First aid kit
70 Emergency rations and water supply
71 Dorsal light
72 Fuselage frames (Z section)
73 Tailplane incidence control rod
74 Lift-hoist tube

75 Controls access cover
76 Rudder and elevator control cables
77 Fin structure (solid section ribs)
78 Fin/fuselage attachment
79 Rudder post
80 Rudder structure (fabric covered)
81 Rubber hinge
82 Trim tab
83 Trim actuator
84 Tailcone

85 Arrester hook fairing
86 Tail light
87 Variable-incidence tailplane
88 Tailplane structure
89 Elevator (fabric covered)
90 Arrester hook (extended)
91 Retractable tailwheel (solid rubber tyre)
92 Tailwheel shock absorber strut
93 Port upper wing structure

94 Port navigation light
95 Interplane 'N' struts
96 Lower wing front spar
97 Lower wing rear spar
98 Spar bracing rib
99 Wing ribs
100 Leading edge construction
101 Wire bracing
102 Retractable landing light
103 Mk XLI bomb rack
104 Mk IV 116-lb (52.7-kg) demolition bomb
105 Fuse unit
106 Wing spar root fitting

107 Flying wire attachment
108 Wing root fillet
109 Port mainwheel (26 in x 6 in/66 cm × 15 cm)
110 Oleo strut
111 Radius arms
112 Fairing door
113 Retraction strut
114 Lock actuator
115 Wheel well
116 Retraction strut axle mounting
117 Retraction chain drive
118 Starboard mainwheel

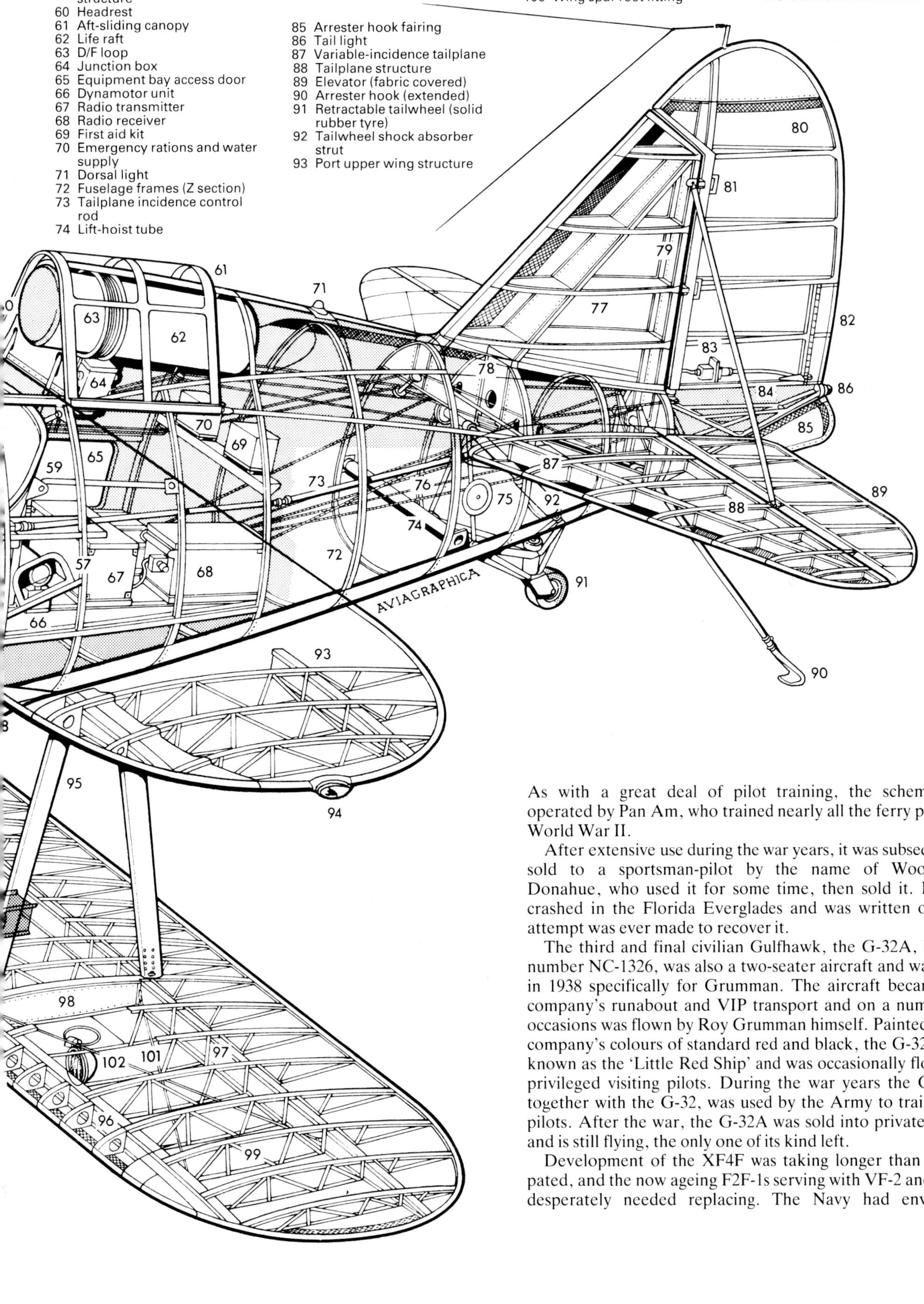

As with a great deal of pilot training, the scheme was operated by Pan Am, who trained nearly all the ferry pilots of World War II.

After extensive use during the war years, it was subsequently sold to a sportsman-pilot by the name of Woolworth Donahue, who used it for some time, then sold it. It later crashed in the Florida Everglades and was written off. No attempt was ever made to recover it.

The third and final civilian Gulfhawk, the G-32A, licence number NC-1326, was also a two-seater aircraft and was built in 1938 specifically for Grumman. The aircraft became the company's runabout and VIP transport and on a number of occasions was flown by Roy Grumman himself. Painted in the company's colours of standard red and black, the G-32A was known as the 'Little Red Ship' and was occasionally flown by privileged visiting pilots. During the war years the G-32A, together with the G-32, was used by the Army to train ferry pilots. After the war, the G-32A was sold into private hands and is still flying, the only one of its kind left.

Development of the XF4F was taking longer than anticipated, and the now ageing F2F-1s serving with VF-2 and VF-5 desperately needed replacing. The Navy had envisaged

6402

An F3F-3 of VF-5 'Screaming Eagles' Squadron at Bethpage, prior to delivery to the US Navy.

forming another squadron, VF-7, with the possibility of another later. So Grumman came up with the idea of upgrading the F3F-2, which would fill the gap until the F4F was ready for service. Although the Navy agreed in principle to the suggestion, they decided that if the improvements were to be acceptable, they would require further test and evaluation before committing themselves to increased production costs. The Navy returned to Grumman one of the F3F-2s that had been delivered to Anacostia as a spare, for conversion to the improved F3F-2, or F3F-3 as it was to be designated. A new streamlined windscreen was fitted, similar to the one that would eventually be fitted on the F4F, and there was a redesigned engine cowling and wing leading edge and fuselage fairing plates. Fittings were also attached to the aircraft to enable wind tunnel tests to be carried out at the Langley Test Facility. While waiting for the tests to be carried out, various propellers were tested. This took over a month to complete, but on 21 June 1938, the Navy ordered twenty-seven upgraded F3F-2 fighters, redesignating them F3F-3s. The Navy wanted to test the aircraft even further before committing themselves to a definite production model, so they decided to evaluate the wing flaps that Grumman had installed on the G-32A. To do this, the G-32As wing had to be removed and fitted to one of the F3F-3s and the aircraft was returned to Anacostia for trials. The F3F-3 was put through a series of exhaustive tests at both Anacostia and at the Naval Air Factory in Philadelphia, where the experimental carrier facility was based. The results were unsatisfactory as far as the Navy were concerned and it was decided that the small improvements shown in the approach and landing speeds were not sufficient to justify the fitting of the heavier wing. The aircraft was returned to Grumman to have the wing removed and the original replaced and also to have some minor modifications carried out.

On 29 October, Grumman sent the XF3F-3 back to the

Navy for Production Service Acceptance Trials. These trials were completed on 14 December, the examiners satisfied that Grumman had fulfilled all the guarantees they had made. Because of the variety of changes that had been made to the F3F-3, the production of the aircraft was delayed somewhat longer than had been originally anticipated and the aircraft carrier *USS Yorktown*, whence the aircraft had been destined, had already sailed. On board the *Yorktown* were the F2F-1s of VF-5 and it was these aircraft that the F3F-3s were to replace. The carrier sailed from Norfolk, Virginia, to San Diego, California, and it was here, in May, that the aircraft were finally transferred. The F3F-3 was accepted with great delight by the pilots, who rated it as the best biplane in the Navy. Although outwardly it was almost identical to the F3F-2 and its performance was only marginally better, the pilots all agreed that it handled better than the F3F-2. It was more manoeuvrable, slightly faster and could make three-point landings under any power or conditions.

The F2F-1s were not disposed of when they were replaced, but assigned to VF-7, although, by the end of 1941, all the biplanes had disappeared from front line squadrons, the last from US Marine squadrons VMF-111 and VMF-211. At the beginning of 1942 there were still twenty-three F2F-1s and 117 F3Fs assigned to various stations in the USA. There were a number of F3F-1s (VF-74) at Norfolk, Virginia, F3F-2s (VF-5) in Miami, and F3F-3s at Corpus Christi, Texas.

It was not until 1943 that the last of the now famous Grumman biplanes were struck from the Navy's register, and although it never fired its guns in anger, the F3F provided a springboard for US Naval aviation. The F4F was a direct result, and the aviation world knows what an impact this aircraft had during World War II.

Technical details F3F

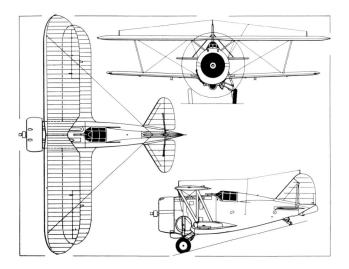

Weight empty	F3F-1 — 2,952 lb. F3F-2 — 3,254 lb. F3F-3 — 3,285 lb.
Weight loaded	F3F-1 — 4,170 lb. F3F-2 — 4,498 lb. F3F-3 — 4,543 lb.
Max. speed	F3F-1 — 215 mph. F3F-2 — 234 mph. F3F-3 — 239 mph.
Range	F3F-1 — 998 miles. F3F-2 — 1,130 miles. F3F-3 — 1,150 miles.
Service ceiling	F3F-1 — 28,500 ft. F3F-2 — 32,300 ft. F3F-3 — 33,200 ft.
Rate of climb	F3F-1 — 1,900 ft. per min. F3F-2 — 2,800 ft. per min. F3F-3 — 2,750 ft. per min.
Engine	F3F-1 — Pratt and Whitney R-1535-84 Twin Wasp Junior, direct drive, single-stage, supercharged, 14-cylinder, radial, air, cooled, rated at 700 horsepower. F3F-2 — Wright R-1820-22 Cyclone, two-speed, supercharged, nine-cylinder, air-cooled engine, rated at 950 horse-power. F3F-3 — As F3F-2.
Armament	One 0.5 in. Browning machine gun. One 0.3 in. Browning machine gun. Two 116 lb. Mk IV demolition bombs.

Wing span	32 ft. (Upper). 29 ft. 6 in. (Lower).
Wing area	260.6 sq. ft.
Length overall	F3F-1 — 23 ft. 3⅛ in. F3F-2&3 — 23 ft.
Height overall	F3F-1 — 9 ft. 1 in. F3F-2&3 — 9 ft. 4 in.

F3F model variations

XF3F-1
Prototype of the last military biplane. Longer fuselage and wingspan than the F2F-1. The first of three prototypes built crashed during tests, then the second was built and that crashed, and the third was built from parts cannibalized from the second. Powered by the Pratt and Whitney R-1575-72 engine.

F3F-1
Production model, but powered by the Pratt and Whitney R-1535-84 engine. The armament was 0.5 in. Browning machine-guns fitted along the top of the engine cowling.

XF3F-2
The last of the F3F-1 series, modified with a new tail rudder. Powered by the Wright XR-1820-22 supercharged engine.

F3F-2
Production model with a three-bladed propeller.

XF3F-3
This was an F3F-2 with a modified engine cowling and fuselage.

F3F-3
Production model, powered by a Wright R-1820-22 engine.

F4F Wildcat

In November 1935, the US Navy's Bureau of Aeronautics announced that they were in the market for a new carrier-based aircraft. To accommodate all the ideas, the Navy initiated a design competition. Grumman reacted immediately and submitted design No. 16 for a biplane, although the market at the time was in favour of monoplanes. The designation XF4F-1 was given to the aircraft, which had an upper and lower wing span of only 27 feet, compared to the 32 feet of the F3F-1. The project got no further than the design stage, because the Brewster Company was awarded the contract for their XF2A-1, which was a monoplane with a retractable undercarriage.

Leroy Grumman was not one to be left behind, so he set his designers and engineers to work building a monoplane. On 28 July 1936, Grumman was awarded a contract for the XF4F-2, which was to be the forerunner of all the F4Fs. The engine chosen to power the XF4F-2 was the Pratt and Whitney R-1830 'Twin Wasp', a two-row, fourteen-cylinder, air-cooled engine. Already a proven engine, it was in service with the Martin 130 'China Clipper' and in the Consolidated PBY. It was also equipped with a single-speed, single-stage supercharger, and developed 900 hp at 12,000 feet. The supercharger was a breakthrough for engine development; prior to this, the higher an aircraft flew, the less horsepower was developed. Essentially the supercharger acted as a pump which sucked in more air and compressed it before vapourized fuel was injected. Experiments were carried out on a two-

speed, two-stage supercharger which would allow an aircraft to operate at an even greater height.

The initial flight of the F4F-2 was made by Robert L. Hall on 2 September 1937. Following tests, the XF4F-2 was flown to Anacostia for further tests. The tests were not very successful, there were persistent engine problems and it was discovered that the bearings in the crankshaft were breaking up. After extensive development, a bearing with a silver-lead surface was used and this solved the problem. Over the next few months, Bob Hall flew the XF4F-2 back to Bethpage periodically for servicing, and it was during one of these flights that he nearly lost his life. The aircraft was at 10,000 feet above Bethpage when several shot bags, which had been placed as ballast in the aft section of the fuselage, caught fire. Fortunately Bob Hall managed to make an emergency landing and the fire was put out, but not before the aircraft had been badly damaged. It was never discovered exactly how the fire had started, but one theory was that the shot bags had somehow become covered in oil or petrol and had been ignited by sparks passing through the fuselage. Although badly damaged by fire, the XF4F-2 was back for tests at

Above: Three F4F-3 Wildcats of VF-5 in overall matt light grey with white and black lettering. The national insignia is half the standard size. This paint scheme was used from 30 December 1940 until 13 October 1941.

Vahlgrem two days later. This time cameras were mounted in the cockpit to film the instrument panel whilst the aircraft was put through a series of dives and spins. The pilot for these tests was a man called McAvoy who worked for the National Advisory Committee for Aeronautics (NACA) as a test pilot. He carried out a number of manoeuvres with both wing guns fitted, with them removed, and with the guns replaced by 1,000 lb. bombs. Some of the pull-outs from the dives registered 8.5 g, which spoke volumes for the strength of the aircraft.

One of the US Navy test pilots, Lt. Carson, flew the XF4F-2 back to Anacostia for further tests, this time in competition with the Brewster XF2A-1 and the Seversky NF-1. The tests began on 1 March and were to last three months, during which all three aircraft were put through an identical test programme. This included take-off and landing tests, simulated carrier landings, stability checks, armament tests and instrument reliability. These were only a few of the large number of tests carried out. Radios were installed and two different propellers tried, one with a diameter of ten feet, the other nine feet nine inches with a spinner.

The tests on the three aircraft were exhaustive and by the middle of March the XF4F-2 had accumulated over sixteen hours of flight time. Already, even at this early stage, comparisons were being made and the maximum speeds were listed as XF4F-2: 290 mph, NF-1: 278 mph, XF2A-1: 268 mph.

At the beginning of April, the XF4F-2 was flown to the Naval Air Factory at Philadelphia for catapult and simulated deck landings and it was here that the XF4F-2 suffered its second serious accident. During a simulated deck landing, the engine suddenly cut-out. Left with no alternative, the pilot made a crash landing on a farm owned by Campbell Soups. Fortunately the pilot was unhurt and the aircraft was shipped back to Bethpage for repair. While the XF4F-2 was being repaired, Grumman were delivering the F3F-2 biplane, fitted with the Wright Cyclone R-1820 engine, to the Navy. In June the same year, Grumman received an order from the Navy for a twin-engined, carrier fighter and it was this aircraft, the XF5F-1, that ultimately led to the development of the F7F Tigercat. In the meantime, the XF4F-2 returned to Anacostia after two weeks of intensive repair work and later that month the Navy made its choice: it chose the Brewster XF2A-1, because, basically, it had been the most trouble-free of the aircraft tested. The Navy ordered fifty four F2A-1s from Brewster and this was regarded as a major setback for Grumman.

Although the Navy had chosen the XF2A-1, they had been impressed by the qualities shown by the XF4F-2 and decided to continue the development of the aircraft by awarding a separate contract to Grumman. One of the improvements made to the XF4F-2 was the fitting of a two-stage supercharger to the engine, enabling the aircraft to maintain power over a wide range of altitudes. The XF4F-2 was lost in April 1938 whilst on a flight test at the Naval Air Factory (NAF), apparently having ran out of fuel. It was later rebuilt as the XF4F-3, with a larger wing span, an increased wing surface, and squared wing tips. The Hamilton-Standard, hydraulically controlled, two-position propeller was replaced by the Curtiss Wright electrically controlled, constant speed propeller, much to the consternation of many US Navy pilots. Curtiss maintained that in the event of an engine malfunction, the propeller would go to full low pitch (high rpm), but the majority of pilots maintained that, in fact, the propeller would almost certainly go to full high pitch (1,400 prm), with the result that the pilot would be unable to maintain flying speed with the gear down. Most pilots hated the Curtiss Electric propeller. A new engine was also designed for the XF4F-3, the Pratt and Whitney XR-1830-76. It had a two-stage, two-speed supercharger, with a rating of 1,050 hp at 11,000 feet and 1,000 hp at 19,000 feet. It was somewhat heavier and more complex than the previous engine, however.

An XF4F-3 undergoing engine tests at Bethpage. Note the tube-sight through the windscreen.

The first XF4F-3 flew on the morning of 12 February 1939. The aircraft then underwent strenuous trials, not only by the manufacturers, but also by Navy test pilots. Three months after the completion of these tests, the aircraft was returned to Bethpage for improvements to the aileron area, which was reduced. After the modifications had been made, the XF4F-3 was flown to the Naval Air Factory in Philadelphia for catapult tests, deck landing trials and night flying evaluation.

The tests were extremely satisfactory, although there were problems with engine cooling, especially at high altitudes. Many ideas were tried, including various propeller spinners, cowl arrangements and variations to the propeller blade shanks. The latter was found to be the most successful, and was ultimately applied to all the F4Fs.

While the XF4F-3 was still going through its assessment stage, the US Navy decided that this was the aircraft that they wanted as a carrier fighter. In August 1939, one month before the start of World War II, a contract was awarded to Grumman for fifty-four F4F-3s.

The US government updated the Expansion Act of 1938, raising the inventory limits for naval aircraft to 3,000, and sanctioning the building of two more aircraft carriers. Grumman was already into production of the F4F-3 by the end of August, and the first production aircraft was ready for testing by February 1940.

There were still problems with the engine at high altitudes and it was not until a fuel tank pressurization system had been installed that these were cured. The tests continued, and the XF4F-3 was even used as a chase plane for the XF5F-1, which was making its initial test flights. The first F4F-3 was sent to Pratt and Whitney for engine tests and evaluation, while the second production model was flown to Anacostia to start Board of Inspection trials. Of all the innovations that had been built into the F4F, one was to cause more problems than any other. Built into the wings of the aircraft were flotation bags that were designed to keep the aircraft afloat in the event of ditching. Problems arose on a couple of occasions when the flotation bags inflated during flight. On the first occasion, the pilot managed to put the aircraft into a dive and rip the bags free from the wings. When the aircraft landed, engineers found that one wing was buckled and the other had ripples in it. On the second occasion, the pilot managed to rip one of the flotation bags free, but not the other. This caused the aircraft to spin out of control and crash, and the pilot, Ensign Howell of VF-42, was killed. After this tragic accident, the flotation bags were removed from all the other aircraft.

Finally, the Navy accepted the F4F-3 and declared it satisfactory for carrier service, although with certain reservations. All the claims of performance were met within the bounds of acceptability. The weight of 5,238 lb. empty was under the initial estimate by 103 lb., the maximum speed of 331 mph was under the original guaranteed speed of 350 mph, and the ceiling of 37,000 feet was found to be as Grumman had stated. Certain improvements were recommended by the Board, but they were the kind of recommendations that would have been made to any new aircraft at that time.

Armament tests were carried out, with satisfactory results. There were, of course, the odd gremlins, like the problem of belt feeding the wing-mounted machine-guns when executing high-g manoeuvres. The four wing-mounted machine guns were found to decrease the maximum speed by 3 mph.

The F4F Wildcat, which made such a lasting impression on the Pacific War, made its first combat appearance, not in the colours of the US Navy, but in the livery of the French Navy. France's interest in the F4F started at the beginning of 1940, when the German Army was making its way across France in a bid to conquer Europe. They ordered 100 F4Fs, designated G-36A and G-36B by the French, on the understanding that a suitable engine would be found, and it was this that was to cause problems, because the engine manufacturers were not yet geared for military demands. Grumman decided to use the Wright R-1820-205A Cyclone, nine-cylinder, single-row, radial engine, developing 1,200 hp and equipped with a single-stage, two-speed supercharger. Hardly had flight testing of the new engine begun in the F4F, when France surrendered to the invading German Forces. The British stepped in immediately, assumed delivery of all the French aircraft and ordered an additional 81 F4Fs for themselves, renaming them Martlet 1s.

The US Navy was experiencing difficulty at this time with the R-1830 engine, so it ordered two Wildcats, designated XF4F-5, to be fitted with the R-1820-40 engine. These two aircraft made extensive tests at Anacostia during the summer of 1940, and although the tests were considered successful, the R-1820-40 engine was not used on the production F4F-3s. Late in 1940, the US Navy ordered an additional F4F-3 to be fitted with a Pratt and Whitney R-1830-90 Twin Wasp engine. It had a single-stage, two-speed supercharger and gave 1,200 hp on take-off and 1,000 hp at 12,000 feet when in high blower. The aircraft was redesignated XF4F-6, and was used primarily as a flying test-bed at Anacostia. The performance and handling characteristics were very similar to the two-stage engine used in the F4F-3.

Because of the pressure on Grumman to produce the Wildcat, a total of 65 F4F-3s were produced with the single-stage engine. They were designated F4F-3As and the majority were assigned to US Marine squadrons, although the British bought a number of them and renamed them Martlet 2s and 3s.

Deliveries of the Wildcat started to become a problem after the fall of France in the June of 1940, and by early December of the same year only twenty-two aircraft had been accepted by the Navy. These aircraft went immediately to the Naval Air Station Norfolk, Virginia, for assignment to the carriers *Ranger* and *Wasp*, and to replace the now ageing F3F biplane.

The first fatal accident involving the F4F happened at this time. Lt. (jg) Johnson was killed whilst on a familiarization flight in the original XF4F-3. It appears he got the flap raising lever confused with the fuel control lever, and consequently shut off the fuel instead of raising the flaps. The aircraft's engine stopped almost immediately, causing the Wildcat to crash into a railway yard at the end of the runway.

Although the F4Fs were armed with four wing-mounted .50 calibre machine guns, they never had the armoured protection of the British aircraft. The RAF and RN aircraft had armoured plating around the most vulnerable parts (including the pilot), and self-sealing tanks.

Early in January 1941 the *Ranger* and *Wasp*, sailed for Guantanamo with two squadrons of F4Fs aboard. The aircraft were still in their distinctive livery of grey fuselage, yellow topped wing surfaces, various coloured cowl rings, and either a black or green tail, depending on which carrier the aircraft came from. Two months later, the order came from the Pentagon to paint all US Naval aircraft light grey overall, and this was to be the end of the brightly-coloured aircraft. The training and familiarization programme carried out aboard the carriers during their winter cruises uncovered a number of minor, yet very important problems. The most important of these was the raising and lowering of the landing gear. While virtually all other aircraft manufacturers had moved on to powered retraction and lowering landing gear systems, F4F pilots had to manually operate their landing gear, and one thing they had to watch most carefully was not to get the cord of the flying helmet caught in the handle. As bizarre as this may sound, it was such an incident that caused the death of one pilot. Shortly after leaving the carrier, the pilot started to wind up the gear (29½ turns), only to discover that his headset cord had caught in the handle. Unfortunately the pilot's head had been pulled downwards and he lost control, with the result that he crashed into the sea.

Even the guns had steel cables running from their bolt mechanisms to four individual handles in the cockpit floor, where a strong upwards pull was needed to cock them. The cowl flaps were also hand cranked, as was the arresting hook. The flaps were the only part of the aircraft not to be manually operated, but were activated by means of a vacuum tank, which was situated behind the pilot's head. It was said that the pilot did everything bar pull the aircraft through the air with his teeth.

By the beginning of February 1941 the Grumman production line was in full swing. March saw the first deliveries to VF-71, when eighteen F4F-3As were flown into Anacostia for familiarization programmes. VF-6 Squadron at NAS La Mesa, California, also received F4F-3As but with the new two-speed engine installed. The first Marine squadrons to be equipped with F4F-3As, VMF-11, VMF-121, VMF-211 and VMF-221, had, by the end of October, received sixty, five Wildcats — as they were now officially known.

Whilst the US Navy and Marine Corps squadrons were still preparing for the forthcoming conflict, across the Atlantic the Royal Navy's Fleet Air Arm was already engaging the enemy. The distinction of the first American aircraft to shoot down an enemy aircraft was to fall to the Fleet Air Arm, on Christmas Day 1940, when a Junkers 88 tried to sneak in and bomb the Royal Navy shore base at Scapa Flow, in the Orkney Islands. The aircraft was intercepted by two F4F-3 Martlets and shot down. The Hamilton-Standard propeller from one of the Martlets (BJ 562) was later presented to the US Navy by the Royal Navy.

The qualities of the F4F Wildcat really became apparent when compared with the ageing, obsolete carrier aircraft that made up the Fleet Air Arm at that time. The Gloster Gladiator biplane was the primary single-seat fighter of the Royal Navy, and although it had given reliable service, it was far too slow. It was supplemented by the Blackburn Skua two-seat, fighter-bomber, and the Fairey Fulmar two-seat fighter. These aircraft were no match for the high performance fighters of the German and Italian Air Forces.

After experiencing the success of the Martlet 1, the Royal Navy ordered 100 F4F-3As, or Martlet IIs as they were known to the British. Although somewhat slower in speed, and less able to match the altitude performance of the two-stage F4F-3, the British requirement for such an aircraft was dictated by circumstances. Grumman developed the 'Sto-wing' with this aircraft, a remarkable innovation that was to revolutionize the capabilities of aircraft carriers.

Up to this time, the wing span of all aircraft on carriers had been dictated by the size of the aircraft carriers, lifts. The F4F Wildcat's wing span allowed for a six-inch clearance at each wing-tip, and, as can be imagined, the amount of manoeuvring required to get the aircraft into position was extremely time-consuming. It also allowed the movement of only one aircraft at a time. The Sto-wing allowed several aircraft to be carried on the lift together, with virtually no manoeuvring required.

The design problem of a folding wing was solved by Roy Grumman, using two paper clips and an eraser. Bending the short ends of the paper clips outwards, he stuck them into the sides of the eraser, which he used to represent the fuselage. Then, by a process of trial and error, he found the position in which the paper clips (Wings) would, by a simple twist, fold flat against the eraser (fuselage).

The Sto-wing depended on the principle of a skewed axis about which the wing hinged, and after that had been perfected the only major problem that remained was the means of securing when unfolded. This was achieved by locking the extended wing into place by means of pins, which in turn were locked into place by a master pin. Roy Grumman's main concern with the Sto-wing was safety. The design of the Sto-wing was such, that in the unlikely event of the wings not locking, they would be forced back against the fuselage whilst the aircraft was moving down the runway, thus preventing the aircraft from taking off. If the wings did not fold back on take-off, they would support the aircraft long enough for it to return to the field. In the case of Grumman

aircraft fitted with folding wings, this is all hypothetical, because there have been no recorded incidents due to wing unlocking.

The Sto-wing meant that for every two fixed-wing aircraft previously carried on an aircraft carrier, five could now be carried. One problem did arise, however: because of the narrowness of the undercarriage, the aircraft had a tendency to be top heavy, and there were several incidents when aircraft toppled over on to other aircraft, especially in a rolling sea, causing a great deal of damage. There does not appear to have been any remedy, other than lashing down.

The Sto-wing concept was so successful that it was incorporated into the later TBF Avengers and Hellcats. Even today, the principle is widely used on carrier-borne aircraft, such as the E-2A Hawkeye.

The first prototype F4F folding-wing aircraft made its initial carrier trials aboard the *USS Yorktown* and was designated the XF4F-4. The wings folded and unfolded hydraulically, but it was soon discovered that the additional weight of the hydraulic system was not acceptable, so the whole sequence of wing folding reverted to manual control by the flight crews.

An F4F-4 on a test flight from Bethpage to Long Island.

A typical example of the cramped maintenance quarters below decks. This F4F Wildcat is undergoing a routine maintenance check.

F4F-4 Wildcats and TBF-1Cs of VC-29 preparing to launch from the escort carrier USS Santee. *Note the 50-gallon drop tank beneath the starboard wing of the F4F-4s.*

The first of the folding-wing Wildcats was retained by Grumman for testing purposes, whilst the remainder were shipped off to Britain. A couple of the aircraft were sent to the Empire Test Pilot School (ETPS) in Wiltshire for evaluation by RAF test pilots. Here, the aircraft was really put through its paces, and although the reports stated that the Wildcat was an extremely good aircraft, there were a number of criticisms. It seemed that there was a carbon monoxide leak into the cockpit and this fault was to appear on a number of subsequent aircraft designs before it was finally rectified. There was also a slight problem with the British radio that had been installed, but this was solved by replacing it with American equipment. Whilst all these tests were being carried out, the rest of the Wildcats were shipped to the Royal Navy base at Hatson on the Orkney Islands, to join No 804 Squadron.

It was at Hatson that the 'Wing-tip' club was formed, after it was discovered that, whilst taxying, the Martlet's wing tip had a tendency to dip into the ground if caught by a sudden crosswind. This was because of the narrow-track undercarriage, which was also incredibly soft, to the consternation of unwary pilots who taxied too fast round the bends of the perimeter track.

Grumman F4F-4 Wildcat cutaway drawing key

1 Starboard navigation light
2 Wingtip
3 Starboard formation light
4 Rear spar
5 Aileron construction
6 Fixed aileron tab
7 All riveted wing construction
8 Lateral stiffeners
9 Forward canted main spar
10 'Crimped' leading edge ribs
11 Solid web forward ribs
12 Starboard outer gun blast tube
13 Carburettor air duct
14 Intake
15 Curtiss three-blade constant-speed propeller
16 Propeller cuffs
17 Propeller hub
18 Engine front face
19 Pressure baffle
20 Forward cowling ring
21 Cooler intake
22 Cooler air duct
23 Pratt & Whitney R-1830-86 radial engine
24 Rear cowling ring/flap support

25 Controllable cowling flaps
26 Downdraft ram air duct
27 Engine mounting ring
28 Anti-detonant regulator unit
29 Cartridge starter
30 Generator
31 Interdooler
32 Engine accessories
33 Bearer assembly welded cluster joint
34 Main beam
35 Lower cowl flap
36 Exhaust stub
37 Starboard mainwheel
38 Undercarriage fairing
39 Lower drag link

40 Hydraulic brake
41 Port mainwheel
42 Detachable hub cover
43 Low-pressure tyre
44 Axle forging
45 Upper drag link
46 Oleo shock strut
47 Ventral fairing
48 Wheel well
49 Pivot point
50 Landing light
51 Main forging
52 Compression link
53 Gun camera port
54 Counter balance
55 Anti-detonant tank
56 Retraction sprocket
57 Gear box
58 Stainless steel firewall
59 Engine bearers
60 Actuation chain (undercarriage)
61 Engine oil tank
62 Oil filter
63 Hoisting sling installation
64 Bullet resistant windscreen
65 Reflector gunsight
66 Panoramic rear-view mirror

67 Wing fold position
68 Adjustable headrest
69 Shoulder harness
70 Canopy track sill
71 Pilot's adjustable seat
72 Instrument panel shroud
73 Undercarriage manual crank

74 Control column
75 Rudder pedals
76 Fuselage/front spar attachment
77 Main fuel filler cap
78 Seat harness attachment
79 Back armour
80 Oxygen cylinder
81 Reserve fuel filler cap
82 Alternative transmitter/receiver (ABA or IFF) installation
83 Battery
84 IFF and ABA dynamotor units
85 Wing flap vacuum tank
86 Handhold
87 Turnover bar
88 Rearward-sliding Plexiglas canopy
89 Streamlined aerial mast
90 Mast support

91 One-man Mk 1A life-raft stowage
92 Upper longeron
93 Toolkit
94 Aerial lead-in
95 Elevator and rudder control runs
96 'L'-section fuselage frames
97 IFF aerial
98 Dorsal lights
99 Whip aerial
100 Wing-fold jury strut
101 Fin fairing
102 Access panel
103 Tailwheel strut extension arm
104 Rudder trim tab control flexible shaft

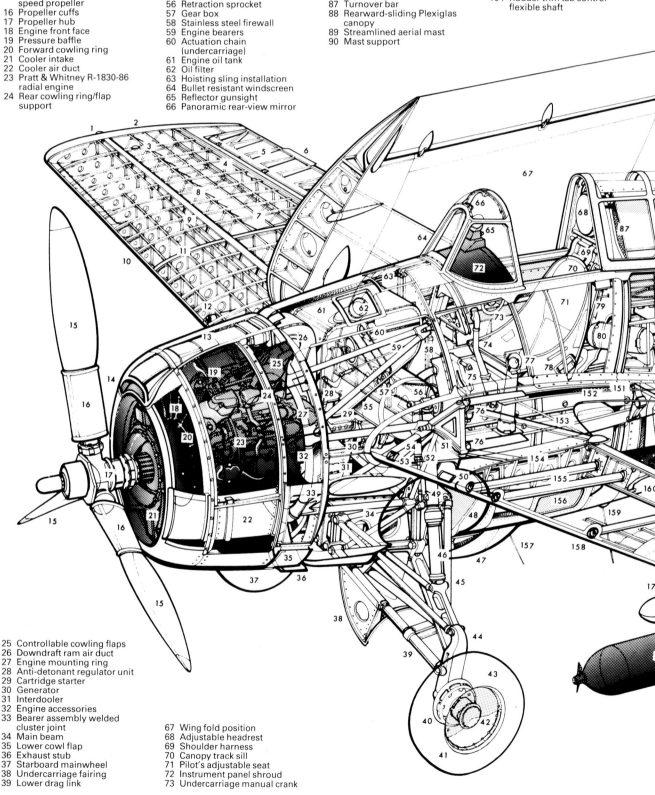

105 Tailplane rib profile
106 Starboard tailplane
107 Static balance
108 Elevator hinge (self-aligning)
109 Fin construction
110 Rudder upper hinge
111 Aerial
112 Insulator
113 Aerial mast
114 Rudder post
115 Rudder construction
116 Aluminium alloy leading-
edge

129 Arresting hook spring
130 Tailwheel shock strut
131 Rear fuselage frame/bulkhead
132 Forged castor fairing
133 Tailwheel
134 Tailwheel centering springs
135 Alclad flush-riveted stressed
skin

158 Outboard gun port
159 ZB antenna
160 Fixed D/F loop
161 Two 0·50-in (12,7-mm)
Browning M-2 machine guns
162 Outboard gun access/loading
panels

163 ABA antenna
164 Flap profile
165 Outboard 0·50-in (12,7-mm)
Browning M-2 machine gun
166 Aileron control linkage
167 Aileron trim tab
168 Port aileron
169 Aileron hinges (self-aligning)
170 Port formation light
171 Port navigation light
172 Wing skinning
173 Bomb rack (optional)
174 Fragmentation bomb
175 Pitot head

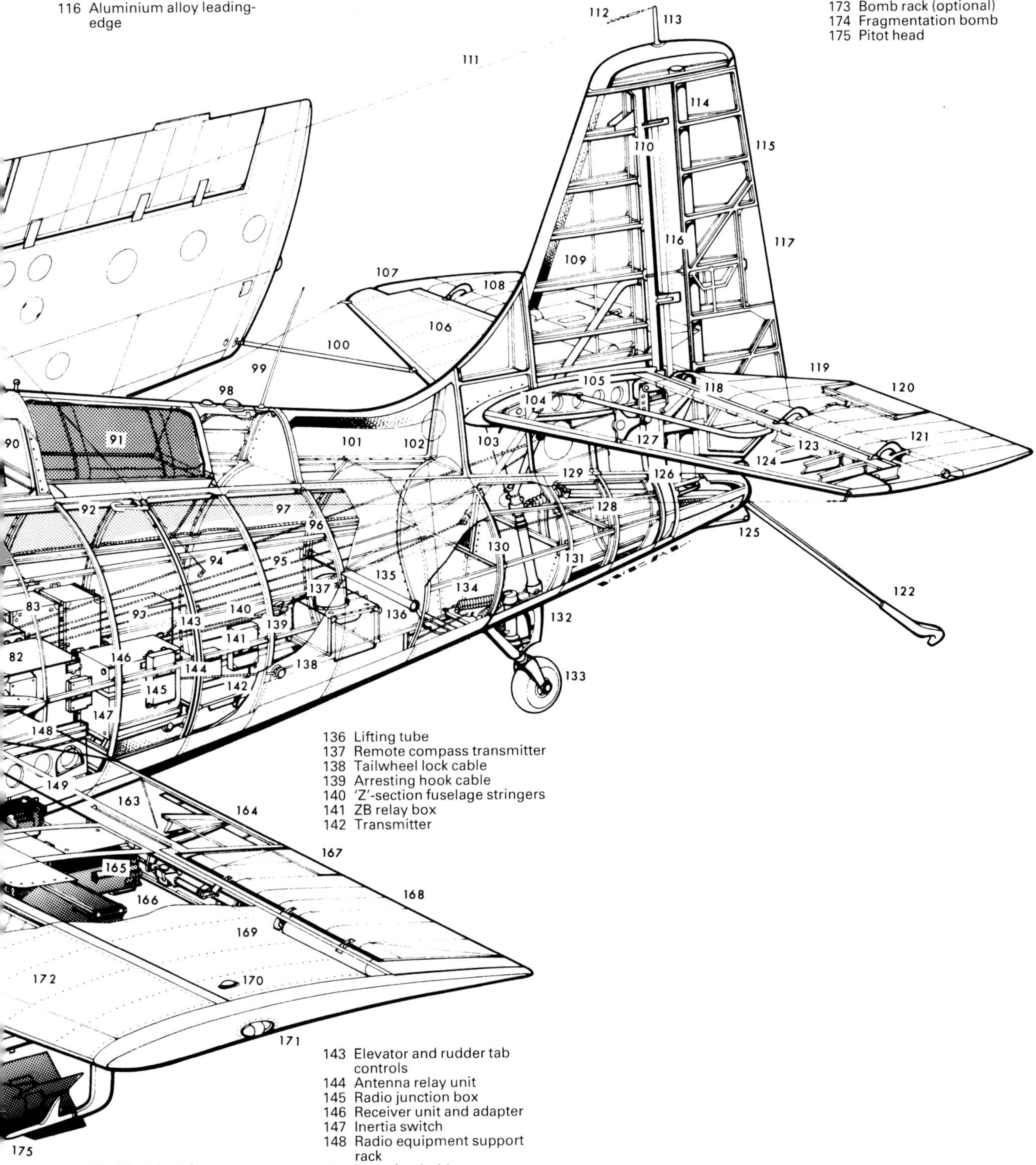

136 Lifting tube
137 Remote compass transmitter
138 Tailwheel lock cable
139 Arresting hook cable
140 'Z'-section fuselage stringers
141 ZB relay box
142 Transmitter

143 Elevator and rudder tab
controls
144 Antenna relay unit
145 Radio junction box
146 Receiver unit and adapter
147 Inertia switch
148 Radio equipment support
rack
149 Entry foothold
150 Reserve fuel tank, capacity
27 US gal (120 l)
151 Fuselage/rear spar
attachment
152 Wing hinge line
153 Main (underfloor) fuel tank,
capacity 117 US gal (443 l)
154 Stub wing end rib and fairing
155 Inboard gun blast tubes
156 Plexiglas observation panel
157 Ventral antenna

117 Rudder trim tab
118 Elevator torque tube
119 Port elevator
120 Elevator trim tab
121 Elevator hinge (self-aligning)
122 Arresting hook (extended)
123 Tailplane spar
124 Rear navigation light
125 Towing lug
126 Rudder torque tube support
127 Elevator control linkage
128 Rudder control cable

An F4F Wildcat landing aboard the USS Ranger *after battle damage had weakened the tail section and caused it to be ripped off after catching a wire.*

There was also a problem with the tailwheel on take-off; even though it was locked in position, it still had a tendency to swing to the left. Grumman solved the problem by replacing the solid rubber-tyred tailwheel with a pneumatic one, which raised it an additional nine inches from the ground, enough to allow extra control on the rudder.

As part of the familiarization programme, the Royal Navy pilots, on occasions, engaged Royal Air Force pilots in mock combat. It was soon discovered that, although it was noticeably slower in the dive than the Spitfire and Hurricane, the Martlet could more than hold its own in a steep climb or in a tight turning circle. Suddenly, the Royal Navy felt it was no longer the poor relation, but as well equipped as the RAF, maybe even more so.

The Martlet IIs were of the fixed-wing variety, and because the development of the Sto-wing was taking so long, the Admiralty decided that they would rather take them than wait. It was claimed by many pilots who flew the Martlets that the aircraft had the best carrier landing characteristics of any aircraft used by the Royal Navy. It was recognized that carrier landings were, and still are, one of the most dangerous aspects of flying, but the Martlet was well suited for it. The slow flying speed, the extremely strong undercarriage that was capable of withstanding what can only be described as a controlled crash, and excellent all-round vision went a long way in making carrier landings safer.

The Martlet also introduced a better form of catapult launching to the Royal Navy. The existing system used a cumbersome cradle that fitted under the aircraft by means of heavy metal spools and claws, but the Martlet had only a small, single steel hook under the belly of the aircraft. One end of a wire strop went around the hook, whilst the other end fitted into the catapult slot on the carrier's deck. The saving of time that this innovation allowed was warmly welcomed by carrier pilots and deck crews alike. It meant that whole squadrons could be airborne in less than half the normal time it would have taken to launch them.

The Wildcat received an enthusiastic welcome from nearly all the Royal Navy pilots who flew it and it served with tremendous distinction, not only in Europe, but in the Far East as well. The little barrel-shaped fighter was eventually replaced by the F6F Hellcat in 1943, but not before it had left an everlasting impression on the Royal Navy's Fleet Air Arm.

In 1942 the number of F4F-4s in the US Navy and the Marine Corps rose to 1,164. At this time, Grumman were considering the use of the Pratt and Whitney R-1200 engine, because the weight of the XF4F-4 was thirty per cent greater than that of the XF4F-3. One of the main reasons for the weight increase was the addition of two .50 calibre machine guns, which increased the firepower to six machine guns. After a great deal of research, however, it was decided that the increased speed would only be in the order of about thirty miles per hour, and this was not sufficient.

Grumman then started looking at the new, more powerful, Pratt and Whitney engine, the R-2800, and decided that this engine needed a larger aircraft to justify it. It was this decision that was to lead to the development of the F6F Hellcat.

Earlier in 1941, the US Navy ordered 100 F4Fs to be converted to long-range photo-reconnaissance aircraft. Although basically an F4F, the aircraft had no armament, the bullet resistant windscreen was replaced by curved plexiglass, and the fuel capacity increased to 685 gallons, using the fixed wings as fuel tanks. The camera replaced the emergency fuel tank that was situated behind the pilot, and an automatic pilot was installed. Two very distinctive fuel dump pipes projected from beneath the tail of the aircraft. Of the 100 F4Fs ordered, only 24 were actually built. These aircraft were designated F4F-7 and the initial flight was made on 30 December 1941.

After evaluation tests at Anacostia, the aircraft underwent a series of flight tests, culminating in an eleven hour, non-stop flight from the east coast to the west coast. The F4F-7 project

was not a great success, but it did serve as a testing ground for future projects of a similar nature.

On the morning of 7 December 1941, the Japanese Imperial Navy launched its attack against Pearl Harbor. During the attack, a flight of Zeros attacked Marine Corps Fighter Squadron VMF-211 and virtually wiped out all their F4F-3s on the ground. This was to be the F4F's introduction to war in US Naval livery. Not one aircraft managed to get into the air, which is what happened on Wake Island the following day when it was attacked. The next four weeks turned novice airmen into experienced fighter pilots, and during the attempted invasion of Wake Island, the F4F Wildcat pilots attacked the invasion force with such venom that it turned the force back. The Japanese suffered the loss of a destroyer, a medium-sized transporter due to strafing, and a number of bombers were shot down. But the price of the battle to the small Marine Force was high: only two F4Fs were airworthy the next day, when the infuriated Japanese sent a force of thirty-three bombers and six Zeros to annihilate the air defences. The two remaining F4Fs managed to shoot down one Zero and damage two others, before they themselves were shot down. With the air defences gone, the Japanese invaded again and this time, after a bitter fight, overran the island.

There were a number of special projects involving the F4F Wildcat. Among them was the conversion of a Wildcat to a Wildcatfish, by attaching floats in place of the undercarriage. The idea behind the project was that a squadron of float-planes could operate from some of the small remote islands dotted around the Pacific, whilst airstrips were being built. The Japanese had had some success with this kind of project, by converting a number of Zeros into floatplanes and re-naming them 'Rufes'.

The US Navy chose the F4F-3 for conversion because of its ruggedness, and it was taken to the EDO Corporation for the work to be carried out. Unlike the Japanese floatplane, which had a central float and two wing-tip floats, the Wildcatfish had two large floats attached to the fuselage and wings. The tests were extremely encouraging, but before the idea could be considered seriously enough to start production, the programme was dropped. The reason was that the construction battalions were transforming the jungle areas into landing strips at such a remarkable rate that the fighter floatplane had become unnecessary.

One extremely unusual project was a proposal to use the Wildcat as a glider. The idea arose out of a need to escort long-range bombers on raids. Because of their limited fuel capacity, fighters could only accompany them for short distances. The suggestion put forward was that two Wildcats would take off and rendezvous with a bomber at a pre-arranged height. Two separate tow lines, one slightly longer than the other, were trailed out from opposite wing roots, each with a specially designed hook on the end. The Wildcats would then position themselves underneath the trailing tow lines and engage the hook fixed to the end of it. After the line

The F4F-3S Wildcatfish. One was produced as an experiment but it was decided not to put it into production.

had been engaged, the pilot could feather his engine and assume the role of glider pilot. In the event of the bomber being attacked, the Wildcat would release from the tow line and defend the bomber. A number of tests were carried out, with encouraging results, but like many unusual ideas put forward during the war, the whole project was quietly forgotten.

The first encounters with Japanese Zeros were quite disastrous for the F4F Wildcat, which suffered badly at the hands of the battle-experienced Japanese pilots, who had been engaged in aerial combat for a number of years with the Chinese, and had learned a great deal. The Zero was superior in speed, rate of climb, range and operating ceiling. But although on the face of it the F4F Wildcat appeared to be completely outclassed, it was of superior construction to the Zero, with armour plating covering all the vulnerable parts, and self-sealing fuel tanks. The armament of the Zero was two rifle-calibre machine guns and two 20 mm cannon which, when compared to the firepower of the Wildcat, was inadequate, so much so that, on many occasions in dogfights with the Wildcats, the Zero made very little impression on its opponent, but when the Wildcat fired and hit the Zero, it virtually tore the aircraft apart. In August 1942 the recovery of a virtually undamaged Zero which had crashed during the Battle of Indway meant that extensive flight tests could be carried out on the enemy aircraft. The preliminary test report showed that as a fighter aircraft its manoeuvrability and speed were far superior to those of the Wildcat, but in a battle situation it was no match for its more rugged and better-armed couterpart.

Eventually, production of all F4F types was shifted to Eastern Aircraft at their Linden factory in New Jersey. This allowed Grumman to continue with the development of the XF6F, which was destined to be the replacement for the F4F. The proposed production rate of the F6F was to be 500 per month.

Eastern Aircraft was a division of General Motors and they were awarded a contract for 1,800 F4Fs, which were redesignated as FM-1s. Production started in April 1942, and by August the first FM-1 had taken to the air. Although

production was slow for the remainder of the year (only twenty were produced), the following year 818 rolled off the assembly lines.

Most of the aircraft built at the New Jersey plant ended up on operational service aboard the new escort carriers, or CVEs as they were known. Over 100 escort carriers were built or converted from merchant ships and they played a major part in the Atlantic and Pacific theatres of the war. Thirty-eight CVEs were transferred to the Royal Navy and it was during the acceptance trials that a problem was discovered: on the shorter flight deck of the CVEs, the weight of the heavily-loaded F4F-3s caused problems when landing. The policy had been to update and improve the aircraft by means of a more powerful engine (possibly the R-2000 or R-2600) which together with other improvements would have made the aircraft heavier still. However, it was decided that in this case the aircraft would have to be made lighter. By combining the new F4F airframe with the more powerful, single-stage 1,350 hp, two-speed supercharged Wright R-1820-56 engine, and fitting only four guns instead of six, Grumman were able to reduce the aircraft's weight considerably, thus solving the heavy landing problem. Two aircraft were converted and sent to NAS Anacostia for the US Navy to evaluate. The Navy soon discovered that the new engine created torque on take-off and landing, so the vertical tail was enlarged to counteract this. The aircraft were redesignated XF4F-8s, and returned the Bethpage for more testing before the design was handed over to Eastern Aircraft for production as FM-2s.

A conference held at Patuxent River, Maryland in October 1944 invited aircraft manufacturers and contractors to participate in a discussion into aircraft requirements. On display was a collection of twenty-three experimental and production aircraft belonging to the AAC and the Navy. Among the aircraft, which included the XF6F-5, XF8F-1, XF4U-4, P-47D, P-47M and P-51D, was an FM-2. Even taking into consideration the bias that existed within the services, and after each of the aircraft had been flown by a variety of military and civilian test pilots, the FM-2 was considered to be the best fighter aircraft to fly under 10,000 feet. The aircraft that took everybody's eye though, was the XF8F-1. Its appearance at Patuxent River was its first time away from Bethpage and as Ralph Clark, now the director of Navy Operations in Washington, recalls, 'Bob Hall flew the XF8F

An FM-2 Wildcat undergoing a full service.

down to Pax River and flew the demonstration flight. As he stepped down from the aircraft afterwards, he said, "Well now the secret's out". The demonstration had astounded everybody there and the Bearcat, as it was to be known, left a lasting impression.

During 1944 and 1945, FM-2s were armed with Napalm bombs and six five-inch rockets, three under each wing. Their role was to provide close air support to the ground forces during the retaking and holding of the islands in the Pacific.

The F4F Wildcat was eventually replaced by the F6F Hellcat. Although by comparison the Hellcat was far superior to the Wildcat, nevertheless the little F4F Wildcat left behind a lasting impression that would ensure it a place in the annals of Naval aviation history.

F4F Wildcat Technical details

Performance	Max. speed 318 mph. Cruising speed 155 mph. Ceiling 39,400 ft. Range 770 miles. Initial climb rate 1,950 ft. per min.		*Type*	Single-seat carrier-based fighter.
			Engine	One Pratt and Whitney R-1830-36 Twin Wasp, 14-cylinder, radial, piston engine.
Weights	Empty 5,758 lb., loaded 7,952 lb.		*Dimensions*	Wing span 38 ft. Wing area 260 sq. ft. Length 28 ft. 9 in. Height 9 ft. 2½ in.
Armament	Six 0.5 in. Browning machine guns and two 100 lb. bombs.			

F4F Model variations

XF4F-1
Designed as a biplane, but never put into production.

XF4F-2
The first of the Wildcats. Powered by the Pratt and Whitney R-1830-66 engine.

XF4F-3
An XF4F-2 with a larger wing area and wing span. Powered by a Pratt and Whitney XR-1830-76 engine with a two-stage, two-speed supercharger.

F4F-3
Production model.

Martlet I
F4F-3 export model. Originally sold to France, but taken over by the British when France fell.

Martlet II
Ordered by the Royal Navy and powered by the Pratt and Whitney R-1830-53C-4G engine. This aircraft was the first Grumman carrier aircraft with folding wings.

XF4F-3A
Originally designated XF4F-6, but redesignated XF4F-3A after it was realized that the production model would be the F4F-3. Powered by the single-stage, supercharged Pratt and Whitney R-1830-90 engine. It was delivered to the US Navy on 26 November 1940, only two weeks after the first test flight.

F4F-3A
This became known as the Martlet III when the first 30, destined for Greece were taken over by the Royal Navy after the Germans had invaded the Greek islands.

F4F-3P
The photographic version of the F4F-3.

F4F-3S
An experimental floatplane version of the F4F-3 which was only the second US Navy floatplane fighter, the first being the Curtiss F-6C-3 in 1929. The F4F-3S was never considered for production.

XF4F-4
An F4F-3 with a number of modifications, such as hydraulically-operated folding wings, a much improved and heavily armoured cockpit, and self-sealing fuel tanks. Powered by a Pratt and Whitney R-1830-86 engine.

F4F-4
Production model, but with manually-operated folding wings.

F4F-4A
This was a project to install a Pratt and Whitney R-1830-90 engine with supercharger, but it never got past the design stage.

F4F-4B
This aircraft was also known as the Wildcat IV and was powered by a Wright R-1820-40B engine.

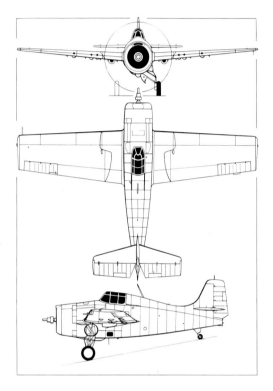

FM-1
The first of the Wildcats to be produced by the Eastern Aircraft Division of General Motors. Almost identical to the F4F-4, except that it only had four machine guns, instead of six. Powered by a Pratt and Whitney R-1830-86 engine.

F4F-4P
Photographic version of the F4F-4.

XF4F-5
Ostensibly these were F4F-3s that were used to test a number of different engines, including the Wright R-1820-40 and the R-1820-54.

F4F-7
This was a basic F4F-3 with large capacity fuel tanks, but no armament. It was used exclusively for long-range photo-reconnaissance.

XF4F-8
This was a prototype of the FM-2, powered by the Wright R-1820-56 engine with a supercharger. Only two were built.

FM-2
Known as the Wildcat VI, this aircraft was produced by the Eastern Aircraft Division of General Motors. More FM-2s were built than F4Fs.

XF2M-1
There were three prototyped designed by the Eastern Aircraft Division of General Motors to test the Wright XR-1820-70 engine. The aircraft was never produced.

TBF and TBM Avenger

At the beginning of April 1940, the US Navy approached a number of aircraft manufacturers to design and build a replacement torpedo-bomber for the ageing Douglas Devastator. The Navy's requirements were far more exacting than previously. Out of all the designs submitted, two were chosen, the Grumman XTBF-1 and the Chance-Vought XTBU-1. Both designs more than met the expectations of the Navy. It is interesting to note, that so precise were the specifications laid down by the Navy, both aircraft were very similar to look at. They were designed to carry a three-man crew of pilot, turret-gunner and radio-operator/tunnel gunner. The aircraft had to be adaptable, able to operate from an aircraft carrier, as well as from a shore base. Both aircraft were to be subjected to rigorous testing under the scrutiny of Navy inspectors.

The first of the two XTBF-1s ordered by the Navy performed uneventfully during weeks of testing until 28 November 1941. Late in the afternoon of Thanksgiving Day, with test pilot Bob Cook and Flight Engineer Gordon Israel aboard, the XTBF-1 took off on a routine test flight. Ten miles from Bethpage, the pilot reported that he saw smoke in the cockpit and bailed out. Gordon Israel in the rear cockpit then jumped, breaking his leg above the ankle against the right horizontal stabilizer. Both men landed safely, but the aircraft was destroyed.

This was not the kind of start Chief Engineer William Schwendler and his engineering team had envisaged when they designed XTBF-1. The loss of the aircraft was a bitter blow to Grumman, and the second prototype was as yet incomplete. For the next two weeks the entire experimental crew worked around the clock, and a 110 hour-week was not uncommon. On 7 December 1941 the second XTBF-1 was ready for static display to some 15,000 guests at the Grumman annual Open House, although the turret was covered with a canvas cover because it was still on the secret list. Grumman had laid on some 300 turkeys, roast beefs and hams, and were ready to serve them when the word came through about Pearl Harbor. The security guards and maintenance men were immediately ordered to bring the occasion to a quiet end. As the last person left the factory, the entire complex was declared secure, and it stayed that way for the duration of the war.

Because of Pearl Harbor, the US Navy was forced to make a quick decision about the replacement dive-bomber. They chose the Grumman XTBF-1 and it went into production immediately, the first production aircraft being delivered on 30 January 1942.

By August 1942, 145 TBF-1 Avengers had been delivered to the Navy. Powered by a R-2600-8 Wright Cyclone 14 engine, developing 1,700 hp, which turned a two-speed,

Above: A wooden mock-up of the XTBF-1. Note the absence of the dorsal fin.

The prototype XTBF-1 at Bethpage in 1941 preparing for a test flight.

Hamilton Standard, three-bladed propeller with a 13 ft diameter, the TBF presented an awesome and powerful sight. Top speed was 271 mph at 12,000 feet, and 251 mph at sea level. The aircraft had a cruising speed of 145 mph and a landing speed of 75 mph. A large landing hook, operated electrically from the cockpit, assisted many an ill-judged landing, bringing the aircraft to a safe halt. The squat, heavy-looking undercarriage was capable of absorbing landings at a 'sink speed' of up to 16 feet per second, which in anybody's estimation was a very hefty thump indeed. It was possible to use the sturdy undercarriage as an airbrake, as many a Japanese figher pilot discovered to his cost. The independently operated, electrically-powered dorsal turret contained a .50 calibre machine gun, and was powered by two synchronized amplidyne motors. It was the brainchild of Oscar Olsen, an electrical engineer who had used a larger version of the motors in his days with General Motors on their larger structures, such as draw bridges and turntable bridges. The turret was manned by the turret gunner, whilst the radio operator/tunnel gunner had a rear-firing, .30 calibre machine gun. The pilot had a .30 calibre machine gun mounted on the starboard engine cowling, synchronized to fire through the propeller, which was to prove ineffective for strafing gun emplacements and other targets. One enterprising squadron commander had a pair of .50 calibre machine-guns mounted illegally on the wing root outside the fuselage. The ammunition belts to feed the guns were fed via the overturn structure by way of the external skin, a remarkable innovation which showed the extent to which people would go to solve problems in wartime. Later models of the TBF-1C and TBM-1C Avengers were equipped with two fixed, wing-mounted, .50 calibre machine guns, in addition to the existing armament.

The Avenger was the first US Navy aircraft to be equipped with rocket launching rails. This was a very useful addition to the aircraft's armament, especially when carrying out torpedo attacks. The Avenger could lay down a devastating barrage of rocket fire, enabling it to reach its target with the minimum of resistance from enemy anti-aircraft fire. In addition to this firepower, the TBF and TBM also carried a variety of torpedoes, bombs, mines, and depth charges. There was even a facility for creating a smoke-screen, achieved by fitting an additional 212 gallon tank in the bomb bay.

A Norden bomb sight was fitted on some of the earlier models, but was discarded by many pilots in favour of glide bombing. This form of bombing was developed after a large number of the aerial torpedoes had proved unreliable, either breaking in half or failing to explode on impact. The pilots found that by dividing at a shallow angle of fifty degrees they could bomb very accurately, and four 500 lb. bombs became the popular load. Since the TBF had no dive breaks, the aircraft achieved some very high speeds whilst diving and frequently exceeded the 'red line' of 371 mph. The Avenger was able to carry either one 2,000 lb. two 1,000 lb., four 500 lb., or twelve 100 lb. bombs and could drop them individually or as a stick.

A maximum of 352 gallons was carried in three self-sealing tanks. The main tank was situated in the fuselage behind the pilot, with two smaller tanks fitted in the fixed wing stubs either side of the aircraft. All three tanks were protected by armour plating. For photographic reconnaissance and scouting misions, an additional 270 gallons could be carried in a special tank fitted in the bomb bay, and a further 100 gallons in drop-tanks. This gave the aircraft a tremendous range, far greater than any other comparable aircraft of the day.

The Avenger started life as the TBF (Torpedo Bomber F), the F being the Navy's designated letter for the Grumman factory. Later, General Motors took over production, and the TBF became the TBM, M being the Navy's designated letter for General Motors. Although it is not strictly true to say that General Motors built the aircraft under one roof, they were all built by the company's own plants, within easy reach of each other at Trenton, New Jersey, where the fuselage and canopies were manufactured and the aircraft were assembled.

The fuselage was constructed in two main sections, fore and aft. It was of a stressed skin, semi-monocoque design, consisting of angle-type frames and stamped bulkheads, covered with a smooth aluminium alloy skin. Channel-type stringers extended along the entire fuselage, to stiffen the skin longitudinally. Special stiffeners were fitted to areas that would have to absorb extra stress, such as the engine mounts, cockpit cut-out areas, where the fore and aft sections joined, wing attachments, gun turret, tail wheel and arrester hook areas. In the event of the aircraft completely turning over, a protective crash tower, called an overturn structure, was built to protect the pilot.

Testing of the TBMs was carried out at a nearby airfield by Grumman test pilots. The hydraulics and electrical assemblies, together with tubes, cables and wires, were manufactured at the Bloomfield, New Jersey plant, while the wings and engine cowlings were produced at Tarrytown, New York. The wings were of the fully-cantilevered type, with a single main spar, pressed aluminium alloy ribs, one centre section and two folding outer panels. Two hinges attached each wing to the centre section main spar, folding about an axis which inclined forward, outward and downward from the centre section, so that the leading edges folded through a downward arc, back against the fuselage. When completely folded, the wings stood on edge with the trailing edges pointing upwards. Folding and unfolding was carried out hydraulically and was controlled from the cockpit. Other parts of the aircraft that operated hydraulically were the automatic pilot, bomb bay doors, cowl flaps, oil cooler flaps, wing gun charges and the retractable landing gear.

The landing gear consisted of a main oleo strut that was braced by a side strut and a drag strut. The wheels retracted upwards and outwards into wells in the outer wings, and an indicator in the cockpit showed the pilot the position of the wheels at any one time. Down locks and up locks, which automatically released when hydraulic pressure began to actuate the gear, were provided for on the main landing gear, and the control handle locked automatically in a down position when the weight of the aircraft was on the landing gear. In the event of the pilot being unable to lower his landing gear, there was a handle in the cockpit that operated a cam, which in turn relieved the hydraulic pressure and released the up locks in the landing gear system. The landing gear then lowered itself partly by its own weight and partly by springs in the hydraulic cylinders. The tail wheel was also hydraulically-operated and retracted and extended simultaneously with the main landing gear; it was secured in the trailing position by the pilot.

The Avenger was probably one of the most reliable of all the aircraft built by Grumman, and although not particularly pleasing aesthetically, created very few problems for its crews. One incident in particular highlighted the need for great care when assembling the aircraft. It happened in November 1942, whilst the chief test pilot for Eastern Aircraft was returning from a test flight. About five miles out from the field, he switched to his reserve tank but nothing

VT-26 Squadron ready to launch from the escort carrier USS Santee.

The enquiry decided that the accident happened because one of the propeller blades had been damaged in the original incident and had come off due to the weakness it had suffered. This caused the torque, created by the missing blade, to rip the engine from its mountings. Fortunately, for the pilot, it happened close to the ground, enabling him to land safely. The aircraft had a new engine and mounts fitted and flew the next day.

By August 1943, 145 TBF-1 Avengers had been delivered to the Navy. The first squadron to be equipped with them was VT-8 — or to be more precise one half of the Squadron. VT-8's CO, Cdr. Waldron, had remained with half of the Squadron and their Douglas TBDs aboard the carrier *USS Hornet,* whilst the executive officer, Lt-Col Larson, took the other half of the Squadron to pick up the TBFs. After completing their conversion course, Larson and his crews, including ground maintenance crews, were transported back to Pearl Harbor with their aircraft to join up with the *USS Hornet.* Before they could get back aboard, the Battle of Midway broke out and the TBFs had to be fitted with ferry tanks so that they could fly out to Midway. They were also carrying the new type of torpedo that they had been testing whilst on the conversion course. Cdr. Waldron and his half of VT-8 had been eliminated at Midway already, so the TBFs were vital to the defence of the fleet.

On 4 June, six Avengers, led by Lt. Fieberling, took off on their first mission to attack the task force of Admiral Nagumo at Midway; these six were the only Avengers to take part in the battle. The task force was sighted at about 0700 hours and the Avengers dived in to attack. As they made their attack, they were jumped by a Japanese patrol of Zeros and came under extremely heavy fire. Although out-numbered three-to-one, they pressed home their attack but managed to drop

TBF-1s from the USS Santee.

only three torpedoes, none of which did any damage. One by one they were destroyed, until only one was left, which managed to limp back to Midway. With only one wheel down, his bomb bay doors jammed open, no flaps, and his radio and compass out of order, the pilot, Ensign Albert Earnest, wounded in the knee, somehow managed to land the aircraft. The turret gunner was dead, the radio man was badly wounded but alive, which is why Earnest decided to land the aircraft instead of bailing out. The Avenger was so badly damaged that it was scrapped. Meanwhile, back at the task force, Douglas SBDs had arrived late at the battle, and because the Avengers and other SBDs had drawn off the fighter cover from the Japanese carriers, they were able to make their dive-bombing runs virtually uninterrupted. They sank four Japanese carriers and turned the tide of the battle. Although this was not a very auspicious start to what was hoped would be an illustrious career, the Avenger went on to distinguish itself throughout the rest of the War.

In all, Grumman built a total of 5,193 Avengers, including 2,311 TBF-1s to TBF-1Cs, and General Motors (Eastern Aircraft) built a total of 4,664 TBM-3s and TBM-3Es. There were twenty-six variations of the TBF and TBM in all, ranging from the TBM-3P, a special photographic reconnaissance aircraft with a trimetrogen camera, to the TBM-1D, -1E, -3C and -3E, which were special radar versions. The TBM-1L and -3L had a searchlight mounted in the bomb bay, the -3N was equipped for night operations, the -3Q for radar countermeasures, and the -3W was another special radar version, although some of these versions did not appear until after the war.

The Royal Navy Fleet Air Arm took delivery of its first TBF-1 Avengers on 1 January 1943. The pilots and crews of No 822 Squadron went to Norfolk, Virginia, to collect them and carry out familiarization programmes. The British called the aircraft the Tarpon 1, but as an inter-allied standardization procedure the American name of Avenger was re-introduced after about a year. After familiarization, the Squadron and their Avengers embarked on the USS Saratoga, which was sailing to support the landings in the Solomon Islands. It is believed that this was the first, and possibly the last, time that a Royal Navy squadron operated from a US carrier.

The Squadron's first engagement with the enemy was during the action in the Coral Sea, in which they distinguished themselves against overwhelming odds. At the end of 1943, eight more squadrons had been formed and shipped to Great Britain on escort carriers, and in 1944 a further five squadrons were activated. In total, 958 TBF and TBM Avengers were shipped to Great Britain under the Lend-Lease agreements.

The Royal Navy's first notable Avenger strike against the enemy was on 1 April 1944, when an Avenger of No 846 Squadron helped to bring about the demise of the German submarine U-355, which was escorting a Russian convoy in the Arctic. Some days later, another Avenger from the same Squadron, with the help of a Swordfish of No 819 Squadron and a Wildcat of No 846 Squadron, sank the submarine U-288. Although it was primarily designed to carry torpedoes, the British used the TBF Avenger for carrying bombs, mines and depth charges. It was also used as a strike aircraft, with rockets attached under its wings. One Avenger was even adapted to carry the 'Highball' bouncing bomb, made famous later for its destruction of the Möhne and Jorpe Dams in Germany. Avenger squadrons were added to Coastal Command, squadrons of Beaufighters and Albacores for the build up to D-Day. In July of the same year, two Avengers were credited with the shooting down and destruction of two V-1 flying bombs. The first was shot down by a dorsal turret gunner and the second by a pilot, using his front guns. This was a tremendous achievement, considering the great speed of the V-1 and the small target it presented. But the Avenger really excelled itself while with the East Indies and Pacific Fleets. On 19 May 1944, the Fleet Air Arm took part in an attack on the Japanese Naval Base at Sourabaya, Java. The

Avengers of Nos 832 Squadron and 845 Squadron, aboard HMS Illustrious, were joined by US Navy Douglas Dauntlesses from the carrier USS Saratoga, and with great daring from all involved, completely devastated the target.

At first glance, the Avenger 1 was remarkably like an enlarged Grumman Wildcat, with its large radial engine and barrel-shaped fuselage. It even had the same solid rubber tail wheel, but that is where the resemblance ended, although there is no mistaking it came from the same family. In 1942, Saburo Sakai, Japan's leading fighter ace, mistook three TBFs for Wildcats, and approached them from the rear. The Avenger pilots and crews had seen him, and as he closed on them, thinking they were easy targets, he was met by a hail of machine gun fire. Though injured and his aircraft badly damaged, he managed to limp back to his base at Rabaul. He lost an eye through the incident and became an instructor.

One of the most important raids of the war in the Far East was carried out on the Palembang oil refineries on 24 and 29 January 1945. Taking part were 238 aircraft, comprising 39 Hellcats, 36 Corsairs, 75 Avengers, 12 Fireflies, 40 Seafires and 2 Walrus amphibians. The attack consisted of two strike forces, codenamed Meridian 1 and Meridian 2, the first strike being on Pladjoe refinery, the second on the refinery at Soengei Gerong.

As the Pladjoe strike crossed the enemy coastline, the aircraft were detected by the air raid warning system and by the time they were fifteen miles from the target they had encountered some fifteen to twenty Japanese fighter aircraft. Diving out of the sun, the Japanese pilots concentrated their attack on the Avengers and it was noticed immediately that the standard of flying was extremely high. This was attributed to the fact that Palembang was the training centre for the 7th Area Air Army and that the majority of the pilots were probably instructors. A fierce battle ensued, driving the enemy fighters off and allowing the Avengers to go through and bomb the oil refineries.

The strike force rendezvoused over a small island some miles to the west, but unfortunately the fighter escort was still engaging the enemy around the target. A number of Japanese fighters were lying in wait, and it was here that the force suffered the majority of their casualties. By 0930 the strike force were back aboard their carriers, with the loss of two Avengers, six Corsairs and one Hellcat. Many other aircraft had been damaged, some severely, but the raid was deemed to have been successful.

Meridian 2, the strike on Soengei Gerong, had its operational plans altered because of the likely threat of an attack on the fleet. It was assumed that the Japanese would be expecting a second attack against their other refinery and

TBM-1s from Natoma Bay CVE-62 over Wotje (in Japanese hands), 9 February 1944.

that they would launch a pre-emptive attack, so it was decided to reduce the size of the strike force and increase the air cover over the fleet.

The Avengers made their bombing runs against tremendous fire from the ground, and the additional hazard of barrage balloons did not make things any easier. After the bombing, the Avengers limped away to rendezvous with their fighter escort, who were having a tremendous battle with Japanese fighters. The strike force returned to the carriers, six of the Avengers having to ditch near the fleet, but their crews were picked up safely. Four Avengers, two Corsairs and a Firefly were lost in the raid. Altogether sixteen aircraft were lost in combat, fourteen from deck crashes, and eleven ditched near the fleet — a total of forty-one aircraft. One thing that became very apparent from the raids was the fragility of the Seafire and the Firefly, compared with the rugged Avenger. The American aircraft seemed to be ideally suited for this kind of work.

The destruction of the refineries was a bitter blow to the Japanese and was to have a lasting effect on their morale and fuel supplies. There is no doubt that it contributed in a large way to the Japanes defeat in that part of the world. As the relentless wave of Allied forces swept across the Pacific and Indian Oceans, Avengers of No 848 Squadron, flying from *HMS Formidable*, attacked the Japanese mainland. This was the first time the Fleet Air Arm had attacked the Japanese on their home ground. Supported by Avengers of No 828 Squadron aboard *HMS Implacable*, they destroyed the airfield at Kokushima. The attacks continued until 15 August 1945, when the last strike against Japan was executed on Tokyo by Avengers of No 828 Squadron.

With the end of hostilities, the Avenger squadrons were disbanded, but reappeared in 1953 when they replaced the ageing Barracudas during the war in Korea. The aircraft were supplied by the USA under the Mutual Defence Assistance Programme and were intended to strengthen the Royal Navy's anti-submarine force during the Korean conflict. The aircraft were the US Navy's TBM-3E and -3C types, that had been superseded by the Grumman S2F-1 Sentinel in 1954. Later that year a number of S2F-1s (designated AS-4 by the British) were delivered to the Royal Navy's carrier *HMS Perseus*, to replace No 815 Squadron's obsolete Barracudas. Later, the following year, the TBMs were themselves declared obsolete by the Royal Navy and were replaced by the Fairey Firefly Mk 5.

A number of other countries were supplied with the TBM Avenger, including TBM-3W-2s to Japan from 1955. The TBM-3W-2s were anti-submarine aircraft, with a radome and electronic sensing equipment. They were supplemented later by the TBM-3S-2s, at first as an addition to the defence force, but later as spares. In 1960, the remaining Avengers were used for target towing, until their retirement from active service in 1962. The Royal Netherlands Navy equipped two squadrons with fifty TBM-3s in 1953. They were used specifically for anti-submarine duties until 1964, when they were retired from active service.

The French had three squadrons of TBM-3W-2s and TBM-3s aboard the aircraft carrier *Bois Belleau*, formerly the *USS Belleau Wood* (CV-24), for anti-submarine duties. The Avengers were in action against the Egyptians in 1957 during the Suez crisis. They were eventually retired from the Aeronavale Flottile in 1963.

In 1956, the United States Forestry Service acquired eight TMB-3Us from the US Navy for a nominal sum. The intention was to use the aircraft as water bombers. After extensive refitting by the Forestry Commission's own workshops, two 400-gallon tanks were fitted into each redesigned bomb bay. The first test drop was made from a height of 100 feet at a speed of 115 mph, swathing an area of 50 feet by 300

A TBM-3W overflying Boca Chica, Key West, Florida.

A TBM-3W about to launch from the USS Franklyn D. Roosevelt.

feet. After many tests, it was decided that one tank carrying 600 gallons would be better than two carrying 400 gallons. With the success of this new firefighter, which gave the Forestry Service access to previously inaccessible places, some private companies began to take an interest. Although it was reasonably economical and successful as a method of firefighting, it was also risky.

In 1958, at an airfield 90 miles south of Los Angeles, an entrepeneur businessman called Jim Venables formed Hemet Valley Flying Services. Starting with two Stearmans, he built up a fleet of firefighting aircraft to ten TBMs and three PBY Catalinas. Securing contracts from the United States Forestry Service and the Californian Division of Forestry, Jim Venables set about make his name synonymous with aerial firefighting. One of his main problems was maintenance; the cost of overhauling the TBM at the time was somewhere in the region of $10,000, and for the PBY Catalina $14,000.

In British Columbia, Jim Venables' Canadian counterpart, Art Sellers, was operating his own aerial firefighting team of TBM Avengers. Rumoured to have the largest stock of Avenger spares in the world, he operated a tanker operation with 40 aircraft, Having bought up the Royal Navy's entire inventory of Avengers, he is able to put eighteen TBMs in the air. Art Sellers believes that his fleet of TBMs will still be flying into the 1990s.

TBF-1 Avenger Technical details

Manufacturer	Grumman Aircraft Engineering Corporation, Bethpage, Long Island, New York.
Model	Torpedo bomber.
Crew	Pilot, gunner and radio/radar operator (later models had wing-mounted radar).
Engine	One 1,700 hp Wright Cyclone 14 R-2600-8.
Dimensions	Wing span 54 ft. 2 in., length 40 ft., height 16 ft. 5 in., wing area 490 sq. ft.
Weight	10,080 lb. empty, 15,905 lb. gross.
Performance	Max. speed 271 mph at 12,000 feet. Cruising speed 145 mph. Initial climb rate 1,430 ft. per min. Max. operating ceiling 22,400 ft. Range 1,215 statute miles.
Armament	One fixed, forward-firing .30 calibre machine gun, one dorsal turret .50 calibre machine gun, one ventral .30 calibre machine gun. Maximum of 2,000 lb. in bomb bay. TBF-1C had two fixed, forward-firing, .50 calibre wing guns.

TBM-3E Avenger

Manufacturer	General Motors Corporation, Eastern Aircraft Division, Trenton, New Jersey.
Model	Torpedo bomber.
Crew	Pilot, gunner and radio operator (later models had radar operator).
Engine	One 1,900 hp Wright Cyclone R-2600-20.
Dimensions	Wing span 54 ft. 2 in., length 40 ft. 11½ in., height 16 ft. 5 in., wing area 490 sq. ft.
Weight	10,545 lb. empty, 17,895 lb. gross.
Performance	Max. speed 276 mph at 16,500 feet. Cruising speed 147 mph. Initial climb rate 2,060 ft. per min. Max. operating ceiling 30,100 feet. Range 1,010 statute miles.
Armament	Two fixed, forward-firing, .50 calibre machine guns, one dorsal turret .50 calibre machine gun, one central .30 calibre machine gun. Maximum of 2,000 lb. in bomb bay.

TBF/TBM Avenger model variations

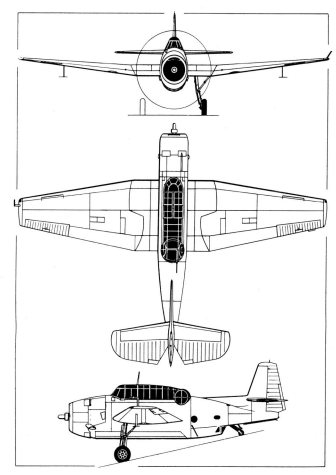

XTBF-1
Prototype torpedo bomber. Two built, the first one crashed during a test flight and was destroyed. Both members of the crew escaped. Powered by a Wright R-2600-8 engine.

TBF-1
Production model. Reputedly called the Avenger after the Japanese attack on Pearl Harbor. The Royal Navy named it the Tarpon.

TBF-1C
As the TBF-1, but with the wing-mounted machine guns removed and replaced by 20 mm cannons. The fuel-carrying capacity was doubled.

TBF-1CP
Same as the TBF-1C, but with trimetrogen reconnaissance cameras installed.

TBF-1D
TBF-1 with RT-5/APS-4 radar installed.

TBF-1CD
TBF-1C with RT-5/APS-4 radar installed in wing pod.

TBF-1E
Experimental TBF-1, used for testing latest radar and avionics.

TBF-1J
Experimental model used for testing adverse weather, lighting and de-icing system.

TBF-1L
TBF-1 with searchlight fitted on a retractable mount.

TBF-1P
Production model of the TBF-1CP, albeit only a small one.

XTBF-2
Prototype with new Wright XR-2600-10 two-stage engine.

XTBF-3
This was the prototype for the Eastern Aircraft Division's TBM-3. Powered by the Wright R-2600-20 two-stage engine.

TBM-1
Eastern's TBF-1 equivalent.

TBM-1C
Eastern's TBF-1C, as were the TBM-1D, -E, -J, -L and -P.

TBM-2
TBM-1 with the Wright XR-2600-10 engine.

XTBM-3
Conversion of TBM-1C with the Wright R-2600-20.

TBM-3
Production model.

TBM-3D
TBM-3 with the APS-4 radar on right wing.

TBM-3E
TBM-3 with strengthened fuselage and RT-5/APS-4 radar in pod under right wing.

TBM-3E2
TBM-3 with additional avionics.

TBM-3H
As the TBM-3, but with the addition of surface-search radar.

TBM-3J
Eastern's version of the TBF-1J.

TBM-3L
Eastern's version of the TBF-1L.

TBM-3M
TBM-3 converted for missile launching.

TBM-3P
Photographic version.

TBM-3Q
A small number of TBM-3s were modified for ECM and EW research.

TBM-3R
Converted to carry between seven and eight passengers.

TBM-3S
Post-war conversion to ASW (Anti-Submarine Warfare) capability.

TBM-3S2
ASW version with updated avionics.

TBM-3U
Target-towing TBM-3.

TBM-3W
AEW version with the APS-20 radar and extra fins mounted on the tail. No armament.

TBM-3W2
Improved version of the TBM-3W, with upgraded avionics.

XTBM-4
Three prototypes with redesigned wing folding systems, and restressed to absorb greater g-forces.

F6F Hellcat

The XF6F started life as a concept for an updated Wildcat. However, after the design engineers had listened very carefully to the suggestions of Wildcat pilots who had flown the aircraft under combat conditions, and had taken into consideration reports on the Japanese aircraft that the Hellcat would eventually face, they ended up with a new type of fighter. This aircraft had virtually everything: increased engine power, more ammunition, extra fuel, improved range, additional armour protection, both for the pilot and the vital areas of the aircraft, and even more important, the ability to meet the enemy over his own territory.

Leroy Grumman and William Schwendler decided that this aircraft had to be produced in the shortest possible time, and this they did, in an incredible eighteen months, without a major problem. They had examined all the best features in the Japanese aircraft that had been captured during the Battle of Midway, including the light construction techniques. These features had given the Japanese some splendid results in terms of performance, but their crews had sustained a very high casualty rate. Grumman had no intention of copying this. He wanted to give the US pilots as much protection, power and armament as possible. In short, what Grumman wanted was an aircraft that would rip through the enemy and return safely to its carrier, ready to fight another day.

Shortly after the Battle of Midway, Leon Swirbul — Grumman's Vice-President at the time — was asked to go to Pearl Harbor to meet some of the Navy's chief men. One of these was John Thach, the master aerial tactician of the US Navy, who had developed the battle techniques of the Wildcat, including the 'Thach Weave' which allowed it to defeat the much faster and superior Japanese Zeke.

The Navy's reason for the meeting was their concern about the choice of the Wright R-2600-16 engine for the Hellcat.

The performance of the aircraft with this engine was extremely disappointing, so much so, in fact, that it was considered unsuitable to fight the Zero. They would have preferred a much more powerful engine and, after a long meeting, it was decided to replace the existing engine with an eighteen-cylinder, Pratt and Whitney R-2800-16 with a Birmann Turbo Supercharger. This revolutionary engine was to increase the power by nearly twenty-five per cent and make the R-2800 probably the most famous of all the radial engines ever built.

On 30 July 1942, the XF6F-3 took to the air. The flight lasted only eleven minutes, but it was enough to convince the Bureau of Aeronautics that the time was right to put the aircraft into production. Also at this time, the F4U-1 was experiencing some serious problems, so the need for the F6F to go into production was intensified. It is a tribute to Grumman engineers and designers that there were very few major criticisms of the XF6F, the most serious being the excessive change of trim between flaps down and flaps up. There was also a slight problem with longitudinal stability, but these faults were quickly rectified. Such was the urgency to build the aircraft that parts of the plant in which the F6F was being assembled were actually being constructed around the production line.

The first F6F-3 Hellcat rolled off the production line at the end of October, and by the end of the year a further ten had been completed. There had been plans earlier in 1942 to have the Vickers Company in Canada undertake additional production of the Hellcat F6F-1 variant and the designation

Above: An F6F-1 on a production test flight from Bethpage. The absence of any markings on these aircraft indicated that they had not been delivered to the Navy or Marine Corps.

Above: An F6F-1 at Bethpage after a pre-delivery test flight.

Top: A pair of production model F6F Hellcats on a test flight during the summer of 1943. The red border around the insignia was used on all aircraft built between July and August 1943, when it was changed to blue in case it was mistaken for a Japanese marking when in combat.

An F6F-3 on a production test flight from Bethpage.

FV-1 had already been assigned to it. The plan did not materialise for one reason or another and all production was concentrated at Bethpage, Long Island.

The US Navy had at this time adopted a new camouflage scheme for the F6F-3. The upper fuselage was painted sea blue, non-specular, and the horizontal upper surfaces, wings and stabilizers sea-blue, semi-gloss. The mid-section of the fuselage was intermediate blue, non-specular, and the lower surfaces of the wings, stabilizers and fuselage were white, and all the colours had to blend evenly. On the later F6F-5s, the aircraft was painted a glossy, high speed darker sea-blue all over. These colours, of course, were pristine when they left the factory, but after a few months of combat and flying on

and off carriers in all weathers, they invariably ended up a dirty blue-grey. Any respraying whilst on board the carriers was a hit and miss affair regarding colour matching.

The US Navy took the first aircraft and subjected them to the most rigorous of tests. This included carrier landings and take-offs under the worst conditions the Navy could conjure up, resulting in a number of problems being discovered in the landing hook assembly. On a few occasions the hook actually pulled out of the fuselage, but modifications were quickly made and the tests completed. One other problem that developed with the early F6F-3s was that the horizontal stabilizers and elevators buckled upwards when the aircraft exceeded 9 g. No one knows how much 'g' was actually pulled as the 'g' indicator only went as far as 9, but the stabilizers were later strengthened, which stopped the buckling.

Within a few weeks the aircraft was accepted by the Navy and the first squadrons were equipped with it. To look at, the F6F Hellcat was not, by any stretch of the imagination, a beautiful aircraft, but everyone who flew her fell in love with her.

The wing area of 334 sq. ft. was the largest wing area of any wartime fighter production aircraft. The fuselage looked like an elongated barrel, was of a semi-monocoque construction, and had a brazier head, or 'button head', riveted aluminium skin, except for the rudder and elevators which were fabric covered. One of the reasons given for using the 'button head' rivet was that it was easier to 'shoot' than the flush rivet, therefore increasing production time and enabling the wartime factory worker to do a better job and learn quicker. The Hellcat had an incongruous, squat, heavy-looking undercarriage, housed in the stub sections of the wings.

Two hundred and fifty US gallons were carried internally in three tanks, one in the, fuselage and one each in the wing stubs, all self-sealing against .50 calibre ammunition. Droptanks held an additional 150 US gallons. These were not self-sealing, because upon entering combat they were dropped.

The outer section of the wing folded back in a swivelling action and lay flat against the aft section of the fuselage. The large, ugly, angular tail completed the picture of the aircraft. Fortunately it was pilots who flew the aircraft, not artists, and they wanted something with strength, reliability and the ability to absorb nearly everything that was thrown at them, and in the F6F Hellcat they had just that. The aircraft's vital areas were protected by heavy armour plate, which added considerably to her overall weight.

The F6F-3 Hellcat first saw service with VF-9 Squadron in the middle of January 1943. The squadron, led by Commander Jack Raby, had just completed a combat tour of duty aboard the *USS Ranger* (CV-4) and had been supporting the North African invasion the previous November, VF-9 had been due to convert from F4Fs to F4U-1 Corsairs, but the Chance-Vought company had run into some serious problems and were unable to supply the aircraft.

The first of the Hellcats, flown by Commander Raby, Lt. (jg) Herbert N. Houck, later to become CO of VF-9, and Lt. (jg) Armistead B. Smith, were flown from Bethpage, Long Island, to Ream Field, near Norfolk, Virginia, on 16 January 1943. Over the next few weeks the squadron pilots flew many delivery flights and it was an incident on one of these flights that was to prove how rugged the aircraft really was. The incident occurred when a four-man delivery team was flying the F6F-3s from Bethpage to Ream Field. The flight, led by Lt. (jg) Casey Childers, was flying over a heavily wooded area, some 30 miles north of Cape May, New Jersey, when Lt. Childers' engine cut out. Given no choice, Childers set up a glide path and made a wheels-up, dead-stick landing amongst the trees. The Hellcat ploughed through the trees, seemingly coming apart in every direction, but when the dust and debris settled, Childers climbed out of the cockpit unharmed and waved to three very anxious pilots circling overhead. Undoubtedly the skill of the pilot, together with the extremely rugged airframe of the F6F Hellcat had saved his life.

The Hellcat first saw action with VF-5 Squadron whilst aboard the *USS Yorktown* on 31 August 1943. Lt. Robert Duncan, on a strafing mission against Marcus Island, engaged a number of Zeke aircraft and destroyed two of them after a hectic battle in which the Hellcat showed its superior speed on a number of occasions. On 4 September 1943, Marcus Island was again attacked by Hellcats and a communiqué from Admiral Nimitz stated that over eighty per cent of its military installations had been destroyed.

At first the Japanese offered very little resistance to the fighter and bomber attacks, but later when they did start to retaliate they discovered that the Grumman Hellcats and

Avengers were more than a match for them. So much so, that one Hellcat squadron, commanded by Commander Bill Dean, shot down 187 aircraft without losing a single aircraft themselves. This remarkable record was matched by Lt. Gene Valencia's flight of four Hellcats of VF-9 when they dispatched fifty Japanese aircraft without even getting a bullet hole in their own aircraft.

By the beginning of September 1943 several other F6F squadrons were operating in the Pacific and the Grumman production lines were working at a rate they themselves never believed possible: they were producing some 500 aircraft per month.

The first major air-to-air combat came on 4 December 1943, when ninety-one F6F-3s were flying close escort on a

Divers position themselves to prepare a US Navy Hellcat for retrieval which has lain twelve miles off the coast of San Diego for 26 years.

Top: A rather ungraceful, but fortunately happy, landing made by 'Lucky 13' on the deck of its carrier, the USS Lexington, after a strike at Kwajalein on 4 December 1943.

Grumman F6F-5 Hellcat cutaway drawing key

1 Radio mast
2 Rudder balance
3 Rudder upper hinge
4 Aluminium alloy fin ribs
5 Rudder post
6 Rudder structure
7 Rudder trim tab
8 Rudder middle hinge
9 Diagonal stiffeners
10 Aluminium alloy elevator trim tab
11 Fabric-covered (and taped) elevator surfaces
12 Elevator balance
13 Flush riveted leading-edge strip
14 Arrester hook (extended)
15 Tailplane ribs
16 Tail navigation (running) light
17 Rudder lower hinge
18 Arrester hook (stowed)
19 Fin main spar lower cut-out
20 Tailplane end rib
21 Fin forward spar
22 Fuselage/fin root fairing
23 Port elevator
24 Aluminium alloy-skinned tailplane
25 Section light
26 Fuselage aft frame
27 Control access
28 Bulkhead
29 Tailwheel hydraulic shock-absorber
30 Tailwheel centering mechanism
31 Tailwheel steel mounting arm

32 Rearward retracting tailwheel (hard rubber type)
33 Fairing
34 Steel plate door fairing
35 Tricing sling support tube
36 Hydraulic actuating cylinder
37 Flanged ring fuselage frames
38 Control cable runs
39 Fuselage longerons
40 Relay box
41 Dorsal rod antenna
42 Dorsal recognition light
43 Radio aerial
44 Radio mast
45 Aerial lead-in
46 Dorsal frame stiffeners
47 Junction box
48 Radio equipment (upper rack)
49 Radio shelf
50 Control cable runs
51 Transverse brace
52 Remote radio compass
53 Ventral recognition lights (3)
54 Ventral rod antenna
55 Destructor device
56 Accumulator
57 Radio equipment (lower rack)
58 Entry hand/footholds
59 Engine water injection rack
60 Canopy track
61 Water filler neck
62 Rear-view mirror
63 Rearward-sliding cockpit canopy (open)
64 Headrest
65 Pilot's head/shoulder armour
66 Canopy sill (reinforced)
67 Fire extinguisher
68 Oxygen bottle (port fuselage wall)
69 Water tank mounting
70 Underfloor self-sealing fuel tank (60 US gal/227 l)
71 Armoured bulkhead
72 Starboard console

73 Pilot's seat
74 Hydraulic handpump
75 Fuel filler cap and neck
76 Rudder pedals
77 Centre console
78 Control column
79 Chart board (horizontal stowage)
80 Instrument panel
81 Panel coaming
82 Reflector gunsight
83 Rear-view mirror

84 Armoured glass windshield
85 Deflection plate (pilot forward protection)

86 Main bulkhead armour-plated upper section with hoisting sling attachments port and starboard)
87 Aluminium alloy aileron trim tab
88 Fabric covered (and taped) aileron surfaces
89 Flush riveted outer wing skin
90 Aluminium alloy sheet wing tip (riveted to outer wing rib)

91 Port navigation (running) light
92 Formed leading-edge (approach/landing light and camera gun inboard)
93 Fixed cowling panel
94 Armour plate (oil tank forward protection)
95 Oil tank (19 US gal/72 l)
96 Welded engine mount fittings
97 Fuselage forward bulkhead
98 Aileron control linkage
99 Engine accessories bay
100 Engine mounting frame (hydraulic fluid reservoir attached to port frames)
101 Controllable cooling gills

102 Cowling ring (removable servicing/access panels)
103 Pratt & Whitney R-2800-10W twin row radial air-cooled engine
104 Nose ring profile
105 Reduction gear housing
106 Three-blade Hamilton Standard Hydromatic controllable pitch propeller
107 Propeller hub
108 Engine oil cooler (centre) and supercharger intercooler (outer sections) intakes
109 Oil cooler deflection plate under-protection
110 Oil cooler duct
111 Intercooler intake duct
112 Mainwheel fairing
113 Port mainwheel
114 Cooler outlet and fairing
115 Auxiliary tank support/ attachment arms
116 Exhaust cluster
117 Supercharger housing

118 Exhaust outlet scoop
119 Wing front spar web
120 Wing front spar/fuselage attachment bolts
121 Undercarriage mounting/ pivot point on front spar

122 Inter-spar self-sealing fuel tanks (port and starboard: 87·5 US gal/331 l each)
123 Wing rear spar/fuselage attachment bolts
124 Structural end rib
125 Slotted wing flap profile
126 Wing flap centre-section
127 Wing fold line
128 Starboard wheel well (double-plate reinforced edges)

129 Gunbay
130 Removable diagonal brace strut
131 Three 0·5-in (12,7-mm) Colt Browning machine guns
132 Auxiliary tank aft support
133 Blast tubes
134 Folding wing joint (upper surface)
135 Machine-gun barrels
136 Fairing
137 Undercarriage actuating strut
138 Mainwheel leg oleo hydraulic shock strut
139 Auxiliary tank sling/brace
140 Long-range auxiliary fuel tank (jettisonable)
141 Mainwheel aluminium alloy fairing
142 Forged steel torque link
143 Low pressure balloon tyre

144 Cast magnesium wheel
145 Underwing 5-in (12,7-cm) air-to-ground RPs

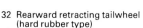

shipping strike at Kwajalein and against airfield on Roi Island. They encountered a force of fifty A6M Zero-Sens, and in the resulting action twenty-eight of the Japanese aircraft were destroyed, with the loss of only three Hellcats. This early combat experience proved that Grumman had built a fighter capable of taking on the best the Japanese had to offer.

Late in 1942, the US Navy decided to create a night fighter squadron to operate from carriers in the Pacific and, ultimately, elsewhere. A radar scanner was mounted in a pod under the starboard wing of the F6F-3, weighing a mere 180 lb. and capable of sweeping an area of four miles. Called the AN/APS-4 (Army Navy/Airborne Pulse Search equipment), the radar was designed so that the pilot could operate it with the minimum amount of distraction from his flying duties. The APS-4 was the forerunner of modern airborne radar sets. Only eighteen F6F-3s were equipped with them, out of a total of two hundred, the remainder of the F6F-3s being fitted with the APS-6 which, although seventy pounds heavier, provided

the aircraft with an increased range of five-and-a-half miles, with the capability of picking up enemy shipping at sixty miles.

With the arrival of the APS-6 radar, the F6F-3 Nightfighter Hellcats became the flying test-beds for all new fighter techniques and equipment. One of the most important innovations of the APS-6 was a radar altimeter that provided exact height information when the aircraft was being flown entirely on instruments. Glare was a problem in the early night fighters and this was overcome by incorporating a flat-faced, bulletproof, glass panel into the windshield and illuminating the instrument panel with red backlighting. For all-round protection, a radar was installed in the tail. It was called the APS-13 and gave the Hellcat a sixty per cent coverage for about 800 yards behind.

Detachments of night-fighters were assigned to the carriers *Hornet*, *Bunker Hill*, *Wasp*, *Essex*, *Yorktown* and *Lexington* during 1944, and the F6F-3Es and -Ns were to make a tremendous impact on the war.

One of the many problems that faced the maintenance

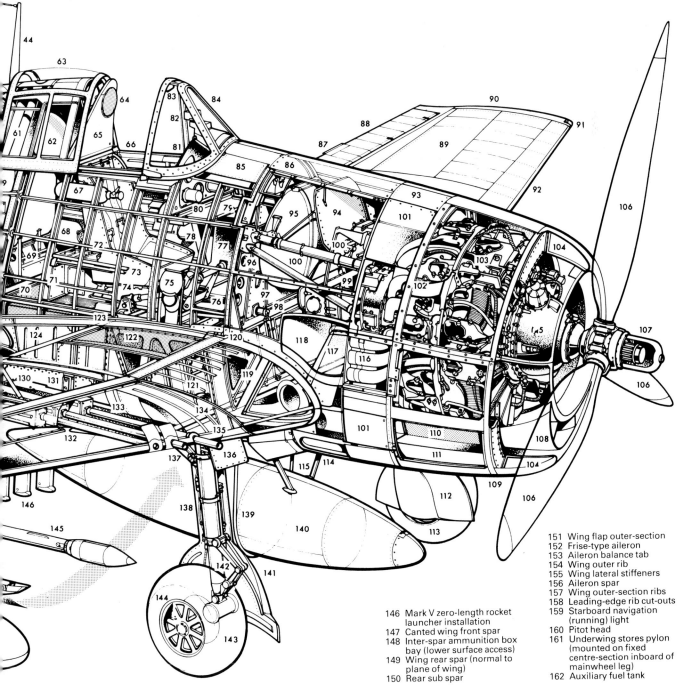

151 Wing flap outer-section
152 Frise-type aileron
153 Aileron balance tab
154 Wing outer rib
155 Wing lateral stiffeners
156 Aileron spar
157 Wing outer-section ribs
158 Leading-edge rib cut-outs
159 Starboard navigation (running) light
160 Pitot head
161 Underwing stores pylon (mounted on fixed centre-section inboard of mainwheel leg)
162 Auxiliary fuel tank

146 Mark V zero-length rocket launcher installation
147 Canted wing front spar
148 Inter-spar ammunition box bay (lower surface access)
149 Wing rear spar (normal to plane of wing)
150 Rear sub spar

An F6F equipped with night fighter gear, August 1945.

crews, was the nightly check of the radar electronics. Under battle conditions the crews had their hands full just carrying out routine maintenance on the aircraft, but with the addition of the F6F-3Ns they were really put under pressure. Up to this point all the night fighter flying operations were carried out on an experimental or casual basis. Because the idea of using night fighters was new, many carrier captains preferred the old, established ways of defending their ships, like using anti-aircraft guns or quick evasive action. But as the war progressed, it became increasingly obvious that the old ways were losing their effectiveness and a solution had to be found. It was decided that a complete, fully operational night air squadron should be formed to operate from carriers.

On 20 January 1944, Lt. Cdr. Turner F. Caldwell was given the job of creating the first full night fighter air squadron, VF(N)-79. After some eight months and about three hundred hours of intensive training, the squadron was ready, and in August the same year, now redesignated VF(N)-41, the squadron split into detachments aboard the light carrier *USS Independence* and other *Essex* class carriers. The first full night Air Group was Air Group 90, aboard the *USS Enterprise* under the command of Cdr. Bill Martin. The Air Group consisted of thirty-one F6F-5Ns and twenty-four TBM-3Es and was a resounding success until the *Enterprise* was hit. The second night Air Group, Air Group 54, was on the *USS Saratoga* under the command of Cdr. Vince McCormick.

At first the detachments were used mainly for daylight fighter sweeps and the occasional dawn or dusk patrol. Then, just after dark one September evening, four Hellcats from the carrier *USS Independence* intercepted a Japanese aircraft that had managed to get within striking distance of the fleet. This

brought home the need for a night fighter patrol just before dawn and after dusk, when the fleet was at its most vulnerable. But the real turning point came on 12 October when Lt. Henry, executive officer of VF(N)-41, picked up on his radar a group of Japanese Bettys (Mitsubishi G4M1s). After a fierce battle, four of the attackers were shot down. Two weeks later, VF(N)-41 pilots were all assigned to regular night flying missions, and by the end of 1944 the number of detachments had increased to thirteen.

In the battle for the Marianas, on 18 and 19 June 1944, the Japanese put up one of their strongest air defences of the war. In less than three hours, 369 Japanese aircraft had fallen to the guns of the Hellcats. The battle was to become known as 'The Great Marianas Turkey Shoot'.

Prior to 1944, the Navy was using the F6F-3, but modifications made during the early part of 1944 produced a faster, smoother Hellcat that could outrun and outclimb any Japanese aircraft at any altitude — the F6F-5 had arrived. One of the major improvements was the spring-tab ailerons, which increased the rate of roll and lowered the lateral control forces required.

In the two ferociously-fought months that were spent retaking the Philippines and surrounding islands, 2,594 Japanese aircraft were destroyed by US carrier-based aircraft, for the loss of 300 US Navy and Marine aircraft. Air Group Two, flying Hellcats and Avengers, accounted for 539 Japanese aircraft and more than 400,000 tons of enemy shipping during this period. In the Pacific War as a whole, approximately 6,500 Japanese aircraft were shot down and of these, 5,000 were accounted for by the Hellcat, at a ratio of 19 to 1.

Right: A division of Marine Corps F6Fs from carriers of Task Force 58 on Iwo Jima in Volcano Islands D-Day +2, with the US fleet in the background. The picture was taken by an aircraft from USS Yorktown.

Meanwhile, on the other side of the world, the F6F-5 Hellcat was creating just as big an impact against the Germans in the South of France. These Hellcats were based on baby flat-tops and were giving close ground support to US Army troops as they fought their way along the coast.

Under the Lend-Lease Agreement between the United States and Great Britain, 252 F6F-3s had been shipped to England to re-equip the Fleet Air Arm. The Hellcat 1, originally named the Gannet 1 by the Royal Navy, entered service with the Fleet Air Arm on 1 July 1943 with No 800 Squadron. After a few months of familiarization training, the squadron was assigned to the escort carrier *HMS Emperor* and carried out anti-shipping strikes off the Norwegian coast. The aircraft was deployed in British waters for a short time before the carrier and her squadrons joined the Pacific Fleet. By the end of 1944, Hellcat squadrons were distributed throughout the British Fleet aboard the carriers *HMS Empress* (Nos 838 and 888 Squadrons), *HMS Khedive* (No 808 Squadron), *HMS Indefatigable* (No 1840 Squadron), and *HMS Indomitable* (Nos 1839 and 1844 Squadrons). Of the 1,182 F6F Hellcats delivered to the Royal Navy, 74 were equipped as night fighters. Search radar was fitted into a radome in the starboard wing, but by the time all the research work had been completed, the war in the Pacific was coming to an end.

The F6F's speed was put to good use when No 888 Squadron was formed into a photographic reconnaissance unit. The Hellcat's speed of 371 mph enabled the squadron to carry out more than 22 missions, between February and March 1945, over Northern Sumatra, Penang and the Kra Isthmus.

The Royal Navy's first major action against the Japanese was the attack on the oil refineries in Sumatra, and the F6F Hellcats played an important part in providing escorts for the strike aircraft. The strike itself was carried out by forty-three Avengers from the carriers *Illustrious* and *Indomitable*, accompanied by twelve rocket-firing Fireflies of *Indefatigable*'s No 1770 Squadron. In the ensuing battle, a total of fourteen enemy aircraft were destroyed in air-to-air combat and thirty-four on the ground. The Fleet Air Arm lost seven, the majority due to landing accidents caused by battle damage.

Meanwhile back in England, one of the few Hellcat squadrons still based there was escorting the strike against the German pocket battleship *Tirpitz* in the Norwegian Altenfjord. The strike was to be carried out by Fairey Barracudas from the 8th and 52nd Torpedo Bomber Reconnaissance Wings. Hellcats from Nos 800 and 804 Squadron (*HMS Emperor*) and Wildcats from Nos 891, 896, 882 and 898 Squadrons (*HMSs Purser* and *Searcher*) provided the escort. The *Tirpitz* was hit fourteen times by armour-piercing bombs, putting the mighty battleship out of action for three months. She was eventually towed south to Tromsø for repairs and it was there that RAF Lancaster bombers found her. The *Tirpitz* was bombed again: this time she capsized, and one of the biggest threats to Atlantic convoys was disposed of. Of the fourteen squadrons of Hellcats in the Fleet Air Arm, ten were in action in the Pacific.

In the meantime, Grumman had been upgrading the F6F, but such was the quality of the first aircraft that all subsequent improvements were relatively minor. After the F6F-3 and -3N, came the F6F-5, of which 7,780 were built. A number of these aircraft were on lend-lease to New Zealand, and it was on these aircraft that the 'mixed battery' of guns was fitted. They consisted of three 4.5 calibre and three 2.2 calibre machine guns, instead of six .5 calibre. The idea was not a success and was not adopted by anyone else.

The improvements made by Grumman to the F6F-5 provided a stronger windshield and canopy that had less tendency to scratch, the rear-view windows were removed, the tail was strengthened, and spring-assisted tabs put into ailerons. Shortly after the delivery of the F6F-5, Grumman produced a modified version of the aircraft, the F6F-5N. Of

One of Grumman's female production test pilots prepares to test fly the F6F-3N.

the 1,434 built, eighty were shipped to Britain with the APS-6 radar installed in the radome under the starboard wing. An unknown number of photographic reconnaissance F6F-5Ps were built for the British, with a top speed of 410 mph and a climb rate of 3,150 feet per minute. An F6F-6 was built, but it was a purely experimental model, used to test a four-bladed Hamilton Standard propeller and a 2,450 hp Pratt and Whitney R-2800-18W engine with water injection. Although the test flights were carried out and the results encouraging, it was never adopted. In all, some 12,200 F6F Hellcats were produced by Grumman in an incredible three years. Nearly all the Lend-Lease Hellcats that survived the war were returned by Britain to the USA, although there were a couple of exceptions. As late as 1953, Capt. J. A. Ivors, RN, the commanding officer of RNAS Lossiemouth, Scotland, was still using an F6F-3 Hellcat as his personal aircraft. The aircraft eventually went to the Fleet Air Arm Museum at RNAS Yeovilton in Somerset.

The end of the war in Europe and the Pacific did not see the end of the Hellcats in action. In October 1950, *Aeronavale* (French Navy) F6F-5 Hellcats were aboard a French aircraft carrier when it arrived off the coast of French Indo-China. They were surplus US Navy F6F-5s, and were part of a massive arms and materials shipment given to France by the Americans. The aircraft were used by the *Armée de l'Air* in their *Escadrilles* 1/6 Corse, 11/6 Normandie Miemen and 11/9 Auvergne. They were to replace the Bell P-63 Kingcobras, but served less than a year with the *Armée de l'Air* before being replaced by F8F Bearcats. The *Aeronavale* used the Hellcats to replace ageing Seafires. The Hellcats stayed with the Navy until 1954, when the French involvement in Indo-China ended. Other countries, such as Argentina and Uruguay, had the Hellcat in operation with their Navies until 1961. These aircraft were supplied through the US Mutual Aid Programme and were the last Hellcats to see operational service.

There was a little-known unit called Guided Missile Unit 90 that, during the Korean conflict, used F6F-5K drones as missiles. The aircraft were packed with explosives, and with a Douglas AD-4Q flying as a control aircraft, they made a number of very successful attacks against the North Koreans.

Several F6Fs are still flying, but they are in private hands. Fortunately the public can still see them flying at air shows.

On 15 June 1946 the US Navy's aerobatic display team made their first public appearance. The Blue Angels, as they were to be known, were formed by Commander Roy M. 'Butch' Voris, an ace with VF-2. The team decided on the best aircraft available at the time and chose the Grumman F6F Hellcat, and up to 1968 used Grumman aircraft exclusively.

F6F Hellcat technical details

Model	Fighter (primarily carrier-based)	*Weight*	9,238 lb. empty, 15,413 lb. gross.
Crew	One.	*Performance*	Max. speed 380 mph, cruising speed 168 mph, initial climb rate 2,980 ft. per min.
Engine	2,000 hp Pratt and Whitney R-2800-10W.	*Armament*	Six fixed, forward-firing, .50 in. guns or two 20 mm and four .50 in. guns.
Dimensions	Wing span 42 ft. 10 in., wing area 334 sq. ft., length 33 ft. 7 in., height 13 ft. 1 in.		

F6F Hellcat model variations

XF6F-1

The first of a new breed of fighter, powered by a Wright R-2600-10 engine with the new three-bladed Curtiss Electric propeller. This aircraft was later modified and redesignated the XF6F-4.

XF6F-2

The second of the prototypes, originally built to take the Wright R-2600-16 engine but fitted with the Pratt and Whitney R-2800-10 instead. This was a considerably more powerful engine and the aircraft was redesignated the XF6F-3.

XF6F-3

See XF6F-2.

F6F-3

First production model of the Hellcat, but with modified landing-gear fairings and a three-bladed Hamilton Standard Hydromatic propeller instead of the Curtiss Electric propeller. The F6F-3 Hellcat was designated Gannet I by the British Royal Navy, but later reverted back to the name Hellcat.

F6F-3E

The first of the APS-4 radar-equipped Hellcats, the radar housed under the right wing.

XF6F-3N

Designation of the last night fighter with the APS-6 radar system, housed under the right wing.

F6F-3N

Production model of the night fighter. The Royal Navy version was designated the Hellcat NF-1.

F6F-3P

These were modified F6F-3s used for photo-reconnaissance.

XF6F-4

This was the original XF6F-1 before it was fitted with the Pratt and Whitney R-2800-27 engine.

F6F-5

The standard F6F-3, but with a number of modifications, a more aerodynamic fairing, reinforced ailerons and tail structure and a flat windscreen. Attachments were fitted to the wings to carry bombs.

F6F-5D

These were radio-controlled drones used during the Korean War.

F6F-5K

These were radio-guided flying bombs used in conjunction with the F6F-5Ds during the Korean War.

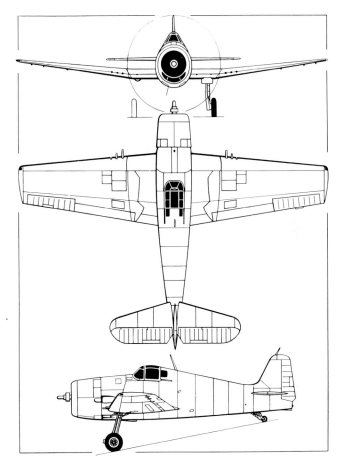

F6F-5N

Modified F6F-5s with the APS-6 radar system, eighty of which were given to the Royal Navy, which designated them Hellcat NF-11s.

F6F-5P

An updated F6F-3P, the -5P had the cameras mounted at the rear of the cockpit, thus leaving the wing armaments unaltered.

XF6F-6

Standard F6F-5 with the uprated Pratt and Whitney R-2800-18W engine and a four-bladed propeller. Two were built.

F7F Tigercat

Although the F6F Hellcat and the TBF/TBM Avenger were having a certain amount of success against the Japanese Zero, one thing that they lacked was superior speed. The US Navy decided it needed aircraft that would have the speed of the Zero, the manoeuvrability of the F6F Hellcat, and the durability and range of the TBF/TBM Avenger. Such a design came to mind almost immediately in the shape of the discarded XF5F-1, or Skyrocket, designed by Gordon Israel, and its updated version, the XP-50. Neither had progressed further than the prototype stages.

The XF5F-1 had a relatively short, slim fuselage, flanked by an unusually broad wing, on which were mounted, ahead of the fuselage, two, large Wright R-1820-40 Cyclone engines. At the rear of the fuselage, two horizontally-mounted stabilizers made up the tail and completed the design of this unusual aircraft.

The initial tests of the XF5F-1 were very satisfactory and the Navy were impressed with the aircraft's performance. It had a top speed at sea level of 383 mph, 50 mph faster than the Wildcat, and a service ceiling of 33,000 feet. The XF5F-1 was given the name Skyrocket after it had displayed an incredible rate of climb of 4,000 feet per minute. But for all this, there were problems: the pilot's vision for carrier landings was one of the major ones, and the general stability of the aircraft caused some concern, although this was remedied later.

The aircraft was intended for carrier use, and the outboard wing panels could be folded up, reducing the wing-span from 42 feet to 21 feet. The initial test flights, which were reasonably successful, were flown by Bud Gillies, but although modifications were made to improve the pilot's view for deck landings, there were a number of accidents.

The US Navy's interest began to wane, and after the last accident, which was a belly-up landing, the Navy abandoned it. The project was not completely forgotten, however, and the US Army, which had been observing the tests, suddenly declared an interest. They did not have the deck landing problems of the Navy and the undercarriage was modified to a tricycle landing gear. This version was called the XP-50, and the test pilot, Bob Hall, worked continuously on its development. Then one fateful day, Bob Hall decided to carry out some altitude tests. Whilst flying over Long Island Sound, one of the turbo-superchargers exploded, cutting all the hydraulics to the landing gear. Although Bob Hall managed to get the main gear down, he could not lower the nosewheel. After all attempts to get it down had been exhausted, he decided to bail out of the aircraft, which he accomplished by jettisoning the canopy and sliding along the fuselage to the

Above: F7F-3N night fighter on test flight over Bethpage. Note the extended nose for the radar and the radar operator's position over the wings.

tail, then just stepping off. By doing this, he eliminated the possibility of hitting one of the projecting tail surfaces, which he could otherwise have done.

The cause of the explosion would have remained a mystery, had it not been for a young boy fishing off the beach at City Island. He had observed the XP-50 flying high in the sky, when suddenly he saw a puff of smoke then, some minutes later, a splash off shore. After waiting until low tide, he recovered what turned out to be the complete turbine wheel, minus its blades. Fortunately, the boy had the presence of mind to take it to a newspaper, the *New York Daily News,* who having heard of the accident, contacted Grumman. It was discovered that the bolts holding the two halves of the turbine wheel together had stretched, allowing them to separate.

Despite this setback, the US Army retained its interest in the XP-50 and asked Grumman to build another prototype. This put Grumman in a quandary because their production lines were working at capacity, and they would only build another one if the Army would give them a firm order for at least 1,000 aircraft. This the Army refused to do, and that was the end of the XP-50.

The concept of a twin-engined, carrier-borne aircraft was ahead of its time, and although the XP-50 did not really achieve a great deal, it did supply Grumman with information which was to prove invaluable with later aircraft.

Grumman eventually produced a design for a twin-engined,

Grumman test pilot Bud Gillies about to climb into the XF5F-1 for its first test flight.

single-seat fighter with a tricycle undercarriage, designated the XF7F-1 and known as the Tigercat. It was powered by two Pratt and Whitney R-2800-22W, two-speed engines, that turned two Hamilton Standard, constant-speed, fully feathering, three-bladed propellers and the armament consisted of four .50 calibre, fixed machine guns in the nose and four Hispano 20mm fixed cannons, mounted in the wing roots. In addition to 2,000 rounds of ammunition, it could carry two 2,000 lb. bombs or one 2,150 lb. torpedo, plus an assortment of rockets fitted in racks under each wing. This made the Tigercat the most heavily armed fighter aircraft in the world at that time, and an ideal aircraft for ground support. At its critical altitude of 19,500 feet, it was capable of a maximum speed of 429 miles per hour. It had a climb rate of 4,200 feet per minute, a range of 1,160 miles (later versions of the F7F had a range of 1,900 miles) and a service ceiling of 42,000 feet. The aircraft weighed 15,274 lb. empty and 20,107 lb. gross. The weight was to cause problems later when its suitability for carrier operations was being evaluated.

The initial test flights, in December 1943, were carried out successfully, but the first pre-production XF7F-1 crashed during low-level trials at Patuxent River. The second production aircraft completed all its trials without a hitch and at the Eight Day Fighter Conference, held at Patuxent River in November 1944, it gave a good account of itself against some stiff competition. A variety of pilots from the Army and Navy flew the Tigercat and all agreed that it was one of the most agreeable aircraft they had ever flown.

The aircraft was found to be particularly sensitive to off-

Of the 250 produced, a proportion were converted to F7F-3N, -3P and -3D variants. There was a proposal for an F7F-3E, carrying electronic equipment, but this never got past the suggestion stage. The F7F-3 itself was a single-seat fighter, with an additional 85-gallon fuel tank in place of the radar operator. The plexiglass rear canopy was removed and the fuselage guns replaced, as in the F7F-1. All the armament was removed and provision was made in the aft section of the fuselage to instal five cameras which pointed from either side of the aircraft, and three apertures, complete with sliding doors, were cut into the bottom of the fuselage. This system was called the Tri-Metragon installation and was extremely successful. In place of the radar operator's position, an SCR-269 radio compass was installed. Later, a number of F7Fs were used as drones and drone controllers.

A nose-on view of the F7F-1 showing the slimness of the fuselage.

With the last delivery of the F7F-1, production of the F7F-2N commenced. The F7F-2N was ostensibly a radar search aircraft and, as such, had a much improved radar, the AN/APS-6 Search Radar, and a larger radome, which increased the overall length of the Tigercat. The radar operator was accommodated by reducing the size of the mid-fuselage reserve fuel tank and placing him above it. His plexiglass canopy protruded much higher than that of the pilot, giving the impression that a cockpit had been stuck on as an afterthought. It looked quite a crude affair. Even the fuselage guns had to be removed to help accommodate the radar operator, although an assortment of air-to-air surface weaponry, such as eight five-inch HVAR (High Velocity Aircraft Rockets) or three 'Tiny Tim' rockets under each wing, was retained; the R-2800-22W Double Wasp engines were replaced by R-2800-34Ws. The same configuration was used later for the F7F-3D, when the drone controller was housed in the radar operator's seat. (Incidentally, the F7F-3K was used as a drone.) The sixty-fifth F7F-2N was delivered to the Marine Corps on 8 March 1945 and later that month the first of the F7F-3s left the factory.

An F7F-3N with the Mark 13 torpedo beneath the fuselage. Note the rocket launching struts for eight five-inch HVAR's beneath the wing.

One final variant of the F7F, the F7F-4N, was the only Tigercat to be modified satisfactorily and accepted for carrier operations. The main landing gear struts were redesigned and lengthened for better impact absorption, and the inner wing panels were strengthened. There was a small radome, similar to that on the F7F-1. Only twelve F7F-4Ns were built and all were delivered after the war, to be used primarily for test work. Of the 1,650 F7F Tigercats ordered, only a handful were ever delivered. Of those that were, the vast majority, 175 in all, were in fact delivered to the Marine Corps, and of these, twenty-six were assigned to the Marine Night Fighter Squadron, VMF(N)-533 at Eagle Mountain Lake, Texas. Whilst the crews were on training and familiarization programmes, World War II came to an end and further contracts for the F7F were cancelled.

At the beginning of 1945, two F7F-2Ns were sent to England for test and evaluation. One went to the Aeroplane and Armament Experimental Establishment at Boscombe Down in Wiltshire to test its suitability for carrier operations. The other went to the Royal Aircraft Establishment at Farnborough, to test its recovery capabilities when landing on one engine, and the use of the power-boosted rudder. Designated TT-348 and 349 respectively, both aircraft were subjected to a thorough evaluation, and to quote from the report from Boscome Down:

> Despite the following criticisms of the F7F Tigercat, it is nevertheless considered to be a most attractive aircraft. The aircraft possesses a combination of good and bad deck operating characteristics, with the former predominating.
>   The good features are:
> Unobstructed view forward and sideways.
> Negligible change of lateral and directional trim, with power or speed, flaps and undercarriage down.

The F7F-2N on a test flight.

No bouncing during take-off and landing runs.
No take-off swing.
Large reduction in stalling speed with power assistance.
Good lateral stability at the stall, flaps and undercarriage down.

The bad features:
Inadequate elevator control engine off, requiring high speed or power approaches to obtain the necessary control.
Lack of lateral and directional control, making single-engine deck landings impracticable, although these controls were adequate for normal (two engines) landings.
Excessive longitudinal changes of control column position with power.
Draughty with cockpit hood open.

However it was noted, and pilots should be warned, that roll was produced by application of the rudder, the roll being in the same direction as the application of the rudder. It is doubtful whether the aircraft as tested would be satisfactory for service use for carrier operations, on account of the inadequate elevator control and deck trials would be necessary before a definite decision could be made.

Although there were no plans to build more F7Fs, the Marine Corps was still using the aircraft as a front-line fighter, in fact VMF(N)-533 actually arrived in Okinawa the day before the Japanese surrender, on 14 August 1945. Throughout September of 1945, the F7F-2Ns of VMF(N)-533 Squadron carried out night patrols over Okinawa. That October, part of the squadron was assigned to reconnaissance patrols in China, providing air support for the repatriation of Japanese troops.

In June 1950 the North Koreans invaded South Korea, with the call-up of reserve marine corps pilots, a second squadron was formed with F7F-3Ns, VMF(N)-542. Even though the majority of the pilots had had no experience flying F7Fs, the squadron left for Japan aboard the aircraft carrier *USS Cape Esperance* and by the end of September were in action flying support missions for land bases in South Korea.

The Tigercat's first encounter with the enemy was against the Russian-built Polikarpov PO-2, flown by North Korean pilots. Although these aircraft were old, fabric-covered biplanes, their slow speed made them difficult to engage in conflict. They were used by the North Koreans for harassing missions, carrying out small bombing raids on the airfields. When the Tigercats were scrambled to intercept them they found that they were virtually at stalling speed before they could get a shot at them. But in reality, the PO-2 was no match for the superior firepower of the F7F and a large number were destroyed.

The F7F-3Ns carried out a campaign against the main enemy supply routes that ran close to the front line, attacking columns with napalm, fragmentation bombs, rockets and the 20 mm cannons that were mounted in the wing roots of the F7F.

The arrival of the MiG-17 tolled the death knell for the piston-engined aircraft, which were no match for the higher speed and greater manoeuvrability of the jet fighter. This decision was brought to a head in 1952 when F7F-3Ns of VMF(N)-513 Squadron were asked to support B-29 bombers of the USAF on their regular raids over North Korea. It was hoped to cut down the losses the USAF were sustaining on these raids by using the Tigercats in a defensive role. That July, VMF(N)-513 made four aircraft available for these missions, but they were lost and the USAF declared the Tigercat to be completely ineffectual against the North Korean jets. They even seemed to be losing their edge when giving air support to the ground troops. This was the end of the road, not only for the F7F, but also for many other World War II-vintage aircraft, and in November 1952 the F7F-3Ns were replaced by the Douglas F3D-2 jet fighter.

Marine Corps F7Fs giving close air support during an amphibious training exercise at Marine Corps School, Quantico.

One of the F7F's more important roles outside the theatre of war was the armament trials at the Naval Ordinance Station, China Lake. Trials were carried out there on the development of aircraft rockets and launchers. A number of firing runs were carried out from different angles and heights, with the intention of developing ballistic data for use in computer sight settings, and ultimately in converting the information into tables that would cover the firing envelope of the aircraft. The dives varied from 10 to 50 degrees and the ranges from 1,000 to 2,000 yards, all of which were recorded on film from cameras mounted on the ground, although the latter also received some of its information through a camera fitted to the gunsight of the aircraft.

With the Tigercat making its first appearance at the end of World War II and its last at the beginning of the Korean War, the aircraft never really had an opportunity to show off its combat capabilities and it was relegated to service with the reserve units, and even there was quickly replaced. A few found an extended lease of life as forest fire borate bombers, but the remainder were scrapped. One Tigercat, however, did find a new lease of life, when in 1948, after being in storage for two years at the NAF (Naval Air Facility) Weeksville, North Carolina, it was removed for modification.

In 1950 it was sent to Cherry Point for a year, and from there to the Marine Night Fighter Training Squadron VMFT(N)-20. It was retired from the military in 1953 and placed in storage at Litchfield Park, where George F. Kreitzberg purchased it and equipped it as a fire bomber. For nearly twenty years the F7F Tigercat flew as a fire fighter, then in

1980, after having been retired for a year or so, it was purchased by Performance Aviation of Oakland, California. It was flown to Oakland, where a passenger seat was installed behind the cockpit. In 1982, it was restored to its original dark blue Marine colour scheme, thus completing a full cycle.

Although the Tigercat did not leave its mark in the manner of the other Grumman 'Cats', it should be remembered for its contribution to the advancement of aircraft design.

An F7F-3D drone controller. Note the controller's cockpit at the rear of the pilot's. The drone is on the pylon beneath the starboard wing.

F7F-2N Tigercat Technical details

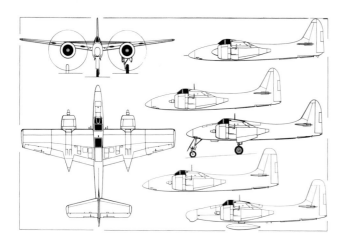

Propellers	Two Hamilton Standard three-bladed hydromatic.
Dimensions	Wing span 51 ft. 6 in., length 45 ft. 6½ in., height 13 ft. 9in.
Weight	Empty 16,028 lb. TOGW 21,690 lb.
Performance	Max. speed 450 mph, cruising speed 190 mph. Service ceiling 40,600 ft., range 1,850 miles. Initial climb rate 6,000 ft. per min.
Armament	Four .50 calibre, fixed machine guns. Four 20 mm fixed cannons. Two 1,000 lb. bombs *or* One 2,150 lb. torpedo Eight five-inch HVAR rockets *or* two Tiny Tim rockets (500 lb. warhead)
Build numbers	XF7F-1 — 03549 to 03550
	F7F-1 — 80259 to 80293
	XF7F-2N — 80261
	F7F-2N — 80294 to 80358
	F7F-3 — 80359 to 80608
	F7F-4N — 80548, 80609 to 80620.
Note	XF7F-2N was modified from third F7F-1 production model. The first F7F-4N was a modified F7F-3 with BuNo. 80548.

Model	Fighter (Day and Night)
Crew	One (The F7F-3N and F7F-4N were modified to carry two).
Engine	Two Pratt and Whitney R-2800-22s, developing 2,100 hp.

F7F model variations

XP-65
The USAAC version of the F7F. Originally designed as a fighter for both the Navy and the USAAF, it was soon realized that the land-based version was no good as a carrier-based fighter.

XF7F-1
The first of the carrier-borne fighters, powered by two Pratt and Whitney R-2800-22W engines with three-bladed propellers.

F7F-1
The production models were identical to the prototypes.

F7F-1N
A small number of F7F-1s were fitted with an experimental radar.

XF7F-2N
Prototype of the two-seat night fighter with the AN/APS-6 radar housed in the nose.

F7F-2N
Again the production model was identical to the prototype.

F7F-3
Basically an F7F-1, but with Pratt and Whitney R-2800-34W engines, larger fuel tanks and increased armour plating.

F7F-3D
These were a small number of F7F-3s modified as drone-controllers.

F7F-3K
These were F7F-3s modifed as radio-controlled drones.

F7F-3E
A few of the standard F7F-3s were used for testing new radar and electronic equipment.

F7F-3N
This was a two-seat night fighter version of the F7F-3.

F7F-3P
A number of -3s and -3Ns were converted as photo-reconnaissance aircraft. The cameras were carried in the nose.

F7F-4N
Similar to the -3N, but with heavier landing-gear and strengthened inner wing panels.

F8F Bearcat

Design No. G58 started life as a replacement for the Hellcat. What Chief Engineer William Schwendler envisaged was a shipborne fighter that would out-perform the Japanese A6M-5 Zeke fighter, with the maximum of performance for the minimum of weight in the low and medium altitude ranges.

A typical Grumman design, short, barrel-shaped and powerful, and powered by a Pratt and Whitney water-injected R-2800 E engine, the Bearcat had twice the rate of climb and roll of the Hellcat. By using flush riveting and a much heavier aluminium skin, which enabled Grumman to minimize the drag, the Bearcat's top speed was 50 mph faster than the Hellcat, and this made the Bearcat the fastest and most powerful fighter aircraft in the world at that time. The weight of armour plating for pilot protection was such that the normal six machine guns were replaced by only four .50 calibre Brownings, carrying 1,200 rounds of ammunition. The four machine guns were considered more than adequate to take care of the extremely lightly-armoured Japanese aircraft. The Bearcat could also carry four five-inch rockets, or two Tiny Tims (500 lb. warhead rockets).

Two XF8F-1 Bearcats were ordered for evaluation by the Navy and nine months later, in August 1944, Grumman's chief test pilot, Bob Hall, took off on the first test flight. The enthusiasm in his report left no doubt in the minds of the Grumman engineers that they had created an exceptional aircraft. That October, the XF8F-1 was flown to the Naval Air Test Centre at Patuxent River, Maryland. There, at the Joint Fighter Conference, the aircraft was put through its paces again, and without exception, all who flew it expressed pure delight at the aircraft's handling qualities and perform-ance. An incredible climb rate of 4,800 feet per minute, a maximum speed of 341 knots at sea level and 368 knots at 17,300 feet, were among its outstanding features. The F8F

had a bubble canopy, which afforded the pilot an all-round, uninterrupted view. This was the first time that a bubble canopy had been fitted to a Navy aircraft.

Shortly after the Joint Fighter Conference, an order for 2,023 F8F-1s was placed with Grumman, and on 5 February 1945, General Motors were contracted to build an additional 1,876 aircraft. These F8F-1s were to be designated F3M-1s, to differentiate them from the Grumman-built ones, and the contract called for an estimated 100 per month by June. The aircraft was to be powered by a 2,100 hp Pratt and Whitney R-2800-34W engine, with a two-speed supercharger.

It was the Grummans intention to phase out the Hellcat, replacing it with the Bearcat by January 1946. Testing continued at the Bethpage plant, while Pratt and Whitney were developing an engine that would increase the range and endurance of the Bearcat without affecting its performance. The fuel carried was increased from 162 gallons to 185 gallons in the internal tank, 150 gallons in the centerline fuselage tank that could be jettisoned when empty, and 200 gallons in wing-tip tanks. The engine turned a massive 12 ft. 7 in. diameter, four-bladed propeller that appeared to shave the deck or runway when landing and taking off. Made by Aero Products, the constant-speed propeller was an outstanding feature of the Bearcat. Its armament was the same as that of the XF8F-1.

Five months after the first test flight, and only three months after the first production Bearcat was started, the initial carrier trials aboard the USS Charger were carried out. After a total of nine landings and take-offs by two Bearcats, the results were better than even the Navy had expected. The

Above: The second of the F8F Bearcat prototypes, the XF8F-2, at Bethpage.

Grumman F8F-1 Bearcat cutaway drawing key

1 Aeroproducts constant-speed propeller
2 Propeller hub pitch change mechanism
3 Propeller fixing bolts
4 Engine cowling ring
5 Cowling ring fasteners
6 Reduction gear casing
7 Engine magnetos
8 Detachable engine cowlings
9 Cowling frames
10 Pratt & Whitney R-2800-34W Double Wasp eighteen-cylinder two-row radial engine

11 Exhaust collector pipes
12 Oil cooler
13 Stainless steel fireproof bulkhead
14 Cowling air flap
15 Starboard 0·5-in (12,7-mm) Colt-Browning machine guns
16 Ammunition feed chutes
17 Ammunition tanks (300 rounds per gun)
18 Machine gun barrels
19 Blast suppressing muzzles
20 Mk 9 HVAR 5-in (12,7-cm) rocket projectiles
21 Aileron hinge control mechanism
22 Wing fold hinge joint
23 Wing folding bar socket fitting
24 Starboard navigation light
25 Starboard aileron
26 Formation light
27 Outer wing panel folded position
28 Aileron tab
29 Starboard flap
30 Oil tank (14 Imp gal/64 l capacity)
31 Induction air duct

32 Water injection tank (13 Imp gal/60 l capacity)
33 Hydraulic distribution unit
34 Engine bearer struts
35 Armoured cockpit bulkhead (29·3-lb/13·3-kg weight)
36 Engine control runs
37 Access plate
38 Instrument panel
39 Rudder pedals
40 Fuel feed pipe
41 Trim controls
42 Pilot's side console panel

43 Engine throttle and propeller controls
44 Control column
45 Oxygen regulator
46 Mk 8 Mod 6 illuminated reflector gunsight
47 Windscreen panels
48 Rearward-sliding cockpit canopy
49 Headrest
50 Head and back armour (49·4 lb/ 22,4 kg weight) see 54
51 Safety harness
52 Canopy sliding rail
53 Pilot's seat
54 Back armour (see 50)
55 Cockpit rear bulkhead
56 Bag type main fuel tank (154 Imp gal/700 l capacity)
57 Fire extinguisher
58 Radio transmitter
59 Dynamotor

60 Radio equipment racks (AN/ARC-1 VHF transceiver, AN/ARR-2A VHF homing and R-23/ARC-5 range receiver)
61 Battery
62 Roll-over crash support arch
63 Fuselage skin plating
64 Handhold
65 Tailplane control cables
66 Whip aerials
67 Formation light
68 Fin root fillet fairing
69 Starboard tailplane
70 Starboard elevator
71 Elevator tab
72 Torque shaft rim tab control
73 Fin front spar attachment
74 Rudder trim control
75 Tailfin construction
76 Sternpost
77 Aerial cable

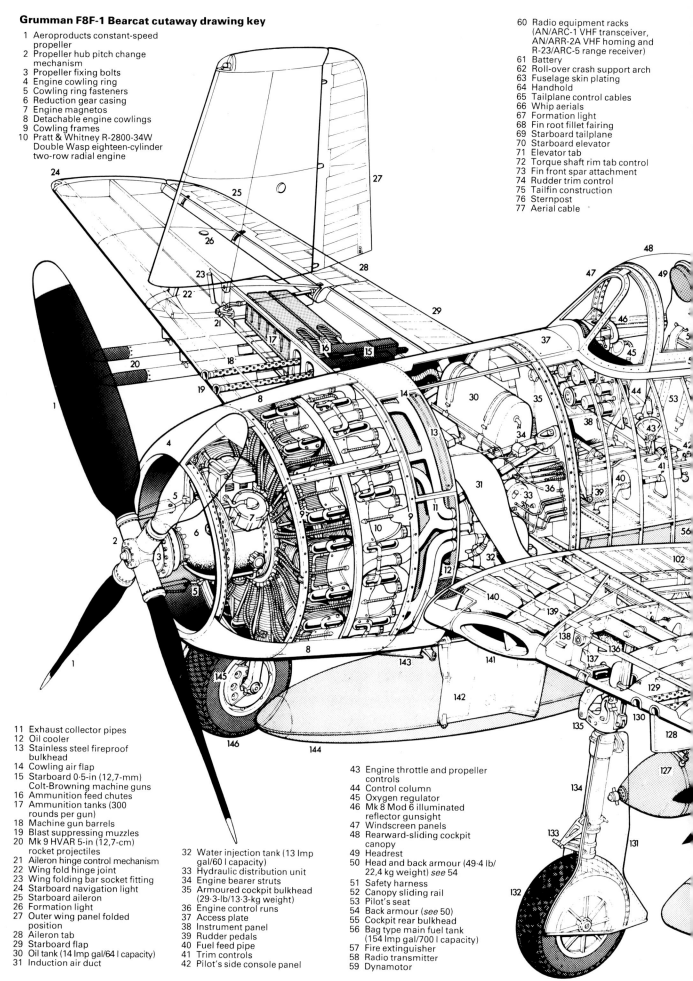

78 Fin tip fairing
79 Rudder balance
80 Rudder construction
81 Rudder tab
82 Arrester hook shock absorber
83 Arrester hook guide rails
84 Elevator tab
85 Deck arresting hook
86 Elevator construction
87 Tailplane construction
88 Elevator control horns
89 Tailplane attachment joints
90 Tailwheel bay
91 Retractable tailwheel
92 Tailwheel leg fairings
93 Shock absorber strut
94 Retraction jack
95 Rear fuselage bulkhead
96 Fuselage frame-and-stringer
   construction

97 Remote compass transmitter
98 Whip aerial
99 Ventral access door
100 Footstep
101 Port flap construction
102 Wing root strengthened
    walkway
103 Wing rib construction
104 Hydraulic flap jack
105 Port gun bay
106 Two 0·5-in (12,7-mm) Colt-
    Browning machine guns

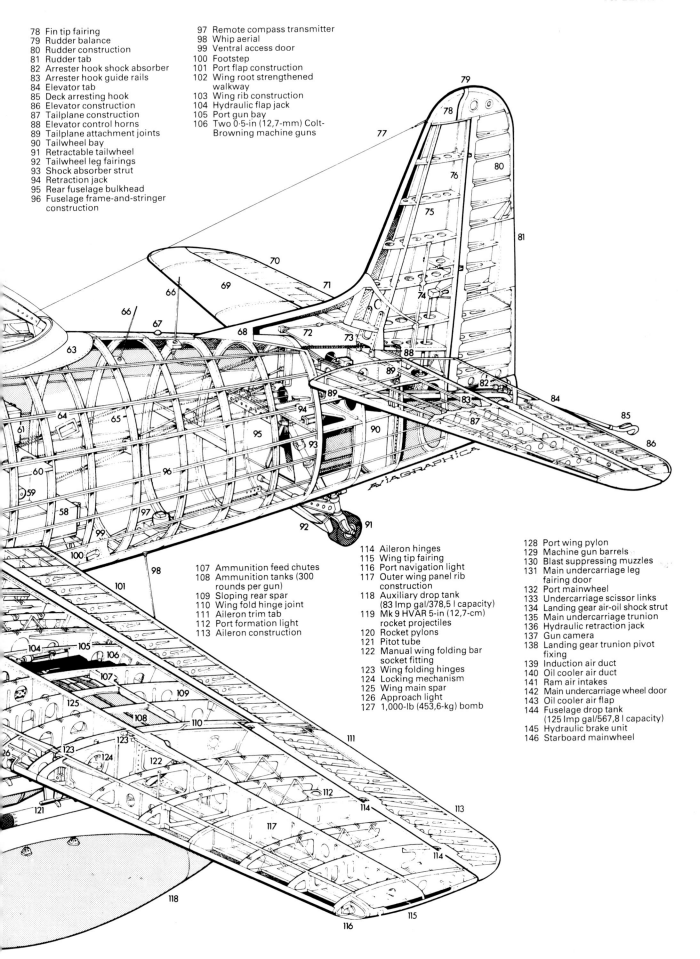

107 Ammunition feed chutes
108 Ammunition tanks (300
    rounds per gun)
109 Sloping rear spar
110 Wing fold hinge joint
111 Aileron trim tab
112 Port formation light
113 Aileron construction

114 Aileron hinges
115 Wing tip fairing
116 Port navigation light
117 Outer wing panel rib
    construction
118 Auxiliary drop tank
    (83 Imp gal/378,5 l capacity)
119 Mk 9 HVAR 5-in (12,7-cm)
    rocket projectiles
120 Rocket pylons
121 Pitot tube
122 Manual wing folding bar
    socket fitting
123 Wing folding hinges
124 Locking mechanism
125 Wing main spar
126 Approach light
127 1,000-lb (453,6-kg) bomb

128 Port wing pylon
129 Machine gun barrels
130 Blast suppressing muzzles
131 Main undercarriage leg
    fairing door
132 Port mainwheel
133 Undercarriage scissor links
134 Landing gear air-oil shock strut
135 Main undercarriage trunion
136 Hydraulic retraction jack
137 Gun camera
138 Landing gear trunion pivot
    fixing
139 Induction air duct
140 Oil cooler air duct
141 Ram air intakes
142 Main undercarriage wheel door
143 Oil cooler air flap
144 Fuselage drop tank
    (125 Imp gal/567,8 l capacity)
145 Hydraulic brake unit
146 Starboard mainwheel

field servicing and maintenance was not up to the standard required.

At the end of the French Indo-Chinese conflict, 150 F8F Bearcats were handed over to the Royal Thai Air Force, where they stayed in service well into the mid-sixties. One squadron of Bearcats was given to the 514th South Vietnam Fighter Squadron.

Back in the United States, the US Navy disbanded their Bearcat squadrons at the end of 1955. The remaining F8F Bearcats in the United States were sold for scrap, but some were rescued by museums and civilians. Bearcats were raced at the Reno Air Races, and what racers they turned out to be! In 1969, Darryl Greenamyer in his F8F-2 set a new world record for a piston-engined aircraft, with a speed of 480 mph. The first Reno Air Race was won by a Bearcat and, since that day in 1964, the F8F Bearcat has won an incredible nine times.

F8F Bearcat technical details

Model	Fighter.		
Crew	One.		
Engine	2,100 hp Pratt and Whitney R-2800-34W Double Wasp, 18-cylinder, two-row, radial, air-cooled engine.		
Dimensions	Wing span 35 ft. 6 in., length 28 ft. 3 in., height 13 ft. 10 in., wing area 244 sq. ft.		
Weight	Empty 7,017 lb., combat 9,116 lb.		
Performance	Max. speed 423 mph, cruising speed 315 mph, climb rate 6,500 ft. per min., ceiling 41,300 ft., range 1,416 miles.		

Armament　　Four .50 calibre, Colt-Browning, wing-mounted, machine guns. (On later models four 20 mm cannon were fitted). Two 100 lb. bombs or four five-inch rockets.

Fuel　　Internal fuel 185 gals. One centreline fuel tank 150 gals., and two wing tanks 200 gals.

Various detail changes were made to the different types of Bearcat, but basically the aircraft stayed the same, right up to the last F8F.

F8F Bearcat model variations

XF8F-1
Prototype of the carrier-based, single-seat fighter. Powered by a Pratt and Whitney R-2800-22W engine with a four-bladed propeller. Break-away wing-tips were fitted for high g-forces, but later removed because they were found to be unsuccessful.

F8F-1
Production model of the prototype, but powered by a Pratt and Whitney R-2800-34W engine with a four-bladed propeller.

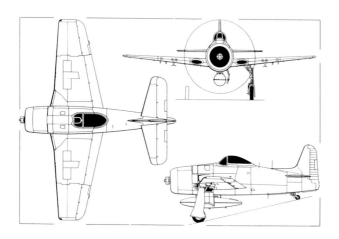

F3M-1
This was the designation that was to be given to the aircraft produced by the Eastern Aircraft Division of General Motors, who had an order for 1,876 Bearcats, but the end of the war brought about a cancellation before production had begun.

F8F-1B
Production model of the F8F-1C.

F8F-1C
Designation given to one F8F-1, when the machine guns were removed and four 20 mm cannon were installed.

F8F-1D
F8F-1B converted to drone director.

XF8F-1N
Experimental night fighter with the APS-19 radar fitted under the right wing.

F8F-1N
Limited production model of the XF8F-1N.

F8F-1P
Experimental photo-reconnaissance aircraft with the camera windows aft of the cockpit.

F8F-2
Similar to the F8F-1, but with the Pratt and Whitney R-2800-30W engine, with automatic engine control and enlarged tail fin and rudder.

F8F-2D
Experimental remote-controlled manoeuvring aircraft.

F8F-2N
As the F8F-2, but with the APS-19 radar mounted on the bomb rack under the right wing.

F8F-2P
Photo-reconnaissance fighter with cameras mounted aft of the cockpit.

G-58A
Also known as the Gulfhawk IV. Only civil version, built for Gulf Oil and flown by their demonstration pilot, Major Al Williams.

The Amphibians

The first amphibian built by Grumman was the XJF-1, which, in reality, was a redesigned Loening XO2L. Although the XJF-1 was similar to the XO2L in appearance, the performance of the XJF-1 was far superior, also the undercarriage folded up flush with the hull, the latter being one of the many innovations attributed to Grumman. The landing gear was hand-cranked up and down and was self-locking when in the down position. A red light on the instrument panel gave the pilot warning if the engine was throttled below 1,200 rpm without the wheels being lowered.

The XJF-1 first took to the air in April 1933. Powered by a 700 hp Pratt and Whitney R-1535-62 engine, the aircraft reached a speed of 164 mph at a height of 21,500 feet and had a range of 800 miles. It had a wingspan of 39 feet, an overall length of 32 ft. 7 in., and a gross weight of 4,831 lb. It was constructed of aluminium alloy, with the exception of the engine mountings, landing gear, high-stress fittings and brace wires, which were steel. The fuselage was of a riveted mono-coque construction, very simple in design but extremely rugged, and very easy to maintain. The wings, ailerons, elevators and rudders were covered in fabric and painted in a silver dope.

The US Navy took delivery of the first XJF-1 late in May 1933, and for nearly a year it underwent exhaustive evaluation tests at NAS Anacostia. The Navy awarded Grumman a contract for twenty-seven JF-1 aircraft, to be designated 'Ducks'.

The first production model JF-1 came off the assembly line in April 1934 and was tested by Roy Grumman personally. A new engine, the Pratt and Whitney R-1830-62, had been installed and, although the speed remained the same as the XJF-1, the service ceiling dropped to 18,000 ft. The aircraft was an instant success and was assigned to squadrons as soon as it came off the production lines. Interest in the Duck was shown by the US Coast Guard and they placed an order for fifteen. This model was designated the JF-2 and had a number of modifications, including a nine-cylinder, single row, Wright R-1820-102 engine producing 750 hp, plus additional communication and signalling equipment.

Deliveries of the JF-1 and the JF-2 were completed in 1935, one of the JF-2s being sent to the US Marine Corps for trials and evaluation, but nothing materialized. While the JF-2s were being completed, an order for five more Ducks for the US Navy was received. Designated the JF-3, they were virtually the same as the JF-1s and carried exactly the same armament. They were delivered in November 1935, one to each of the five major naval reserve bases.

The upper wing surfaces of the JF series were painted a yellow ochre and the service markings were painted on the fuselage as appropriate, e.g. US Navy, US Marines or US Coast Guard. The US Marine JFs had vertical stripes painted on the rudder, in addition to the lettering on the fuselage, while the US Navy had the name of the aircraft's base painted

Above: A J2F-1 being brought up to the flight deck of an unknown carrier.

on the fuselage. It is interesting to note that the main centre float was designed and built by Grumman some years earlier and was known as the Model B Float. The float was initially fitted on the Vought 02U4 amphibian and was the first to have a retractable undercarriage.

There is very little recorded information about the early JF amphibians, perhaps because there was little to write about: they were not involved in any spectacular or tragic operations and were totally reliable aircraft.

After the last JF-3s had been delivered, it was six months before the production lines began to move again. In March 1936, the US Navy decided that, although the JF-1s satisfied their early needs, they really wanted an updated version that could carry more equipment and would widen the scope of the aircraft. The Grumman designers produced an updated version of the JF-1 and submitted it to the Navy, who approved it and ordered twenty-nine. The design of the aircraft was hardly altered, just enough to allow for additional photographic equipment, smoke tanks, target towing facilities and more powerful radio sets. The main centreline float was redesigned and lengthened by one foot and was the only dimension to alter. The first J2F-1 was delivered to the Navy at NAS Anacostia on 3 April 1936, the same day as its maiden flight. All twenty-nine aircraft were delivered to the Navy within one year, ready to be assigned to squadrons.

Whilst interest in the J2F continued, eight JF-3s, or G-20s as they were to be known, were built and sold to Argentina at the beginning of 1937.

The US Marine Corps received their batch of amphibian aircraft, the first in their history, in the spring of 1938. Twenty J2F-2s were delivered. They were identical to the J2F-1, with the exception of the propeller. The J2F-2s were fitted with the two-position, adjustable pitch, Hamilton-Standard propeller, which increased the aircraft's performance very slightly. With the start of hostilities in Europe, VMS-3 of the US Marine Corps, stationed at Charlotte Amalie in the Virgin Islands, was placed on active duty status. Called the Neutrality Patrol, the squadron of nine J2F-2s had additional armament fitted: two extra bomb racks and a second flexible machine gun, mounted on the aft ring mount.

At the beginning of 1939, twenty more J2F-3 Ducks, were ordered by the Navy. Although basically the same as the J2F-2s, and carrying the same armament, some were fitted out as executive-type aircraft, with a blue and silver exterior finish. They were used widely as VIP transport for high-ranking military officers, and occasionally to transport personnel from ship to shore bases. The Hamilton-Standard constant-speed propeller was fitted, which gave added performance. The remainder of the J2F-3s were delivered to the Navy to strengthen existing squadrons.

As increased patrols of the shoreline and oceans were ordered, so another thirty two J2F-4 Ducks were purchased. The Duck could operate from the smallest of bases or inlets, without the need for elaborate docking facilities, thus making the aircraft an invaluable part of the defence network. The J2F-4s were basically the same as the J2F-3s, although there were some modifications to the cockpit instrumentation.

With the war in Europe moving into its second year, the threat to the United States increased. Grumman received an order for a further 144 Ducks, designated the J2F-5. Such was the need for the aircraft, that the first one was tested and delivered the same day. A new engine had been installed, a Wright R-1820-50 that produced 950 hp. There were a few minor alterations to the design, a long, cord cowl and the protruding oil filter made flush with the fuselage fairing. The armament remained the same, one .30 calibre machine gun, two 100 lb. bombs, or two 325 lb. depth charges.

When the United Stated entered the war in December 1941, the strain placed upon the aircraft industry was enormous. Grumman were already heavily committed to the production of the FF-1, the F2F, and the F4F Wildcat, contracts were pending also on the J4F Widgeon and the JRF

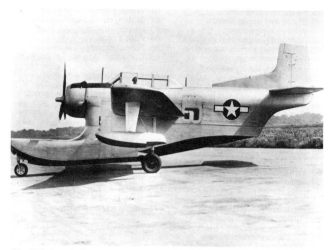

The XJL-1, a single wing prototype with retractable tricycle undercarriage. Only two were built but were never put into production.

Goose. The F6F Hellcat and the TBF Avenger were about to go on the production line, so Grumman decided that they would have to subcontract out to other manufacturers, and the Duck was the first to go.

A brand new company called the Columbia Aircraft Company, of Valley Stream, New York, was formed and took over the full production of the J2F. The aircraft was redesignated the J2F-6 and a total of 330 were built. The only difference from the J2F-5 was the updated R-1820-54 Wright engine, although the J2F-5 was slightly lighter. The top speed of the J2F-6 was 190 mph and the stalling speed 70 mph.

Although it was insignificant when compared to other, more glamorous, aircraft that appeared during World War II, there are many pilots and crewmen who owe their lives to the Duck. One advantage the Duck had over other rescue aircraft was its ability to operate virtually anywhere, irrespective of the weather. The rugged airframe enabled it to withstand some horrendous beatings from the sea whilst picking up downed aircrew. There are confirmed stories of Ducks rescuing aircrew and bringing them out lashed to the lower wings, because the small area in the fuselage was already full. There are countless tales of heroic rescues, more than enough to fill this book.

During operations in the Pacific Theatre many of the J2F Ducks were painted black, enabling them to be used for covert missions at night. This role was later taken over by the now famous PBY Catalinas, or Black Cats as they became known.

At the end of the war, the Ducks were no longer required, so the contracts were cancelled and the Columbia Aircraft Company closed down. Grumman designed a tricycle under-carriage for the J2F-6 Duck and two prototypes were built, both with single wings. Redesignated XJL-1s, they were delivered to the US Navy for evaluation, but were rejected, so heralding the end of a great aircraft.

At the end of the war a surprising number had survived, and these were quickly snapped up by South American governments for a number of uses. Some found their way into the forestry services, where they were used for agri-cultural spraying and fire-fighting. The Canadians purchased a number for their fisheries patrols with great success. The Duck was even immortalized on the screen, in the film *Murphy's War*, which starred Peter O'Toole.

During the late 1930s, another amphibian, the Grumman Goose, made it appearance. The G-21, as it was officially known, was a twin-engined, high-winged monoplane, designed as a private amphibian, but it was extremely expensive to run. It was regarded by those who could afford to own one as a real status symbol. The G-21 Goose was a luxurious, high-speed aircraft that could operate with safety from small fields, lakes and harbours.

The first G-21 production model. It was later named the 'Goose'.

Grumman had been encouraged to build the Goose when a syndicate of very wealthy businessmen, led by Wilton Lloyd-Smith, had investigated the possibility of having a small private aircraft that would transport them from their Long Island estates to Wall Street, the financial district of New York. The fact that Wall Street was on the waterfront made an amphibian the obvious choice. The added advantage of the Goose having a retractable undercarriage, together with a speed of 200 mph and a range of 800 miles, made it the perfect commuter/business aircraft. Among the notables who purchased the Goose as well as Wilton Lloyd-Smith, were Marshall Field, owner of a chain of department stores; the banker, Henry Morgan; C. W. Deeds of United Aircraft; Colonel McCormick of the *Chicago Tribune*; Captain Boris Sergievsky of Sikorsky Aircraft; and Lord Beaverbrook, the British newspaper magnate, who was to eventually own two.

An eight-seater G-21 Goose was delivered to Wilton Lloyd-Smith on 3 July 1937, the first of a total of 300, eight of which were purchased from their owners by the US Navy at the beginning of World War II.

Like the J2F Duck, the Goose was of an all-metal construction, with the exception of fabric-covered outer wing panels and flight controls. It was powered by two Pratt and Whitney R-985 Wasp Junior engines, rated at 400 hp, with Hamilton-Standard twin-bladed propellers. A total of 220 gallons of fuel was carried in integral tanks, situated in both wings. The aircraft had dual controls and the landing gear was raised and lowered with a chain-driven, hand-cranked screw arrangement, as in the J2F. The first military Grumman Goose, the XJ3F-1, went to the US Navy for evaluation in 1938 and was an immediate success, with the result that they ordered an additional ten, designating them JRF-1s and JRF-1As. The latter were modified for aerial photography and target towing. During the war years, the US Navy acquired more than 250 JRFs and the Royal Navy were given fifty under the Lend-Lease Programme. These were equipped with navigational training equipment and designated JRF-6Bs. The name 'Goose', incidentally, was given to the aircraft by Grumman and retained by the Royal Navy when they replaced their ageing Armstrong Vickers Walruses.

The US Navy was not the only branch of the armed forces to have the Goose: the Army Air Force purchased twenty-six and gave them the designation OA-9; the US Coast Guard acquired ten designated JRF-2 and JRF-3, while the Royal Canadian Air Force purchased a number as coastal reconnaissance aircraft. A modified flying-boat version of the Goose, the G-21B, was ordered by the Portuguese government. These were armed with two .30 calibre machine guns (bow and dorsal) and had provision for two 100 lb. bombs under the wings. The removal of the undercarriage reduced the weight by 300lb. This was the only true seaplane ever built by Grumman.

The G-44, or Widgeon, as it came to be known was also produced at this time. It was of a very similar design to the G-21 Goose, but was much smaller, and had a number of very distinctive features which highlighted the differences. For instance, the wingspan for instance, was nine feet less, and the length of the fuselage was reduced by 7 ft. 5 in. The wings were a very angular shape, as was the tail section. The aircraft was of an all-metal construction, with the exception of the ailerons, which were fabric covered. The hull consisted of five watertight compartments, covered by a riveted aluminium-alloy skin. The undercarriage and tail wheel was of the old, tried-and-tested, Grumman retractable type.

Designed primarily as a commercial aircraft, considerable numbers were sold to private buyers prior to World War II, but immediately after the attack on Pearl Harbor all the aircraft were requisitioned by the military, the US Navy taking the lion's share. The US Coast Guard purchased twenty-five; seven went to the Royal Navy, which renamed it the Gosling; and a few went to Brazil. Even the US Army Air Corps purchased a number. In 1941, the RCAF took delivery of the J4F, also naming it the Gosling, and used it as a search and rescue aircraft.

The Gosling was powered by two 200 hp L440 C-5 Ranger in-line, air-cooled, inverted engines. It had a top speed of 153 miles per hour and a cruising speed of 138 miles per hour, with a range of 800 miles. Towards the end of the war, Grumman started producing the Widgeon for the commercial market; when the war was over it started receiving war-surplus J4Fs for refurbishment. Thirty Widgeons were built by a French company under licence from Grumman. These were called Super Widgeons and were fitted with two 275 hp Lycoming engines, which gave the aircraft a top speed of 170 miles per hour. Today, a number are still flying and continuing to provide the kind of service they did back in 1944.

A J4F-1 Widgeon on patrol. Note the depth bomb beneath the starboard engine.

Between 1937 and 1945 a total of 345 J4Fs were built, a large number of these surviving the war to be sold to an ever-increasing number of charter aircraft companies and mini-airlines. The largest users of the Goose in this capacity were Chalk's International Airline, which began operating out of Miami across to the Bahamas in 1962; several airlines in south east Alaska; and Antilles Air Boats in the US Virgin Islands.

The G-73 Mallard was designed primarily for the commercial operator. Built to carry between ten and twelve passengers, it was able to operate on both land and water, and made its first flight on 30 April 1946. Powered by two 600 hp Pratt and Whitney R-1340-S3H1 engines, with Hamilton-Standard three-bladed, constant-speed propellers. The Mallard had a top speed of 215 mph, could cruise at 180 mph and had a range of 1,200 miles. It was the first Grumman amphibian to

A G-73 Mallard overflying Long Island Sound.

be equipped with a tricycle undercarriage and, as with previous amphibians, the main landing gear folded up flush with the fuselage. The fuselage was designed as a flying-boat hull and was extremely strong, far stronger, in fact, than most land-planes. It was designed to reduce hydrodynamic drag, and produced relatively little spray on calm water take-offs. The cockpit had dual controls of the wheel type, fitted on a single pedestal, and the aircraft was flown by a two-man crew. The cockpit layout was similar to other Grumman monoplane amphibians and other flying-boats, in that the engine controls, including the throttles, were located above the pilots' heads. The control column could be detached to allow access to the nose compartment for the purpose of conducting docking operations or handling mooring lines. Dual radio controls were fitted for the first time in a small commercial aircraft, providing another safety aspect. The cabin of the Mallard could be arranged to suit individual needs, although the standard arrangement was two cabin areas, the forward one containing two large facing divans, with room enough for a card table or desk to be accommodated, and the aft section having four standard airline seats, two on each side. To the rear of the section was a dressing room with full toilet facilities.

A number of safety devices were fitted: dual hydraulic brakes, two hydraulically-driven pumps, with an emergency

A UF-2G of the US Coast Guard on a test flight prior to delivery.

hand pump, and an automatic fire detection and extinguishing system. The heating system was operated by ram-air pressure whilst in flight, and defogging and anti-icing equipment was provided for the windshield. The Mallard was the first amphibian to be awarded a full scheduled Air Carrier Operations rating and among the first operators of the aircraft were Twentieth Century Fox Studios and the Texaco Oil Company. Of the fifty-nine Mallards built, about thirty-five are still in use.

While the Mallard was making its mark, Ralston Stalb at Grumman was working on an amphibian that was to have an even greater impact on the aviation world, the XJR2F-1, later designated UF-1. Known universally as the Albatross, it was designed primarily for utility transport work. The US Coast Guard realized that the Albatross had a great potential for Air Sea Rescue work, and it was credited with saving nearly 1,000 lives during the Korean conflict.

The Albatross was the largest of all the Grumman amphibian family, a high-winged, all-metal, twin-engined aircraft, powered by two Wright R-1820-76 engines, with single-stage, two-speed superchargers and Hamilton-Standard three-bladed, constant speed, controllable pitch, reversible propellers. Like the Mallard, the Albatross had a tricycle undercarriage which retracted hydraulically, flush into the fuselage. It carried a total of 1,709 gallons of fuel, 340 gallons in each of the two main tanks, 209 gallons in the right float tank and 212 gallons in the left one, with an additional 304 gallons in two drop tanks under the wings. This gave the Albatross an endurance time of around twenty hours, and a tremendous range.

The external rack beneath each wing was normally used to carry drop tanks, but on ASW modified aircraft the rack could carry mines, bombs, or even gun pods. One role the Albatross was ideally suited for was the para-rescue or para-drop. Provision was made for a jump platform, static line cable and a bail out signal system. The jump platform was designed for easy stowage and folding, and, when not in use, folded flat against the left wheel well. It was ideally suited for delivery of medical equipment and supplies, survival gear and life rafts.

The 'B' version of the Albatross had a larger wingspan, a superior single-engine rate of climb, a greater range and higher cruising and stalling speeds than the '4'. The longer wing had to be compensated for by enlarging the aileron, fin and stabilizer areas. Over 150 such conversions have been carried out successfully to date and extremely economically.

Another of the more important roles of the Albatross was that of an ASW operations aircraft, fitted with wide sweep-angle and long-range radar. The Albatross could also carry magnetic airborne detection systems, electronic counter-measures equipment, sonobuoys and sonobuoy receiver equipment, sound signal depth charges and marine markers. The aircraft also had a facility to enable several crews to be accommodated for in-flight ASW training. The ASW version had a 600 lb. station facility under each wing. This enabled it to carry a variety of armament, including the Mk. 43 Model 1

An SA-16B on a pre-delivery test flight.

Torpedo. Every Albatross had the additional facility of JATO (Jet Assisted Take-Off) units. These could be mounted easily, even when airborne, being fitted to the main cabin door (port-side) and the emergency cabin door (starboard side), both doors opening inwards.

In 1970, Grumman carried out a feasibility study to try and ease the ever-growing commuter problem into New York. The proposal was that amphibian aircraft could handle up to 5,000 passengers a day, landing them near to the financial district of New York, and that turbo-prop versions of both the Mallard and the Albatross would be considered, if the seating for both was extensively reorganised. Licence-building the famous Japanese Shin Meiwa PX-S flying-boat, and the development of a four-engined turbo-prop Super Albatross was also considered, but neither came to fruition.

The Albatross has been sold to more countries than any other aircraft manufactured. As well as Canada and Japan, Argentina, Brazil, Chile, Ecuador, Greece, Iceland, Indonesia, Italy, Mexico, Norway, Pakistan, Peru, the Philippines, Spain, Taiwan, Thailand and Venezuela have purchased the aircraft.

In 1982, Grumman completed the conversion of an HU-16B to a twenty-eight seat, passenger aircraft for a commuter airline company. Redesignated the G-111 Albatross, the aircraft plies between southern Florida and Nassau in the Bahamas. Of the 464 Albatrosses built for the Navy, Air Force and Coast Guard, some 200 are still in existence, although not all are in flying condition. So impressed were they with the G-111 conversion, that Grumman obtained fifty-seven Albatrosses to convert to passenger-carrying aircraft to sell worldwide. They will be powered by two Wright 982-C9-HE3 engines, with two Hamilton-Standard three-bladed, constant-speed, reversible, auto-feathering propellers; the amphibian, once thought as 'archaic', is starting to make a comeback.

Grumman HU-16B/D (UF-1) Albatross cutaway drawing key

1 Starboard navigation light
2 Anchor light
3 Wing tip fairing
4 Ventral UHF aerials
5 Leading edge de-icing boot
6 Retractable landing lamp
7 Elevator hinge control
8 Starboard aileron
9 Aileron tab
10 Fixed portion of trailing edge
11 Starboard outer wing panel
12 Three-segment split trailing edge flap
13 Nacelle tail fairing
14 Starboard wing fuel tank (total internal capacity 675 US gal/2550 l)
15 Engine exhaust duct
16 Accessory equipment compartment
17 Wright R-1820-76A nine-cylinder radial engine
18 Engine cowling panels

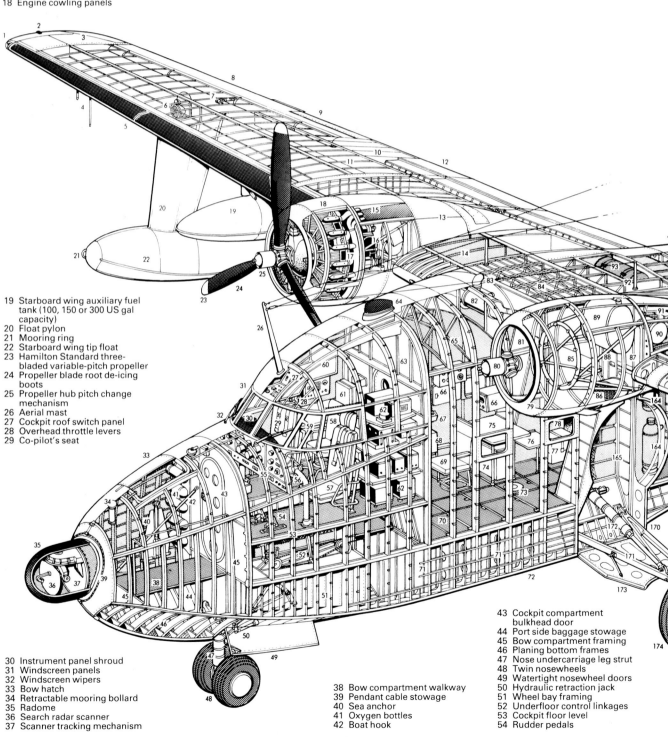

19 Starboard wing auxiliary fuel tank (100, 150 or 300 US gal capacity)
20 Float pylon
21 Mooring ring
22 Starboard wing tip float
23 Hamilton Standard three-bladed variable-pitch propeller
24 Propeller blade root de-icing boots
25 Propeller hub pitch change mechanism
26 Aerial mast
27 Cockpit roof switch panel
28 Overhead throttle levers
29 Co-pilot's seat

30 Instrument panel shroud
31 Windscreen panels
32 Windscreen wipers
33 Bow hatch
34 Retractable mooring bollard
35 Radome
36 Search radar scanner
37 Scanner tracking mechanism

38 Bow compartment walkway
39 Pendant cable stowage
40 Sea anchor
41 Oxygen bottles
42 Boat hook

43 Cockpit compartment bulkhead door
44 Port side baggage stowage
45 Bow compartment framing
46 Planing bottom frames
47 Nose undercarriage leg strut
48 Twin nosewheels
49 Watertight nosewheel doors
50 Hydraulic retraction jack
51 Wheel bay framing
52 Underfloor control linkages
53 Cockpit floor level
54 Rudder pedals

55 Instrument panel
56 Control column
57 Pilot's seat
58 Direct vision opening side window panel
59 Radio operator's swivelling seat
60 Cockpit roof ditching hatch
61 Chart case
62 Radio and electronics equipment racks
63 Cockpit rear bulkhead
64 D/F loop aerial
65 Cabin roof frame construction
66 Radar navigator's instrument displays
67 Drift sight
68 Directional gyro
69 Radar navigator's swivelling seat
70 Cargo loading floor panels
71 Boat hull frame construction
72 Fuselage chine member
73 Bilge access cover
74 Sextant stowage
75 Chart table
76 Folding seat
77 Parachute stowage
78 Cabin window panel
79 Port engine cowling
80 Port propeller hub
81 Cowling nose ring

97 Port split trailing edge flap
98 Flap hydraulic jack
99 Life raft stowage (2)
100 Starboard side emergency exit hatch
101 Cabin rear bulkhead
102 Aft equipment bay
103 Water tank
104 Bilge pump
105 Equipment bay rear bulkhead
106 Sea rescue platform stowage
107 Fin root fillet construction
108 Anti-collision light
109 Leading edge de-icing boots
110 Starboard tailplane
111 Starboard elevator
112 HF aerial cables
113 Tailfin construction
114 VOR aerial
115 UHF aerials
116 Fin tip fairing
117 Rudder construction
118 Rudder tab
119 Sternpost
120 Elevator hinge control

121 Elevator tab
122 Port elevator construction
123 Tailplane tip fairing
124 Leading edge de-icing boot
125 Tail navigation lights
126 Tailplane rib construction
127 Tail assembly attachment main frames
128 Parachute flares
129 Trailing aerial winch
130 Trailing aerial fairlead
131 Engine work platform stowage
132 Fuselage hull boat tail
133 Chemical toilet
134 JATO bottles
135 Hinged JATO bottle rack, internal loading
136 2-segment main cabin door
137 Waste water tank
138 Sea rescue platform
139 Port flap outer segment
140 Fixed portion of trailing edge
141 Aileron tab
142 Port retractable landing lamp
143 Aileron shroud
144 Fixed tab
145 Port aileron construction
146 Wing tip fairing
147 Anchor light
148 Port navigation light
149 Ventral UHF aerials
150 Port wing tip float construction
151 Tip float overload fuel tank (200 US gal capacity)
152 Mooring rings

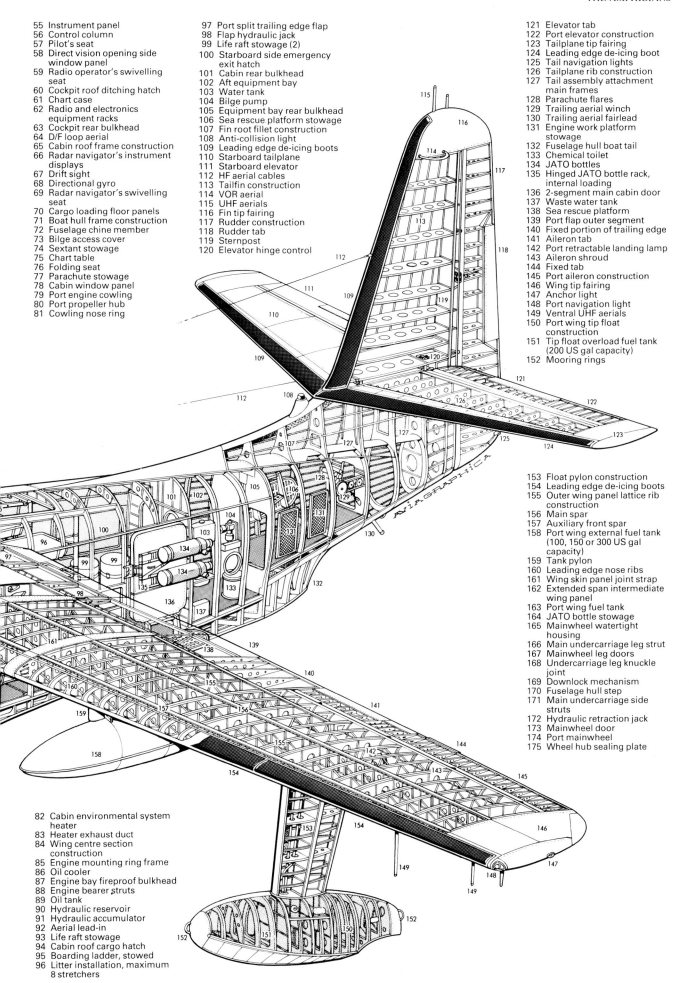

153 Float pylon construction
154 Leading edge de-icing boots
155 Outer wing panel lattice rib construction
156 Main spar
157 Auxiliary front spar
158 Port wing external fuel tank (100, 150 or 300 US gal capacity)
159 Tank pylon
160 Leading edge nose ribs
161 Wing skin panel joint strap
162 Extended span intermediate wing panel
163 Port wing fuel tank
164 JATO bottle stowage
165 Mainwheel watertight housing
166 Main undercarriage leg strut
167 Mainwheel leg doors
168 Undercarriage leg knuckle joint
169 Downlock mechanism
170 Fuselage hull step
171 Main undercarriage side struts
172 Hydraulic retraction jack
173 Mainwheel door
174 Port mainwheel
175 Wheel hub sealing plate

82 Cabin environmental system heater
83 Heater exhaust duct
84 Wing centre section construction
85 Engine mounting ring frame
86 Oil cooler
87 Engine bay fireproof bulkhead
88 Engine bearer struts
89 Oil tank
90 Hydraulic reservoir
91 Hydraulic accumulator
92 Aerial lead-in
93 Life raft stowage
94 Cabin roof cargo hatch
95 Boarding ladder, stowed
96 Litter installation, maximum 8 stretchers

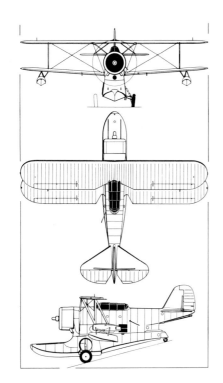

Technical details J2F-6 Duck

Type	Two/three-seat utility amphibian.
Engine	900 hp Wright R-1820-54 Cyclone 9 engine.
Dimensions	Wing span 39 ft., wing area 409 sq. ft., length 34 ft., height 13 ft. 11in.
Weights	Empty 4,400 lb. Max. 7,700 lb.
Performance	Max. speed 190 mph, cruising speed 155 mph, ceiling 25,000 ft., range 750 miles.
Armament	Provision for two 325 lb. depth bombs.

G-21 Goose

Type	Light amphibian transport for seven passengers.
Engine	Two Pratt and Whitney R-985 radial engines.
Dimensions	Wing span 50 ft. 10 in., wing area 377.64 sq. ft., length 39 ft. 7 in.
Weights	Empty 6,700 lb. Max. 12,500 lb.
Performance	Max. speed 243 mph, cruising speed 200 mph, ceiling 20,000 ft., range 1,600 miles.
Armament	None.

G-44 Widgeon

Type	Light amphibian transport for five passengers, or for coastal/anti-submarine patrol.
Engine	Ranger L-440C-5, six-cylinder, in-line piston engine.
Dimensions	Wing span 40 ft., wing area 245 sq. ft., length 31 ft. 1 in., height 11 ft. 5 in.
Weights	Empty 3,189 lb. Max. 4,500 lb.
Performance	Max. speed 153 mph, cruising speed 138 mph, ceiling 14,600 ft., range 920 miles.
Armament	None.

G-73 Mallard

Type	Twin-engined, amphibian transport for ten passengers.
Engines	Two Pratt and Whitney R-1340-S3H1 Wasp, nine-cylinder, radial piston engine.
Dimensions	Wing span 66 ft. 8 in., wing area 444 sq. ft., length 48 ft. 4 in., height 18 ft.
Weights	Empty 9,350 lb. Max. 12,750 lb.
Performance	Max. speed 215 mph, cruising speed 180 mph, ceiling 23,000 ft., range 1,380 miles.
Armament	None.

HU-16D Albatross

Type	Search and rescue and general purpose amphibian.
Engines	Two Wright R-1820-76A or 76B Cyclone nine-cylinder, radial piston engines producing 1,425 hp.
Dimensions	Wing span 96 ft. 8 in., wing area 1,035 sq. ft., length 61 ft. 3 in., height 25 ft. 10 in.
Weights	Empty 22,883 lb. Max. 35,700 lb.
Performance	Max. speed 236 mph, cruising speed 150 mph, ceiling 24,610 ft., range 2,850 miles.
Armament	None.

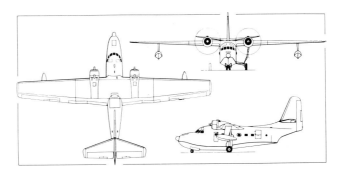

Model variations
JF/J2F Duck

XJF-1
Prototype model of the utility amphibian.

JF-1
Production model. Twenty-seven ordered by the US Navy. Powered by a Pratt and Whitney R-1830 Twin Wasp engine.

JF-2
Second production model. Fourteen ordered by the US Coast Guard. Powered by the Wright R-1820 Cyclone engine.

JF-3
Four JF-2s from the US Coast Guard transferred to the US Navy's inventory.

J2F-1
Third production model, but no significant difference to previous models.

J2F-2
As above.

J2F-2A
Nine ordered by the US Marine Corps (VMS-3 Squadron), the only difference to previous models was the provision of machine guns and underwing bomb racks.

J2F-3
As the J2F-2.

J2F-4
As the J2F-2.

J2F-5
This was the first model to be officially known as the Duck, and was powered by a Wright R-1820-50 engine. It was also the last Duck to be built by Grumman.

J2F-6
A version of the -5 built by Columbia Aircraft Corporation, Long Island, New York. Powered by a Wright R-1820-54 engine. Over 300 were built, and they were used on virtually every type of operation, e.g. rescue, target-towing, patrol, photo-reconnaissance; the only exception being strike operations.

XJL-1
This was a single-wing version of the Duck, with a tricycle undercarriage. It was designed by Grumman but built by Columbia. Two prototypes were built but it was never put into production.

G-44 Widgeon

G-44
Highly successful eight-seat, twin-engined amphibian. The prototype was flown on 28 June 1940; ten were sold even before the first production model came off the assembly line. Powered by two Ranger L-440C5 engines.

OA-14
Designation given to the G-44 by the USAF.

J4F-1
Part of third production batch, all for the US Coast Guard. One of them sank the *U-166* of the Passes of Mississippi during World War II.

J4F-2
Part of third production batch, this for the US Navy. Fifteen of the 131 built were given to the Royal Navy under the Lend-Lease Agreement and became known as the Goslings. The name later reverted to Widgeon.

G-44A
This was an improved version of the G-44, with a deeper keel and a revised hull. Powered by two Avco-Lycoming 90-435A engines.

SCAN-30
Forty-one G-44As were built under licence by the *Societé de Construction Aero-Navale (SCAN)* in France.

Super Widgeon
This was another conversion by McKinnon Enterprises. The cabin area was improved, as was the hull, and the fuel capacity was increased. Powered by two Avco-Lycoming GO-80-B1D engines.

G-21 Goose

G-21
Twin-engined amphibian, powered by two Pratt and Whitney R-985 radial engines. Built mainly for commercial use.

G-21A
This was an uprated version of the G-21, built to accommodate seven passengers. Production was continued throughout the war, although the engines were changed towards the end to Avco-Lycomings.

G-21C
This was a G-21A model converted by McKinnon Enterprises, who replaced the Avco-Lycomings with Pratt and Whitney PT6A Turboprop engines.

G-21D
As the G-21C.

G-21G
Also known as the Turbo-Goose, again converted by McKinnon Enterprises who uprated the cabin area, instruments etc.

HU-16D Albatross

XJR2F-1
The first prototype of the Albatross.

JR2F-1
This was the US Navy's designation after acceptance.

PF-1A
A small number were assigned to ASW duties, but later reverted back to JR2F-1s.

SA-16A
The designation given to the Albatross by the USAF, who used it for SAR (search and rescue).

UF-1
A number were ordered by the US Navy for SAR and utility work.

UF-1G
Designation given to the US Coast Guard version.

UF-1L
Designation given to three purchased by the US Navy for Arctic/Antarctic research.

UF-1T
Five ordered by the US Navy for training purposes.

UF-2
Later known as the HU-16D, this was an updated version of the JR2F-1.

UF-2G
The Coast Guard improved version of the JR2F-1, later known as the HU-16E.

SA-16B
This was the USAF's improved version of the JR2F-1, later known as the HU-16B.

SHU-16B
Two SA-16Bs were produced for evaluation for the export market.

G-111
The only civilian version of the Albatross. In 1980 Grumman were granted certification of an HU-16B and featured a new wing centre section, seating for twenty-eight passengers and other improvements. Powered by two Wright R-1820-76A Cyclone nine-cylinder, radial engines.

AF-2 Guardian

Two-thirds the size of the legendary DC-3, the Grumman AF-2 was the largest, single-engined, piston-driven aircraft ever to fly off the deck of an aircraft carrier. Its overall weight was 24,800 lb., only 1,000 lb. less than the DC-3. Having two versions, the AF-2 Guardian potentially represented one of the most deadly of all hunter/killer aircraft combinations ever produced.

At the beginning of 1944, Grumman produced a design that met the requirements of the US Navy in a replacement for the TBF/M Avenger. The Navy had wanted an aircraft that was half jet and half piston-engine, so Gruman produced the XTB3F-1, which had a 2,300 hp Pratt and Whitney R-2800-34W piston engine and a Westinghouse 19XB-2B (J30-WE-20) jet engine. The jet engine was intended for use as a back-up booster, and, in the event it was required, during critical combat situations. It was situated in the rear of the aircraft and produced 1,600 lbs. of thrust. The air intakes were situated in the leading edges of the wing and ran the length of the fuselage. Because of problems with the jet engine, all the run-up tests were conducted on the ground and the engine was never powered up during a test flight. It was later removed, mainly because of the collapse of the inlet duct linings.

Nevertheless, the Navy accepted Gruman's proposal for a new, high-speed, torpedo-carrying scout bomber, and ordered three prototypes. The aircraft carried a wide variety of armament, including two 20 mm cannons in the wing fold

joints; one 2,150 lb. torpedo, internally; or two 1,000 lb. bombs, and provision was made for bomb racks and rocket launchers under each wing.

The XTB3F-1's most distinctive feature, besides an enormous wing span, was the big square vertical tail, that appeared to dominate the aircraft. The first XTB3F-1, flown by Grumman test pilot Pat Gallo, crashed during Navy trials. In January 1947 the Navy decided that the other two were to act as an ASW (anti-submarine warfare) team — a hunter and a killer. This new proposal led to the redesignation of the aircraft, to XTB3F-1S and XTB3F-2S, and also a complete redesign.

ASW missions required low-altitude searches at a slow speed, with sophisticated search and detection equipment, whilst being armed with enough bombs, mines or torpedoes to destroy the submarine, when found. The Navy and Grumman agreed that it would take two aircraft to carry out a mission of this kind, so it was decided to modify the second and third prototypes accordingly: one to carry out the search and the other to destroy: XTB3F-1S, also known as 'Fertile Myrtle', possibly because of the large radome slung under the belly of her fuselage, was chosen to become the search aircraft. The Westinghouse turbo-jet engine was removed and replaced with the APS-20 search radar with its bulbous underbelly radome. Electronic surveillance equipment was

Above: An AF-1S on a test flight. Note the magnetometer boom extending from the tail.

89

installed and provision was made for additional fuel to be carried. The jet exhaust was in the rear of the aircraft beneath a fairing and radar countermeasure (RCM) antennas were installed. The XTB3F-1 was originally designed as a side-by-side two-seater and the second seat was removed and two new crew positions were created inside the fuselage. An RCM operator was added later, and provision was also made for the inclusion of sonobuoys and sonobuoy receivers. This aircraft was redesignated the AF-1S.

The other aircraft, the XTB3F-2S, was basically the same as the -1S, except that it was the attack version and had a small radar and searchlight combined, mounted on the starboard wing, plus a sonobuoy receiver and combination periscope and bombsight. As the 'killer' half of the team, it was designed to carry six five-inch HVAR rockets, four 500 lb. bombs or four Mk 54 depth-charges (two under each wing) and an ASW homing torpedo in the modified bomb bay. With the modifications complete, it was redesignated the AF-2S.

In October 1947 the Navy authorized the production of sixteen AF-1Ws and fourteen AF-2s, but defence budget problems cut this number down from a combined total of thirty to twenty-three. The aircraft were then flown to the Naval Air Test Centre at Patuxent River for tests by Grumman and Navy pilots. On 4 October 1949, the prototype suffered a propeller failure during a test flight; the test pilot managed to bale out but the Hamilton Standard representative, who was on board, did not, and was killed in the ensuing crash. The trials continued with the "killer" AF-2 taking part in carrier suitability trials at Patuxent River from 27 September to 6 December 1949, and these tests highlighted a problem with the propeller scraping the deck during arrestment rollout. The 13 ft. 6 in. propeller was replaced with the 12 ft. 2 in. type used on the F8F Bearcat. It was also noticed that, during run-out, the aircraft's tail bounced and rose higher than normal, which partly accounted for the propeller clipping the deck. To

An AF-2W of VS-37 on patrol in the Pacific.

combat this, a new hook-suspension system was designed and this resolved the problem.

The first production models were assigned to the fleet in September 1950 and the first squadron to receive one AF-2S and one AF-2W was VS-24. The initial production of the aircraft was extremely slow. Pilots from the Naval Air Test Centre carried out the first carrier landings aboard the *Wright* (CVL-49) on 26 and 27 November. One month later, VS-24 went aboard the *Palau* (CVE-122), under the command of Commander H. S. Jackson, and became the first operational AF squadron. In all, 153 AF-2Ws and 193 AF-2Ss were built between 1950 and 1953, but by the end of production a further 40 AF-3Ss had brought the total to 386.

An AF-2S escorting the US submarine SS319 into harbour.

Preparing the AF-2S for launch aboard the USS Wright.

Known to the various squadrons as the 'Guppy' (AF-2W) and 'Scrapper' (AF-2S), the hunter/killer teams operated from ASW aircraft carriers. As with most strike carrier aircraft at the time, the idea was to attack predetermined targets with the maximum amount of firepower and return to the carrier for rearming and refuelling. In the meantime, the carrier would move safely out of range of any retaliatory attack and prepare for the next sortie. The role of the AF was to create a protective screen around the fleet by hunting and destroying enemy submarines that came within a 500 mile radius. The "Guppy" would carry out the search pattern, usually at an altitude of between 1,000 and 1,500 feet, and at a speed of around 135 knots. It would hope to locate either the submarine on the surface, or the snorkel. After making contact, the pilot would then summon up the 'Scrapper',

The AF-2W at the bottom of the picture was the hunter. Distinguishable from the AF-2S (killer) by the large radome beneath the fuselage. The final version has two finettes (auxiliary vertical fins on the horizontal stabilisers) fitted to the tail.

An AF-2S and AF-2W of a hunter-killer team.

whilst staying on station and tracking the submarine. When the 'Scrapper' was close enough to take over, it switched on its own wing-mounted, APS-431 radar, descended to between 500 and 200 feet and tracked the submarine itself. When contact was made, the radar operator would manoeuvre the aircraft to within two miles and the bombardier, looking through a periscope mounted in the belly of the aircraft just aft of the trailing edge of the wing, would call out the attack vectors, if necessary with the help of the port wing-mounted, AVQ-2 searchlight. The four wing-mounted, Mk 54 depth charges would be released at preselected intervals.

The AF-3S was the final version of the 'killer' model, and was virtually identical to the AF-2S, except that it had MAD (Magnetic Anomaly Detection) installed, which greatly improved the potential for submarine location and subsequent destruction.

The AF was an ungainly-looking aircraft. With its enormous wing span and long fuselage and high, heavy, rugged-looking undercarriage, its size belied its capability. Both AFs had fabric-covered control surfaces, with the exception of the flaperons. Because of the low speed requirement for its search operation, the AF-2W had large control surfaces which required a boost system. The leading edge of the wing was slotted and the Pratt and Whitney R-2800-48W engine was canted three degrees to the right to help counter the torque created by the large propeller in high power and low speed conditions. In addition, the engine was also canted three degrees downwards to ensure good visibility for the pilot during landings and take-offs. The aircraft carried a total of 620 gallons of fuel; the main tank, situated in the fuselage,

directly behind the pilot, held 170 gallons, each wing tank held 75 gallons, and provision was made to carry two 150 gallon drop tanks under each wing.

Although the AF, or Guardian as it came to be known, was a thoroughly reliable aircraft, a large number of accidents were recorded because of its size and the narrowness of the CVE/CVL decks. Unlike today's angled decks, most carriers had straight decks then, so when other aircraft were parked up forward, extra barriers had to be erected across the deck to ensure their safety. This, of course, made the landing area shorter and barrier crashes were not uncommon. Also the aircraft handlers were used to aircraft half the size and weight of the AF, and inevitably accidents occurred during parking operations. At one point, the problems got so bad, that one squadron commander refused to allow an AF to be moved unless the pilot was in the cockpit.

From the initial conception of the TB3F project, Grumman were always aware that the Navy were only using this project as a stop-gap until a firm replacement was produced. But this did not materialise and from 1945 to 1954 the AF Guardian was the Navy's front line ASW aircraft. Although this span covered nine years, only three years were spent with the fleet on squadron service and in 1954 they were replaced by Grumman S2F-1 Trackers. The last of the AFs were turned over to the Naval Reserve's squadrons, but most ended up in the breaker's yard.

Of the 386 AFs built, five did manage to escape the breaker's yard; two AF-2s and three AF-2Ws. They were acquired by a civilian aerial fire-fighting organization, the Aero Union Corporation, and three were converted to flying tankers, whilst the remaining two were retained for spares. From 1957 to 1974 the AFs fought fires all over the United States, dropping 800 gallons of 'Firetrol' at a time. But in 1974, two of the AF tankers, along with a number of TBM Avenger tankers, were scrapped after the US Forestry Service had declared that no more single-engined tankers would be used for fire-fighting. The sole survivor was restored to its original condition and displayed at air shows around the United States; it now resides at the Naval Air Museum at Pensacola, resplendent in the colours of VS-25.

Not once did the AFs drop a depth charge in anger, nor release a torpedo. They caused a great deal of problems to the handlers aboard the carriers, and sometimes to the pilots who flew them. But one thing is certain, the AF paved the way for future ASW aircraft and the Navy became richer for it.

Running engine tests on the AF-2W.

Above right: A hunter-killer team about to launch from the USS Wright.

AF-2S technial specifications

Model	Anti-submarine search or strike aircraft.	*Performance*	Max. speed 317 mph at 16,000 ft., initial climb rate 1,850 ft. per min. Service ceiling 32,500 ft., range 1,500 miles.
Crew	AF-2S two; AF-2W four.		
Engine	One 2,400 hp Pratt and Whitney R-2800-48W.		
Dimensions	Wing span 60 ft. 8 in., wing area 560 sq. ft., length 43 ft. 4 in., height 16 ft. 2 in.	*Armament*	AF-2S only: one 2,000 lb. torpedo, or two 2,000 lb. bombs, or two 1,600 lb. depth charges.
Weight	14,580 lb. empty, 25,500 lb. gross.		

AF Guardian model variations

XTB3F-1
The first of three planned prototypes. All the aircraft were unique, inasmuch as they had one piston engine and one jet engine, although the jet engine was only ever run-up on the ground and never used in the air. The -1 was powered by a Pratt and Whitney R-2800-34W and the Westinghouse 19XB-2B jet engines.

XTB3F-2
The -2 was powered by the Wright R-3350 and a Westinghouse 24C-4B jet engine.

XTB3F-2S
The third prototype was built without the Westinghouse jet engine, and the space created was used to accommodate another crew member.

AF-2S
This was the 'killer' part of the 'hunter/killer' partnership with the AF-2W. It had six underwing pylons capable of carrying HVAR rockets and depth charges. Beneath the starboard wing an AN/APS-31 radar was carried, whilst under the port wing an AN/AVQ-2 searchlight was mounted.

AF-2W
The 'hunter' part of the team also had a searchlight under the port wing, but was easily distinguishable from the -2S by the large radome under the fuselage.

AF-3S
Similar to the AF-2S, but with additional ASW equipment. This included a magnetic anomaly detector, boom-mounted on the starboard side of the fuselage.

F9F Panther/Cougar

Although they had already experimented on the XTB3F-1 torpedo-bomber (later to become the AF-2 Guardian submarine hunter and killer), with a mixture of jet and piston engine with little success, Grumman's true entry into the jet age was on 21 November 1947, when their XF9F-2 took to the air with Grumman test pilot Corwin (Corky) Meyer at the controls. Corky Meyer flew the XF9F-2 from Bethpage to Idlewild (later becoming John F. Kennedy International Airport) in New York, because there was some question about the braking system on the aircraft and Idlewild offered a very long runway compared to the relatively short one at Bethpage. As it turned out, the flight was an uneventful one and the aircraft turned around after landing at Idlewild and returned to Bethpage. Although this was officially the first flight, it wasn't the first attempt! A week previously, Corky Meyer was taxying the aircraft out for its first flight when he decided to take a short cut across a patch of grass. The weight of the aircraft was too much for the grass and the wheels sank up to the hubs, and, even with full power on, Corky Meyer was unable to get the aircraft out. It was decided to send for a tow truck to pull the aircraft clear, but in doing so the nosewheel buckled, with the result that the flight was put back a week. The aircraft completed a number of test flights before making its official press debut, all of them carried out without serious problems.

The XF9F-2 was fitted with the Rolls-Royce Nene engine,

two of which had been brought over from England for testing. After a great deal of discussion, the Grumman team were granted a licence to build the Nene engine in the United States, and they returned to Bethpage with the installation drawings. The licence to build the Nene engine was given to the Taylor Turbine Corporation, in fact who later relinquished this right to the Pratt and Whitney Corporation.

The XF9F-1 was designed primarily for use on board aircraft carriers from where it would be launched by catapult. The design of the aircraft was quite advanced for the time: it was to have been 46 ft. long, with a wingspan of 64 ft. 2 in. (30 ft. folded) and have four Westinghouse 24C turbojet engines, mounted in nacelles, underslung from each wing. The main landing gear retracted between the jet engine nacelles. Designed to carry one pilot and one radar operator in a side-by-side configuration, the role of the aircraft was to have been primarily the destruction of ground and waterborne targets at night. The armament, four 20 mm cannon with 1,000 rounds of ammunition, was located below the jet units and on either side of the main landing gear. All the fuel was carried in three self-sealing tanks, located in the fuselage behind the cockpit. A total of 1,530 gallons would have given the aircraft a radius of 350 miles at a speed of about 650 mph at sea level.

Above: An F9F-3 on a production test flight.

As design progress was made on the XF9F-1, it became increasingly obvious that there were going to be serious problems with the four-engined aircraft and the project was dropped, much to the relief of the Grumman team. A new design with a single, newly-developed Rolls-Royce engine, producing 5,000 pounds of thrust was built, and designated the XF9F-2. Two prototypes were ordered and, although there were many who thought that a swept wing should have been incorporated into the design, it was decided that the straight wing was, for the moment, ideal.

The aircraft had been designed with a great deal of thought given to ease of maintenance, and one innovation was the sliding nose. Fitted on rails, when released by a lever in the nose-wheel well, the nose exended some three-and-a-half feet, giving easy access to either the armament, or, in later models, the photographic equipment. At the other end of the aircraft, the whole tail section could be disconnected from the fuselage at the wing-flap line. The difference this made for the maintenance crews aboard the aircraft carriers, whose space was extremely limited, was tremendous. It also meant that squadron aircraft would only be down for half the time of other aircraft. The aircraft was of a very advanced design for 1946: a pressurized, air-conditioned cockpit; an automatic radio direction finder; and a quick-release, one-piece, bubble canopy were only a few of this aircraft's innovations.

Grumman, in the meantime, had been having discussions with Allisons regarding a back-up engine, or an alternative to the Nene. A third prototype was ordered and this was powered by an Allison J33-A-23 engine, which produced some 4,600 pounds of thrust and was already in service with the US Air Force.

Production of the third prototype continued without problems and the initial contracts called for forty-seven F9F-2s with J42-P-6 engines and fifty-four F9F-3s with the Allison J33-A-8 engine. In late September 1948, three Rolls-Royce Nene engines, or XJ42-TT-2s, as the Navy called them, were delivered to Grumman for test purposes. Also at that time, Martin Baker ejection seats were tested in the armament test-stand facility, with a view to fitting them as standard equipment in all production models. None of the prototypes was ever fitted with the ejection seat. Trials were also carried out with wing-tip fuel tanks, initially on the basis that the additional fuel would give the F9F either extra range or operational flexibility when over the target. It was discovered that the detachable, but non-jettisonable, tanks improved the aileron response significantly, and so it was decided to fit them as a permanent fixture. None of the prototypes had them, nor the first twelve off the production line, but all subsequent F9Fs had them. A total of 567 F9F-2s were built, the majority of which saw action in Korea, either with the US Navy or the Marine Corps.

Serious flight testing began in the early part of 1948, including the testing of the four nose-mounted cannon and the final design of the ejection seat installation. Two major problems came to light that needed immediate attention: longitudinal instability in the landing mode, and lateral snaking or 'Dutch rolls' at all speeds. To combat the snaking, baffles were installed in the fuel tanks, which solved the problem, and increasing the tail surfaces corrected the instability.

Comparison flights were later made with the North American FJ-1 Fury and, overall, the XF9F-2 was superior in all aspects of simulated combat conditions. A maximum Mach .85 was reached during structural dive tests; because of the severe buffeting experienced at this speed, the operational maximum was reduced to Mach .83. One major problem dogged the engineers throughout testing and that was poor lateral control with the aileron boost. To correct this, the complete control system had to be redesigned.

With this obstacle overcome, Grumman received an order for an additional 317 F9Fs, 244 of which were F9F-2s, whilst the remaining seventy-three were F9F-3s. It was discovered,

during flight testing, that there was a rather unusual problem associated with the F9F's short landing gear arrangement. The Panther squatted in a tail-low position, and during the long engine run-ups on board carriers, the caulking between the planks of the flight deck burned. A similar problem occurred on asphalt runways. The temperature from the tail pipes was in excess of 1,000 degrees Farenheit and, to solve the problem, an exhaust deflector was fitted on carrier aircraft and a concrete run-up area built for the ground-based aircraft.

In October 1948 the first F9F was delivered to the NATC for carrier suitability testing. Various design changes were made: the introduction of a roller-type arrester hook and a revised, accordion-shaped, tail pipe installation being among these. However the aircraft suffered a flame-out and crashed whilst on a test flight. The problem was caused by a fuel system malfunction. With the necessary fuel system modifications made, the XF9F-3 was delivered to the NATC to complete the carrier suitability tests.

The first production Panther flew on 24 November 1948, and the second in December the same year. Problems were experienced again, with the fuel system, causing delays in the flight tests, and the order for F9F-2s reverted to F9F-3s. Of the 418 on order, 364 were to be fitted with the J42 engine. Carrier trials continued throughout January 1949, with greater emphasis being placed on carrier landing techniques, flight tests with the wing-tip tanks, and fuel dumping.

With the necessary major redesign changes completed, the modified F9F-2s began their carrier trials again, on the USS Franklin D. Roosevelt, in May, only to be halted once more because of arrester-hook problems. In the meantime, the first F9F-3 Panthers were delivered to VF-51, under the command of Cdr. Pete Aurand, the first to a fleet squadron. Even then trouble seemed to dog the F9F. On delivery, one aircraft was lost completely after an emergency landing in a field, and another was lost after an engine flame-out just short of touchdown. Fortunately, there were no injuries in either accident, and all other aircraft were delivered safely. During the familiarization programme, a number of minor problems came to light, but this was par for the course with any new aircraft.

The Panther completed its carrier suitability trials at NATC by September and was cleared for carrier operation, even though the early F9F-3s were discovered to be under-powered. VF-51 carried out its initial carrier qualifications on board the USS Boxer in mid-September.

An F9F-2 on a production test flight.

The Panther continued to create interest, even though there were problems with the initial production order. The F9F-3s were the first to be delivered, then the -2s, with the Pratt and Whitney J42 engine, followed closely by the -4s and -5s. The

improved Allison engine, the J33 with 6,450 pounds of thrust, was fitted in the F9F-4, and the Pratt and Whitney J48 (this was the Rolls-Royce Tay engine built under licence) was installed in the F9F-5. There were some other differences between the F9F-2, -4, and -5, the fuselage was progressively lengthened and the vertical tail surfaces increased. The -2 and -3 could not be converted to -6s and -5s, but the -4 could be converted to -5s. The F9F-2B had provision for six rockets and two 1,000 lb. bombs under each wing. This was accomplished with a conversion kit and was so successful that the kits were issued for all F9F-2s, and VMF-115 was the first squadron to have them.

The first F9F-5 prototype made its maiden flight on 21 December 1949 and all the tests were successful. Uprated J48-P-8 engines were installed in all the production F9F-6s and -8s, which were known as Cougars. The Navy expressed a need for photo-reconnaissance aircraft and, with the help of the Grumman designers, developed a version of the F9F-2 the F9F-2P. This was achieved by modifying the nose section (which was, as explained earlier, detachable), removing the guns and ammunition and installing cameras. Later, a version of the F9F-5 was developed by Grumman specifically as a photo-reconnaissance aircraft. As more and more squadrons were equipped with the F9F Panther, the old fuel problem reappeared. This time it was discovered that one of the problems was in the fuel tank, with the baffles tearing loose. But the fuel control solenoid problem took some time to find, with the result that all the aircraft had to be grounded for a period because of a number of engine fires, some of them fatal. The problem was discovered to be failure of the engine fuel nozzles, allowing unrestricted fuel into the combustion chamber until it burned through. The fitting of a new type of fuel nozzle cured the problem.

The transition from flying piston-engined aircraft to jet aircraft must have been a difficult, yet exhilirating one. One such pilot, Ensign (now Lt. Cdr.) R. P. Youngjohns, who experienced this, tells how he first encountered and flew the F9F-2:

The first thing we found out was that the F9F had a very slow throttle response with the engine, compared to the propeller aircraft we were used to. After a few approaches, I began to get the hang of it. The power was slow to respond so you had to set up early, but once the feel of the throttle became more comfortable, landings became smooth. Downwind was about 125 knots and final approach was about 118 to 121 knots, with power about eighty-five to ninety per cent, if I remember correctly. The aircraft itself was very steady throughout the landing pattern. In-flight speed was limited to about Mach .85 because we had no hydraulic elevators and anything over that would cause control problems. The aircraft was not designed for speed when compared with later models; besides, the engine wouldn't give you the required power, plus the straight wings, tip-tanks and human power on the controls. Only in a dive could you approach the outside of the envelope on speed, so we were limited on aerobatics. If we approached speed limits, we had to put out the speed brakes. Also, as speed brakes were not used for landings, you had to be right on top of your speed requirements.

The F9F-5 was an improvement over the F9F-2. The engine was better, there was more controlability, improved instrumentation, and a slightly higher speed. We had the J48 engine, which was a quantum jump over the F9F-2 and F9F-4. The F9F-4 had the same engine as the T-33, talk about a dog! A contest was held to determine the paint scheme we were to use on the tail. A design was made, one aircraft was painted and the air group commander, Cdr. Heber Badger, was asked for his approval of our marvellous effort. His comment was: 'Its very pretty, but it is the same as the Cuban Air

Force'. Needless to say, the tail was painted over in a hurry.

The squadron was officially commissioned on 1 June 1955 and we were told that we were to get rid of the Panther as we were to receive a new aircraft. The big question was, would it be the F7U Cutlass or the F9F Cougar? Some of the pilots were already at the F7U school, but then the decision was finally made, it was to be the F9F Cougar. We all gave a huge sigh of relief! The Cutlass was, as far as were were concerned, an experimental aircraft, that had poor controls and a poor performance record. It wasn't long before we had fourteen, brand new, blue Cougars. As far as Grumman products go, it was like moving from a Chevrolet to a Cadillac. It was well built, had the new state-of-the-art in centrifugal flow in the new J48 engine, those new-fangled controls called 'flaperons' and powered stabilizers, or 'flying tail' as it was sometimes called. It was capable of supersonic speed — mind you, you had to be going straight down at high altitude on a cold day above 30,000 feet. The aircraft was well built, a typical 'Grumman Ironworks' aircraft. It could take a lot of punishment and was very forgiving. Acceleration was slow but once you were at speed, the aircraft was highly manoeuvrable. There were problems: the instrumentation was completely inadequate when instrument flying, the gyro-horizon was only two-and-a-half inches wide, though the radio magnetic indicator was large — about four inches. The RMI was in the centre of the instrument panel and the gyro-horizon to the side of it. The airspeed indicator was to the left of the RMI and the engine instruments were located around the navigation and flight instruments. It took a while to get used to flying on instruments! Because of the slow engine acceleration, it was decided to use speed brakes on landing, in order to keep the power in the 'quick response range' — seventy-eight to eighty-five per cent. Some new instruments were included, such as the angle-of-attack-indicator. No one knew how to use it or to maintain it, so we never used it — talk about seat-of-the-pants-flying! The navigational radio was the standard 'coffee grinder' VHF, tied into the RMI. We also had UHF direction finding capability. Our weapon systems included four .50 calibre machine guns in the nose and four wing station racks for bombs/rockets/fuel drop tanks. The maximum size drop tank was 150 gallons and performance fell off dramatically with a full wing load at altitude, a maximum of about 1,500 pounds per side.

Take-off rotation was about 128 knots with full flaps and flying tail disengaged. The flying tail automatically cut off with flap down, but upon raising the flaps, the tail was re-engaged by pushing down a plunger in the cockpit. Maximum range was at about Mach .78 with maximum endurance at Mach .50. Fuel was ample for about one-and-a-half hours of flight, with a maximum of two hours and thirty minutes to flame-out. With 500 pounds of fuel, power was unreliable and maximum power was unavailable. A stall warning device was located in the wing and caused the control stick to vibrate when the stall was approached. In the level carrier attitude for landing, using speed-brakes, the nose attitude was such as to cause this device to engage. It became rather unnerving to have the stick vibrating, indicating how close to a stall you were during the carrier approach. The answer was to just disconnect the darn thing.

The air conditioning was pretty good, except you had to be at 'full hot' for take-off, otherwise the cockpit would fog up. On let-down, particularly instrument penetrations, the heat had to be turned up full at least five minutes ahead of time. Otherwise, with speed brakes out, seventy per cent power, 250 knots and 4,000 feet per minute descent, the canopy would fog up and there you

An F9F-8 on a production test flight, fitted with expendable wing fuel tanks and Sidewinder missiles.

would be, blind and madly wiping the canopy so you could see out. The aircraft had some minor idiosyncrasies — on a 360 degrees roll, the aircraft rolled around the inside wing, due to the flaperons rather than the nose. Until we got the hang of it, this caused some interesting problems in formation flying, especially formation rolls!

As a weapons platform, the F9F-8 was an excellent attack aircraft, being limited to total stores carried and time on station. It was a steady platform and you could be really accurate. It was not unusual to have a fifty-foot CEP, or less, in high altitude dive bombing, which consisted of rolling in at 23,000 feet (over the target, roll inverted at 250 knots, extend the speed brakes and pull the nose through until your pipper on the gunsight was centred on the target, power to eighty per cent, accelerate to 450 knots, release at 15,000 feet and pull out pulling four g's, boards in, climbing back to altitude with a 180-degree turn). Rockets were a snap, 450 knots, 5,000 feet, 30 degrees dive, pipper on target, fire and out at 15,000 feet. Strafing, same thing, so was the low-level bombing. Air-to-air combat — highly manoeuvrable below 35,000 feet. Altitude of choice was below 30,000 feet as the controls were more responsive, above that you would lose flying speed too fast, plus control effectiveness and acceleration capability. Maximum ceiling was about 43,000 feet for a number of reasons — flying speed and stall speed at this height were nearly identical (220 knots indicated), the diluter oxygen system would

not be life sustaining if pressurization was lost, and the engine fuel control tended to do alarming things, such as the RPM increasing above one hundred per cent (up to 103) all on its own, engine surge and EGT increasing up to 800 degrees. This was guaranteed to get your attention! The ejection seat was not state-of-the-art. There was a zero lanyard attached but the seat was figured to be safe only above 1,200 feet (and that was right side up). There were two ways to eject, pull the canopy release handle first and then eject, or eject through the canopy. If you tried the first and the canopy didn't go all the way, you were stuck!

If I give the impression that the Panther and the Cougar were not amongst the world's best fighters, all I can say is that they were ahead of the McDonnell FH-1 Phantom, the Chance Vought F6U-1 Pirate, the North American FJ-1 Fury and given the choice again, the Grumman aircraft without hesitation would be the first.

With the further involvement of the United States in the war in Korea, production of the F9Fs was increased and the testing of improved models, such as the F9F-4 and -5, was brought forward. By the end of 1952, 1,382 production aircraft had been delivered to the Navy. After delivery to the NATC for BIS (Board of Inspection and Survey) trials, the aircraft were delivered to the Fleet for carrier trials and this turned out to be a most dramatic and spectacular event.

The trials were carried out aboard the aircraft carrier *USS Midway* and the Panther, with Commander George Duncan at the controls, made its approach to the carrier's deck. Just seconds from touchdown, the Panther suddenly sunk low and hit the ramp at the end of the flight deck. The rear of the cockpit under the leading edge of the wing took the impact, with the result that the aircraft burst into flames. As luck would have it, the forward section of the fuselage broke off and was sent tumbling down the deck with the pilot still strapped inside. A battered Commander Duncan was quickly pulled from the wreckage very much alive to the surprise of everyone who had witnessed the accident. The accident set the carrier trials back some months, and it was August before another F9F-5 was available. Other trials were being carried out by the Navy regarding the exterior finish of the aircraft. One hundred Panthers were ordered from the production line with only an anodic film covering the metal skin. These aircraft were intergrat with other F9Fs on squadron duty so that comparisons could be made with regard to corrosion. No findings were ever published and the Navy still paint all their aircraft, so one has to assume that any comparisons were inconclusive.

The F9F Panther first saw action on 3 July 1950, when the aircraft carrier *USS Valley Forge* launched the Panthers of Air Group Five. The mission was a complete success, the aircraft destroying two Yak-9 fighters and a number of enemy ground targets. On 9 November, the first jet-versus-jet encounter in combat was recorded. An F9F-2 Panther of VF-111, flown by the CO Lt. Cdr. W. T. Amen, encountered a MiG-15 and shot it down.

Ordnance men loading an F9F-2 Panther with bombs for an air strike in Korea.

The first few months of the Korean conflict were fought by US Navy carrier squadrons, and it was not until December that the US Marine Corps entered the war, flying combat missions from carriers. The first Marine squadron, VMF-331, flying F9F-2s in the fighter/bomber role, flew its first combat mission late in December. Up to this point the Navy had flown only fighter combat roles, but in April 1951, VF-191 flew the first Navy bombing mission from the carrier *USS Princeton*. From that moment, all F9F Panthers flew as fighter/bombers and as the pilots were to find out later, the sturdiness of these aircraft was to be of paramount importance.

At this time, the J48 engined, F9F-4s and -5s came into service but were dogged with problems, with the result that in January 1952, all F9F-5s with the J48 engine were grounded. Meanwhile, some of the F9F-4s powered by the J33-A-16 engine were having their own problems. They too were grounded in January 1952, with bearing and inducer failures. The J48 engine was partially redesigned and reinstalled in the F9F-5s, but they were grounded again with fuel nozzle problems some months later. By June all the problems were solved and the F9F-4s and -5s were returned to the fleet for squadron duties. Of the 109 F9F-4s produced, most went to USMC squadrons.

The F9F-4 was a slightly larger version of the F9F-2 and was capable of carrying a total of 3,465 lb., which increased the overall weight of the aircraft to 21,250 lb. Its fuel capacity was increased from 923 gallons to 1,003 gallons, and had additional launch racks for rockets and bombs. Development also started on an autopilot system, known as GEG-3, which was installed in the F9F-5P. None of the other fighters had autopilots and the reason given for choosing the F9F-5P

was that it gave the pilot more time to concentrate on operating his cameras. Tests were also carried out at the same time on the use of 150 gallon fuel tanks, mounted externally on the inboard wing racks. There was still concern about the stall warning and stalling speed characteristics. A small fence was positioned at the wing's leading edge, just outboard of the engine inlets. This appeared to solve the problem, so the device was fitted to all F9F Panthers. As more and more F9F-4s and -5s were produced, they slowly took over the tasks performed by the F9F-2s, which had already distinguished themselves, but the truce was signed before they could replace them completely. By the end of 1952, the F9F-5 had been replaced by a new version designated the F9F-6 Cougar. But such was the reliability of the Panther, that the Navy continued to find new roles for it rather than discard it. F9F-2Ds and F9F-2KDs were used extensively, either as drones or as controller aircraft in the Regulus missile programme.

Meanwhile, the US Navy was working on a system that would give the F9F-4, increased lift, and after extensive wind tunnel tests, the Navy came up with the first super circulation Boundary Layer Control (BLC). Bleed-air from the engine was ducted to nozzles that extended laterally ahead of the flaps, blowing air over the upper surfaces of the deflected flaps. This gave increased maximum lift to the F9F-4, with the result that it was installed on other aircraft, including the McDonnell Douglas Phantom and the Lockheed F104.

An F9F-4 of VMF-115 making an emergency landing.

With the Cougar replacing all the Panthers, the F9Fs were reassigned to the Advance Training Units which gave novice pilots their first taste of a jet fighter. A number of reserve squadrons were issued with them and the Marine Corps retained two squadrons (VMA-223 and VMF(AW)-314) of F9F-5s until December 1957. One Navy F9F-2 was actually mentioned in dispatches as having dropped more than 400,000 pounds of bombs and worn out sixteen guns whilst in the process of firing more than 100,000 rounds of ammunition. It had apparently taken part in the first Navy air strike and really epitomized the ruggedness and durability of the Panther.

The F9F-6 Cougar was basically a redesigned F9F Panther, with wings and tail swept back to an angle of thirty-five degrees. The wings had leading-edge slats that operated with the trailing edge flaps, to lower the landing speed. As on the Panthers, a stall fence was positioned fore and aft on each upper wing surface to improve the aircraft's stability at low speeds. The tip tanks were discarded and the wings themselves used as auxiliary tanks, with seventy-eight gallons in each wing, bringing the total carried by the aircraft to 919 gallons. The speed brakes, mounted under the fuselage, were similar to those fitted on the Panther and featured on all subsequent Cougars, as on the four nose-mounted cannon.

An F9F-5 on a pre-delivery test flight.

Between December 1951 and February 1954, 646 F9F Cougars were built but, although they were aboard at least one carrier operating off the coast of Korea, they never saw action. The Cougar, like the Panther, was essentially a day fighter and, because it was unable to carry the type of radar necessary to operate the all-weather, long-range Sparrow missiles, it was restricted to carrying the Sidewinders.

The F9F-6 Cougar was also adapted as a photo-reconnaissance aircraft. A total of sixty F9F-6Ps were built, identical to the standard F9F-6, except for the specially-adapted nose which had camera apertures in the sides. The F9F-6 was also the first swept-wing, high-speed drone. There were two types, the F9F-6D and the F9F-6K2; the D was developed as the drone director and the K2 as either the drone controller or the drone itself. The only distinguishing features were different antenna arrangements and a multi-coloured paint scheme of red, yellow and blue.

The development of the Allison J33-A-16, which produced 6,350 pounds of thrust, provided the F9F-7 with a new power plant. Of the 168 F9F-7s built, only the first 118 had the Allison engine. The last fifty were delivered as F9F-6s and were powered by the Pratt and Whitney J48 engine.

The F9F-7 Cougar flown by LCDR F. X. Brady which set the record of 3 hours 45 minutes and 30 seconds from NAS San Diego to NAS New York, a distance of 2,430 miles.

One rather interesting experiment was carried out using an F9F-7, called 'Flex-deck', and its purpose was to evaluate the possibility of reducing the weight by eliminating the landing gear. A rubberized deck, 375 feet long and 80 feet wide, was secured to air bags underneath it. The bottom of the aircraft's fuselage was strengthened and reshaped slightly but, although a number of landings were successfully made, the idea was never pursued.

The next variant was the F9F-8P photographic-reconnaissance aircraft. Basically the same as the F9F-8, the 20 mm cannon were removed and the nose extended. The elongated nose allowed for the installation of fourteen cameras, which could photograph forwards, sideways and downwards. The nose itself had flat sides and a flattened bottom, and access to the cameras was through a large hatch in the side. The pilot was able to line up and activate the cameras by using a viewfinder that had been installed in place of the gunsight. The special cameras could photograph continuously a ten-mile wide section of the terrain for five hours. One hundred and ten of these aircraft were built.

There was one more variant of the F9F-8, the F9F-8T, later designated the TF-9J. It was a two-seat version of the F9F-8 and was primarily for training purposes. The fuselage had to be lengthened by thirty-four inches to accommodate the extra seat, and two of the four nose-mounted cannon were removed to compensate for the additional weight. Two 150-gallon fuel tanks were carried on the external underwing racks. As late as 1966, TF-9Js were operating from Da Nang in Vietnam as Tactical Air Co-ordinators (TAC) and helicopter escorts. With tiger sharks teeth painted on their noses, they flew many sorties in support of Marine and Army ground forces against the Vietcong.

The ageing Cougars were eventually replaced, but some, instead of going to the scrapyard, were fitted with powerful radio equipment and used as high-performance drones. They were very easily distinguished by their bright orange dayglo finish. One F9F-8T was assigned to the Naval Parachute Facility at El Centro, California. The rear canopy was removed and the aircraft used for ejection seat testing. It was a fitting way for the F9F Cougar to end its career, helping to protect the lives of men like those who had flown her.

An XF9F-9. Note the TF-1 Trader in the background.

An unpainted XF9F-9 about to start on a test flight.

Technical details
Gruman F9F-2 Panther

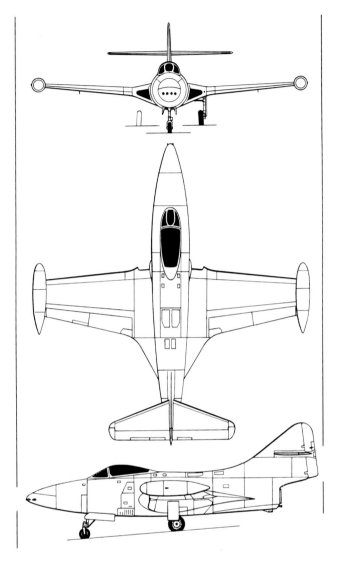

Type	Single-seat, carrier- or land-based fighter.
Engine	Pratt and Whitney J42, producing 5,700 pounds of thrust.
Dimensions	Wing span 37 ft. 11 in., wing area 250 sq. ft., length 38 ft. 1 in., height 12 ft. 3 in.
Weight	9,303 lb. empty, 15,700 lb. gross.
Performance	Max. speed 500 knots, stalling speed 78 knots. Rate of climb 10,000 ft. in 68 secs. Service ceiling 44,000 ft., range 1,175 miles.
Armament	Four nose-mounted M-3 20 mm cannon. The -2B had provision for six five-inch rockets and two bombs.
Fuel capacity	923 gallons, including two 120 gallon wing-tip tanks.

Technical details
Gruman F9F-8 Cougar

	Single-seat, carrier- or land-based fighter.
Engine	Pratt and Whitney J48-P-8A turbo-jet, producing 7,250 pounds of thrust.
Dimensions	Wing span 34 ft. 6 in., wing area 337 sq. ft., length 41 ft. 9 in., height 12 ft. 3 in.
Weight	11,866 lb. empty, 24,763 lb. gross.
Performance	Max. speed 647 mph, cruising speed 516 mph. Initial climb rate 5,750 ft. per min., service ceiling 44,500 ft., range 933 miles.
Armament	Four AIM-9B Sidewinder AAMs or four 500 lb. bombs.

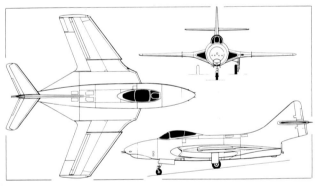

F9F model variations

XF9F-1
Designed as a four-engined, two-seat, night fighter, but progressed no farther than the drawing board.

XF9F-2
This was the first Grumman jet aircraft to come off the production line. Two were built, both powered by the Rolls-Royce Nene engine and used specifically for research and development.

F9F-2
The first production model, powered by the Pratt and Whitney J42-P-6 engine. Top speed 526 mph at 22,000 feet. The -2B carried a Mk 51 bomb under each wing.

F9F-2P
An F9F-2 that was initially converted to a photo-reconnaissance aircraft, and later manufactured as such.

F9F-2KD
An F9F-2P that was converted by the US Navy as a drone director and painted in bright, easily-distinguished colours.

XF9F-3
Same as the F9F-2, with the exception of the engine, which was an Allison J33-A-8.

F9F-3
Same as the F9F-2, except that initially it had the Allison engine but this was changed later to the Pratt and Whitney J42-P-8.

F9F-4
Had a slightly longer fuselage and a straight tail fin and rudder. The engine was an Allison J33-A-16. The armament was the same as in all the previous models, four nose-mounted 20 mm cannon.

F9F-5

Identical to the F9F-4 externally, but the instrument panel had a number of extra instruments. Powered by a Pratt and Whitney J48-P-6 engine. A total of 616 were produced.

F9F-5P

An unarmed, photo-reconnaissance aircraft with cameras fitted in an elongated nose.

F9F-5KD

A small number originally started life as F9F-5Ps but were converted by the US Navy to drone controllers.

F9F-6

The Cougar was the first swept-wing jet that Grumman built. It was powered by the Pratt and Whitney J48-P-8 engine and carried the same armament as the Panther.

F9F-6D

A standard Cougar with specialized radio equipment, making it the first swept-wing, high speed drone.

F9F-6K2

Had the same equipment as the -6D, but was used as a drone director or target. It was distinguished from the standard Cougar by the colourful red, yellow and blue paint scheme.

F9F-6P

A standard Cougar with the armament removed and replaced by nose-mounted gun-cameras.

F9F-7

Externally, identical to the F9F-6. It was powered by the Allison J33-A-16 engine. The cockpit instrumentation was designed for a day fighter.

F9F-8

This was the last of the Cougars and had a much larger wing area, allowing for the provision of six underwing racks. The engine was a Pratt and Whitney J48-P-8A, giving the aircraft a top speed of 714 mph. Adopted by the Blue Angels in 1955. The nose of the aircraft was adapted for in-flight refuelling with the addition of a probe on the tip.

F9F-8B

The same as the F9F-8, but with the provision of a low altitude bombing system. A number of changes were made by the Navy to the cockpit instrumentation: dive and roll indicators, accelerometers beig two examples.

F9F-8P

A standard F9F-8 with all the armament removed and the nose elongated to house fourteen cameras. The performance was identical to that of the -8.

F9F-8T

Designed primarily as a trainer, four of them operated in the Vietnam war as USMC forward air controllers. The engine was the same as for the other -8s.

QF-9J

Equipped with the latest radio control equipment, which converted them into high performance drones, with the capability of making high speed turns.

XF10F-1 Jaguar

As the F9F Cougar and Panther were coming to the end of their illustrious careers, another member of the "cat" family was about to make its appearance, albeit for only a short time. The XF10F-1, or Jaguar, as it was called, was the first variable swept-wing aircraft to be built with production and operational service in mind. It was not the first variable swept-wing aircraft to be built, that distinction fell to the Messerschmitt P-1101 in 1944, which had ground-adjustable variable wings, whereas the first American model, the Bell X-5, a derivative of the Me P-1101, had in-flight adjustable wings.

As fighters went, the XF10F-1 was not a small aircraft. The elongated, barrel-shaped fuselage with its high placed, knife-edged variable swept wing attached looked rather ungainly. The original design of the F10F-1 did not have variable swept wings, but had variable incidence wings, the idea being to reduce the angle of attack of the fuselage for landing visibility with a fixed swept wing. The design went through many changes, including both variable incidence and variable sweep. The mechanics of the design became too complicated, so Gordon Israel, the designer, concentrated on variable sweep.

The 'unswept' wing angle of 13½ degrees was selected for take-offs, landings and low-speed flight. The 'swept' position, selected by the pilot in flight, was an angle of 42½ degrees, and was used for high-speed flight only. The sweep was actuated by a large hydraulic cylinder, situated on the centreline between the wings. This drove the wing pivot forward, pulling the two wings into the fuselage. The external stores racks were fitted on swivelling pylons that kept the racks centralized.

The flaps were to cause a minor problem, because once the wings were 'swept' the inboard ends of the flaps were slotted into the fuselage, rendering them useless. A series of sixteen (eight each side) perforated, paddle-type spoilers, which extended through slats in the wings, provided lateral control.

These spoilers were operated from the control column in the cockpit by means of a mechanical linkage that moved them out of their slots, both above and below the wing, whilst the flaps were up. When the flaps were down, lateral control was provided by small ailerons on the wingtips, but the spoilers could also be extended symmetrically to serve as speed brakes.

The horizontal tail design was unique in appearance and was an attempt by Grumman to achieve an aerodynamically-boosted tail surface. All the pilot really controlled was the forward canard, but the faster the aircraft went, the more power the forward canard had over the slab tail behind it. The fin surfaces were mounted on a streamlined boom, which was hinged to the top of the vertical stabiliser and statically balanced. The double-delta, canard-type, horizontal, high 'T'-tail was controlled via the tab of the servo-plane, this, in turn, deflected the stabilizers when the flaps were lowered, changing the aircraft's trim. In fact the pilot was only directly connected to the springtab, everything else worked from that. The rudder remained under conventional control.

The double-delta tail's main disadvantage was poor control and response from the aircraft at speeds below 110 knots, although when it was flown at Mach .98 in dive tests it handled well. With the wings in the upswept configuration the

Above: The XF10F-1 being readied for ground tests whilst at Bethpage. A good view of the double-delta, canard-type, horizontal, high T-tail.

107

Although, on the face of it, the aircraft was not successful, this belies the enormous contribution it made to future generations of aircraft, in terms of evidence concerning the lateral-directional characteristics of variable-geometric aircraft, the aerodynamic problems of variable-sweep winged aircraft, and the ineffectiveness of manual control systems above Mach One.

The Jaguar was powered by the Westinghouse J40-WE-8 axial-flow engine, which produced 11,600 pounds of thrust with afterburner. The afterburner had not yet been fully developed however, so the engine was able to produce only 6,800 pounds of thrust, which prevented the XF10F-1 from attaining the projected maximum speed of 722 miles per hour. In March 1953, the engine was rejected by the Navy and its development terminated. This provided a good excuse to terminate the XF10F-1 project and the two aircraft, still painted in their all-over dark glossy sea-blue with the leaping Jaguar painted on each side of the fuselage — one only ninety per cent complete — were handed over to the Navy. One was used to test a new crash barrier, whilst the other was used to test the effects of gunfire on a jet-powered aircraft.

The J40 engine, incidentally, was the same as that used to power the McDonnell XF3H-1 and the Douglas XF4D-1. The XF3H was able to convert to the Allison J71 engine (with many subsequent engine problems) and the XF4D-1 converted to the Pratt and Whitney J57, a highly successful engine. The aircraft itself had a very short life, mainly because of aerodynamic trim problems.

The XF10F about to touch down at Edwards Air Force Base after trials.

The designer of the XF10F-1, Gordon Israel, was one of Grumman's most successful designers. Before World War II he had designed the very distinctive stubby racer, the GB Sportster; then, during the war and after, the F7F, F8F, F9F and F10F. He left Grumman shortly after the Navy axed the XF10F-1 project and joined the Lear Corporation, designing the Learstar jet.

XF10F Jaguar Technical details

Type	Single-seat fighter, carrier- or land-based.
Engine	Westinghouse J40-WE-8 producing 6,800 pounds of thrust.
Dimensions	Wing span (unswept) 50 ft. 7 in.
	Wing span (swept) 36 ft. 8 in.
	Wing area 450 sq. ft.
Weight	28,133 lb. max., 20,426 lb. min.
Performance	Max. speed 722 miles per hour envisage but never attained, rate of climb 10,600 ft. per min., range, 1,159 miles, service ceiling 45,800 ft.
Armament	Four 20 mm cannon in the nose and two 2,000 lb. bombs.

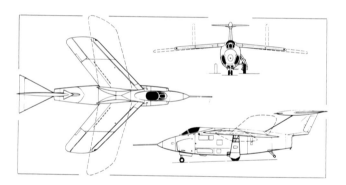

S-2 Tracker, TF-1 Trader and WF-2 Tracer

In 1952, the US Navy decided that it needed a replacement for both the 'hunter' and 'killer' versions of the AF-2 Guardian. The Guardians had given valuable service to the Navy in their anti-submarine role, but although extremely successful, there was a need for a more efficient, all-purpose aircraft. Grumman had anticipated this need and had produced a design for a twin-engined aircraft, equipped with electronic search equipment and a weapons store capable of destroying any submarine or surface vessel. However, at the time when the Navy invited proposals for an anti-submarine aircraft, Grumman were extremely busy, producing the F9F and really did not need the extra business. Approximately twenty-two proposals were submitted from a range of companies, including Lockheed, Curtiss and Douglas. The Grumman package was not very elaborate, nor was it a high-pressure sales pitch, but, much to their surprise, Grumman were awarded the contract.

The design was to become the basis for more than 1,200 air-frames and five different models; the S2F-1 Tracker was one of the most successful aircraft built by Grumman. Over 755 were built, and it was sold to a number of countries, including Brazil (thirteen), Italy (thirty), Japan (sixty) and the Nether-lands (twenty-six). De Havilland of Canada built 100 S2F-1s, designated CS2F-1s, for the Royal Canadian Navy, under licence from Grumman.

The first of the aircraft, designated XS2F-1, was flown on December 1952, with test pilots Fred Rowley and Norm Coutant at the controls. There were only two experimental XS2F-1s; one was delivered to the Navy on 3 July 1953 for evaluation, and the other remained at Grumman for test

purposes. A production order for the S2F-1, or S-2A as the US Navy designated it, was awarded even before the 'X' models had flown for the first time. The production lines got under way with the first delivery to the Navy being made on 19 October 1953. The aircraft was powered by two Wright R-1820-82 engines, which drove two Hamilton-Standard, three-bladed propellers. It carried a crew of four: pilot, co-pilot and two electronic surveillance operators. A retractable radome, the APS-33, was situated on the underside of the fuselage, aft of the trailing edge of the wing, and a MAD (Magnetic Airborne Detection) boom, that could be extended, was located at the rear underside of the fuselage, just under the rudder. Once a snorkel or periscope had been detected by the search radar, there was little chance of the submarine escaping from the Tracker.

The S2F-1 was capable of scouting an area of several thousand square miles on a single flight, and if the search extended into the night, then a 70 million candlepower searchlight, mounted in the leading edge of the starboard wing, aided identification of surfaced vessels. Once the general position of a submarine had been determined, sonobuoys were dropped to pinpoint the position exactly. Thirty-two of the three-foot long expendable detection devices were carried in special launchers, housed in the engine nacelles and they were dropped in predetermined patterns, usually three to a group. The sonobuoys picked up underwater noises and transmitted them back to receivers in the Tracker, which in turn plotted the position and course of the target.

Above: Preparing for the test flight of the XS2F-1.

111

Above: A TF-1Q with MAD (Magnetic Airborne Detection) boom extended.

Left: A TF-1Q, one of the four TF-1s converted into ECM (Electronic Counter Measure).

A TF-1Q on ground engine tests at Calverton. Note the USAF Albatross on the far right of the picture.

The MAD boom was then extended and the target pinpointed; once identified, any one of the complement of weapons carried — homing torpedoes, depth bombs, and five-inch rockets — could be used to destroy it. A number of S2F-1s (S-2As) were later modified with updated electronic equipment and redesignated S2F-1S (S-2B).

In 1955, a variant of the S2F-1, the TF-1 (C-1A), or Trader, made its appearance. Designed as a personnel and cargo

A TF-1 Trader at Calverton prior to a test flight.

transporter, it was essentially a modified S2F-1 Tracker. The more obvious changes were a larger and deeper fuselage; the removal of the retractable radome; the addition of a wide cargo door; and the fairing over the nacelles that held the sonobuoys. In place of the sonobuoys, two life rafts were installed, which could be released from inside or outside the aircraft. Internally, the electronic equipment was removed and replaced by nine aft-facing seats. The seats could be removed and stored against the walls of the fuselage, allowing for quick conversion to a cargo-carrying aircraft. It could also be reconfigured to take three litters and three medical staff. The aircraft was in fact the first purpose-built COD (carrier on-board delivery) aircraft and had additional roles as a carrier-familiarization trainer, a carrier-qualification trainer, and a multi-engine trainer. Its all-weather capability made it one of the most versatile aircraft in the fleet and during its acceptance trials it averaged less than three maintenance man-hours per flight-hour for over 300 hours of operation.

Like the S2F-1, the Trader was of conventional all-metal, semi-monocoque construction. As with all carrier-borne aircraft, space is of primary concern and the TF-1 (C-1) Trader was no exception. The main problem was the wings, and this was overcome by using a 300 psi hydraulic system which folded the wings over the top of the fuselage. Because of the exposed conditions on the decks of carriers, the TF-1's wing-folding mechanism was designed to fold or spread fully in less than 42 seconds in a 45-knot wind blowing from any direction. Take-offs were made by using the steam or hydraulic catapults, although, because of the high perform-ance engines, the TF-1 was able to make free deck take-offs fully loaded from *Essex* class carriers with only a two-knot wind over the deck.

113

F11F Tiger

Initially the F11F-1 was known as the F9F-9, but this was a gimmick to get money for the new aircraft under an existing contract, an administrative manoeuvre to expedite the research and development money flow. The Tiger had no similarity to the Panther/Cougar at all, especially in the area of performance.

The prototype F11F-1 had an area-ruled fuselage, which was unique in its shape because of its resemblance to the Coca Cola bottle, or, as it was variously described, Marilyn Monroe, or 'Wasp Waist'. The area-rule concept was a way of reducing the sharp drag rise which occurs at transonic speeds. It was developed by the National Advisory Committee for Aeronautics (NACA, which later became NASA) at their facility at Moffett Field, and by Grumman.

The F11F-1 and the Convair F102A were the first aircraft to be built using this concept. The design of the Tiger was simplicity itself: the wings, which were 31 ft. 8 in. in span and swept back to an angle of 35 degrees, were machined from single sheets of aluminium, top and bottom. They were also 'wet', as was the vertical tail fin: the wings, tail fin and engine intake duct walls had cavities which served as additional fuel tanks, in an attempt to meet the range and cycle time required. But even with these ingenious additions, it was a short-cycle time aircraft. The wings also had manually operated, folding wing tips that required virtually no main-tenance, compared with the hydraulically-controlled folding wings of the Cougar and Panther. The main landing gear was fuselage-mounted, as were the engine intakes.

The Tiger was powered by a Wright J65-W-18 turbo-jet with afterburners, although the first F11F-1 did not have the afterburner fitted. The engine, in fact, was a British Sapphire built by the Curtiss-Wright Corporation under licence from Armstrong Siddely Motors. It had a thrust rating of some 7,800 pounds and a maximum speed of 850 miles per hour at sea level.

The first flight took place on 30 July 1954, and four months later the first production model was delivered to the Navy for trials. A total of 199 Tiger F11F-1s were built for the Navy, and of these, numbers 44 and 45 were converted to F11F-1Fs, or Super Tigers, as they were known. The first forty-two aircraft were built with short noses, and the remaining 151 with long ones. The long nose improved the fuselage finesse ratio, to help cut down drag. Wing fillets were also added at the fuselage joint to cut down the approach speed for carrier requirements. At one time a suggestion was put forward to instal radar in the long-nosed F11F-1F, but this never materialized.

Amongst the trials carried out by the Navy with the F11F-1, was a 20 mm cannon-firing demonstration off Long Island, New York. The pilot, Tom Attridge, fired his cannon whilst in a shallow dive at 13,000 ft., then increased his dive angle and speed and caught up with the practice rounds that he had fired twelve seconds earlier. At 7,000 ft. the engine suddenly flamed out. After putting out a Mayday call, Attridge set the F11F-1 in a glide back to the field at Peconic, Long Island, but did not quite make it . He carried out a wheels-up landing in a patch of scrubland just south of the airfield, shearing off the wings in the process, but a fire broke out in the aft of the fuselage. In addition to his personal problems, which were a broken shin and several fractured vertebrae, the 20 mm cannon started firing. Fortunately, Grumman had recently

Above: The F11F-1 about to take off from Calverton on one of its numerous test flights.

118

Two YF11F-1s from the Naval Air Test Center (NATC) being hoisted aboard the USS Saratoga *for carrier trials.*

purchased a Sikorsky helicopter and within minutes it was hovering over the crash site. Fifteen minutes later Tom Attridge was in hospital being treated for his injuries.

The cause of the crash was determined as being the fault of defective ammunition which had tumbled in the air, consequently slowing down, one round striking the wind-shield and shattering it, one striking the nose, and another lodging in the engine, causing the flame-out.

The first F11F-1 was delivered to the Navy in February 1957 for operational evaluation. The FIP (Fleet Introduction

Preparing the F11F-1 for a catapult launch off the USS Intrepid.

The F11F-1 about to launch from the USS Saratoga.

The Ag-Cat 1 on an initial test flight.

interchangeable and relatively inexpensive to replace. In the event of a pilot damaging one of the four wing sections, the pilot just replaced that section, and a flap would become an aileron, or an aileron a flap.

Visibility was enhanced by sloping the nose, and because the pilot would have very little time during flight operations to check his instruments, the airspeed indicator and tachometer were placed almost in line with the pilot's vision. This

Hank Kurt, a Grumman test pilot, on a demonstration test flight.

made it unnecessary for the pilot to look down into his cockpit during low-level passes.

The price decided on was $12,995 without the engine and propeller, and $13,995 if the engine had to be supplied. Although this was a high price at the time, it was feasible. Initially, no windshield was fitted, as the crop duster pilots said they did not want one; it would get covered in dust and dirt, and they preferred a pair of goggles which they could quickly wipe clean.

When the time for the first flight came, Joe asked Roy Grumman if they could invite their wives to the ceremony. This was a most unusual request, but Joe Lippert explained that as all the men involved in building the aircraft had given a large amount of free overtime to the project, they thought it would be a nice gesture to their wives, so that they could see what their husbands had been getting up to on those late evenings. Roy Grumman agreed, so on the evening of the flight, all the wives were present to see 'the other woman' in their husbands' lives.

Considering that the aircraft literally flew 'off the drawing board' its first flight was extremely successful, and one month later the second of the experimental Ag-Cats took to the air. The team wanted to take the aircraft down to Texas so that they could demonstrate it to the crop dusters, but Roy Grumman said that he would rather invite some of them to Bethpage to fly it. Three pilots were invited, one from Texas, another from New York State and the other from Washington State. All three pilots were delighted with the handling qualities of the aircraft and its tremendous turning capability. The latter was most important, because stalling in the turn would cause the aircraft to go into a spin or invert and at low altitude that invariably would be fatal. This turned out to be a great selling point; the aircraft was much safer than anyone had anticipated. One of the most important safety features

Production model Ag-Cats awaiting delivery.

built into the aircraft was the design of the cockpit, which was built to withstand a 40 g impact. Before Grumman entered the business of building agricultural aircraft, one out of every ten crop duster pilots would have a serious crash each year; it was to be nine years before the first serious crash in an Ag-Cat.

In the summer of 1958, the Grumman team took the two aircraft on a fact-finding trip down the East Coast. Over 150 pilots flew the aircraft during the trip. They would fly one of the Ag-Cats, first without a load, and then with a full load. All through the tour they received favourable reports from the pilots who flew it.

Whilst down in Texas, Joe Lippert acquired his pilot's licence, and on the day he received it, he flew the Ag-Cat: one of the rare occasions when a designer actually flew his own creation!

Of all the problems that the Ag-Cat had, which incidentally were very few, the one that caused the most concern was the spray patterns that the aircraft put out. The ideal spray was one that gave a paint brush effect down the field and it took a major design alteration to achieve this.

On their return to Bethpage, Joe Lippert and his team heard that the Grumman board had decided that they could not build the Ag-Cat at the Bethpage plant. Originally Roy Grumman had felt that production of the Ag-Cat would keep people busy if sales of military aircraft were slow, but the plant was already in full production with several military aircraft. It was decided to sub-contract the whole project to the Schweizer Aircraft Company of Elmira, New York, whose existing main production line consisted of light aircraft and gliders.

The first Schweizer-built Ag-Cat appeared in 1959 and was identical to the one built by Grumman. The open cockpit remained until 1962, when a large number of pilots decided that they wanted some protection against the increasing use of highly toxic pesticides.

The first production Ag-Cat was sold to one of the crop duster pilots who flew the original experimental model. The only updates initially made to the aircraft were the engines. With the aircraft being asked to carry heavier loads, engines with increased horsepower were requested, so that, at one point, the aircraft had a range of five different engines: the Continental 220, the Gulf Coast 240, or the Jacobs 245, 275 or

125

300. Because of the long engine mount originally installed, all the engines could be accommodated without too much trouble. In the early 1960s, one Californian owner put a 450 hp Pratt and Whitney engine into the aircraft, again mainly because of the increased loads that were being flown. Grumman and Schweizer realized the significance of this, and created the Super Ag-Cat with the Pratt and Whitney 450 hp engine. A second improvement some months later increased the wing span by four feet.

America, at this time, was getting heavily involved in Vietnam and a suggestion was made to militarize the Super Ag-Cat. The idea was to ship the aircraft to the South Vietnamese, under the guise of an agricultural crop-dusting aircraft; on arrival it could be converted to a military aircraft. There were a number of ways that the Ag-Cat could be utilized. Light machine guns could be strapped on the wings; it could be used as a field ambulance with pods strapped to the wings; and small bombs could even be dropped from it. One military duty would have suited the Ag-Cat perfectly, and that was as an observation aircraft. Because of the low-flying capabilities of the Ag-Cat, the aircraft could penetrate areas virtually unseen, and turn in areas only 200 feet in diameter. One Ag-Cat was sent to the Army and placed at their disposal for evaluation. The Army pilots thought the Ag-Cat was a tremendous aircraft and quite capable of doing everything that was asked of it, but they could not recommend the purchase of an old-fashioned looking biplane to the Pentagon, when they were in a jet-orientated world.

At the end of the 1970s, Schweizer purchased the full rights to the aircraft from Grumman and with it a rather special provision from the FAA, known as 'Part 8'. Operators of Ag-planes have a rather unusual arrangement with the FAA, inasmuch as they are given permission to fly any load configuration that they can get off the ground, fly around a field to their own satisfaction and that of the FAA inspector, and land safely. This means that they can basically certificate themselves, although there are certain restrictions. They are restricted from flying over populated areas, or any place that anyone on the ground could get hurt. Today, sales in America have dwindled dramatically, (though the sales of the Cat are nearing 3,000), mainly because the country is at saturation point, brought about by the aircraft's incredible reliability. Sales teams are having to go abroad to sell the Ag-Cat: even Ethiopia, with its agricultural problems, has sent a team of engineers over to the United States so that they can learn to build the Ag-Cat. The intention is to let the Ethiopians build the aircraft under licence. Schweizer will initially supply all the parts.

Thirty years on, the Ag-Cat still remains an undisputed champion of crop-dusting. In thirty years time it probably still will be.

Technical details G-164 Ag-Cat

Type	Aerial agricultural applicator.	*Performance*	Max. speed 131 mph, cruising speed 75 mph, stall speed 62 mph, climb rate 1,400 ft./min. Abrupt manoeuvre speed 103 mph.
Engine	220 hp Continental W-670-6A 240 hp Continental W-670-240 245 hp Jacobs L-4M 275 hp Jacobs R-755-B2M 300 hp Jacobs R-755-A2M		
		Fuel capacity	32.7 gallons. Fuel consumption 12 gallons p.h.
Crew	One pilot.	*Oil capacity*	5 gallons.
Dimensions	Wing span 35 ft. 8 in., wing area 326 sq. ft., length 24 ft. 4 in., weight 10 ft. 9 in.	*Hopper capacity*	217 gallons.
		Hopper load restriction	1,200 lb.

G-164A Super Ag-Cat technical details

Type	Aerial Agricultural applicator.	*Performance*	Max. speed 131 mph with Jacobs engine, 147 mph with Pratt and Whitney. Stall speed 67 mph, climb rate 1,600 ft./min. Abrupt manoeuvre speed 117 mph.
Engine	275 hp Jacobs R-755-B2M 300 hp Jacobs R-755-A2M 400 hp Pratt and Whitney R985. 600 hp Pratt and Whitney R1340.		
		Fuel capacity	46.3 gallons. Fuel consumption 20 gallons p.h.
Crew	One pilot.	*Oil capacity*	5 gallons Jacobs engine, 7 gallons P&W.
Dimensions	Wing span 35 ft. 8 in., wing area 326 sq. ft., length 24 ft. 4 in., height 10 ft. 9 in.	*Hopper capacity*	2,000 lb. or 247 gallons.
		Hopper load restriction	2,000 lb.

Gulfstream

The Gulfstream was the first commercial, land-based aircraft that Grumman ever built, and epitomized the way the Grumman management operated — with instinct, born of experience and judgement. On the face of it, the prospects for a twin-engined, executive aircraft seemed quite remote in the aftermath of the Second World War. This was because aircraft like the Douglas DC-3, the Convair and the Lockheed Lodestar, were no longer required by the military and were easily convertible into executive-type aircraft. Grumman themselves had a couple of DC-3s, four Geese and a Mallard operating as executive transport, but they experienced a need for a specifically-designed, executive aircraft to replace all these conversions.

Initially, a design was considered for a three-engined, medium-range jet, but this was dismissed in favour of the prop-jet or turbo-prop, because it was thought that small jet engines had not been around long enough to prove their reliability. It was also decided that executive clientele would favour the more reliable turbo-prop, which would give the aircraft a greater range, an improved economy and make it more adaptable to flight planning and fuel reserves.

One of the main problems that faced Grumman was that of convincing the commercial market that they were ready to pay £845,000, for an executive aircraft, excluding interior furnishings and avionics, or $1,000,000 for a variant carrying long-range fuel tanks. The price tag was especially pertinent, as it was possible at the time to pick up a DC-3 for only $200,000.

One of the central figures in the Grumman sales team was a former production test pilot and pilot-salesman, Henry Schiebel. Although not an engineer, he knew every aspect of commercial aviation and, what was more important, he knew the right people to talk to. A private survey carried out by Grumman revealed that there were around five hundred companies financially capable of purchasing the Gulfstream, and with a break-even point of around thirty aircraft, the possibilities were there.

Design commenced and the fuselage was the first section on the drawing boards. All the designers agreed that the DC-3 had one of the best all-round configurations fuselage, in the commercial aviation world incorporating safety, comfort and room, so it was used as a yardstick for the Gulfstream. There were two schools of thought regarding the positioning of the wings. One favoured a high wing, but this was poor on crashworthiness and it was hard to see the wingtips when ramp manoeuvring; the other favoured a low wing, which had good visibility, with the additional advantage of being aesthetically pleasing, although neither would have made any significant difference to the aerodynamic performance of the aircraft. A decision was made in a most unusual way: two

Above: Engine tests on the Gulfstream I in painted livery.

127

G-159 Gulfstream technical details

Type	Commercial transport.
Engine	Two Rolls-Royce Dart R. DA 7/2s.
Dimensions	Wing span 78 ft. 4 in., wing area 610.3 sq. ft., length 63 ft 9 in., height 23 ft. 4 in.
Performance	Max. speed 350 mph, cruising speed 305 mph, ceiling 30,400 ft., range 2,621 miles.
Weights	Empty 18,723 lb., loaded 36,000 lb.

Gulfstream IIB technical details

Type	Commercial transport.
Engine	Two Rolls-Royce Spey Mk 511-8X turboprops.
Dimensions	Wing span 77 ft. 10 in., wing area 934.6 sq. ft., length 79 ft. 11 in., height 24 ft. 6 in.
Performance	Max. speed Mach 0.85, cruising speed Mach 0.77, ceiling 45,000 ft., range 4,088 miles.
Weights	Empty 39,100 lb., loaded 66,200 lb.

Gulfstream model variations

G-159 (G-1)
Was going to be originally a version of the TF-1 Trader, making it a high-winged aircraft, but a low-wing design was chosen. Powered by two Rolls-Royce Dart engines. Designed primarily as a commercial transport.

TC-4C
Bombardier/navigator trainer for the A-6 Intruder, purchased by the US Navy. This was a standard Gulfstream with an extended nose to house the radar equipment.

VC-4A
Designation given to the Coast Guard version. Used primarily as a VIP transport.

G-II
The first of the jet-powered Gulfstreams. It had a swept-back, low wing, a 'T'-shaped tail, and was powered by Rolls-Royce Spey Mk 511-8 turbofan engines. It was selected by NASA as the crew training aircraft for Space Shuttle Orbiter astronauts.

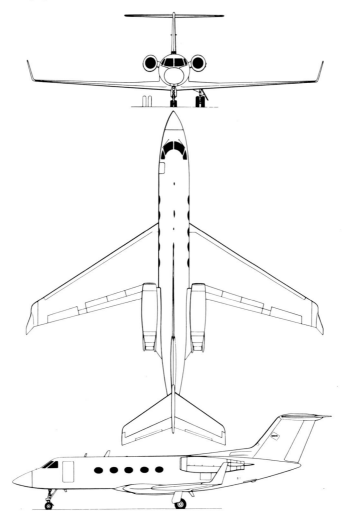

OV-1 Mohawk

The only time that Grumman ever departed from making aircraft for the US Navy was when the US Army invited tenders for a small, two-seat, twin-engined, surveillance aircraft. They wanted an aircraft that would carry the latest avionics and a variety of weaponry capable of attacking ground positions. It was to have STOL (short take-off and landing) capabilities and be able to operate from the roughest terrain or from the smoothest of runways. What they got was the AO-1 Mohawk, a complete battlefield surveillance aircraft that would supply virtually anything in the way of information that any battlefield commander would want; and if necessary destroy it.

The Mohawk was, in fact, a joint production for both the Army and the US Marine Corps, and, although the basic design of the aircraft was the same for both, it met a number of different requirements. The Marine Corps made an unusual proposal that water skis be fitted as an optional extra, thus enabling the OF-1, as they designated it, to land on water and taxi on to the shore at speeds of up to 20 knots. The different requirements of both services caused the Mohawk project to become expensive, $22 million for nine prototypes: so expensive, in fact, that when the mock-up was displayed, the Marines withdrew from the project.

The Army, however, ordered the nine prototypes to be completed. The mock-up had a distinctive 'T'-shaped tail, but Grumman engineers discovered that, in the event of one of the two engines failing, the tail would require a hydraulically-boosted rudder. The aircraft was complicated enough as it was, so by experimenting with different tail designs, engineers came up with a distinctive triple tail. There was an unexpected bonus with the triple tail, it gave a smaller reflection on radar than the larger 'T'-tail.

The first of the nine prototypes made its maiden flight on 14 April 1959 and by the end of the year the last was flying. The short, broad-chord wing and hydraulically-operated leading edge slats, big fuselage, speed brakes and flaps gave the Mohawk its STOL capability, enabling the aircraft to land within 300 feet. Even when carrying more than the recommended weight of 17,976 lb., the Mohawk was able to take off within 900 feet and still clear an obstacle some 50 feet high.

Powered by two Lycoming turboprop engines, with three-bladed, Hamilton-Standard, full-feathering, constant speed, reversing propellers, the Mohawk had a maximum speed of 330 mph, a cruising speed of 280 mph and a service ceiling of 25,000 feet. With drop tanks, it had a range of 878 nautical miles. A sturdy aircraft, the Mohawk was rated at −5g and ×1½g, but could actually pull −7g in an emergency without causing structural damage. During flight testing, very few problems were encountered. The major one was some slight

Above: The fifth YAO-1 prototype.

133

shuddering during flight, but this was cured by smoothing the skin on the vertical tail and adding a counter-balance weight to the centre vertical rudder. The undercarriage was extremely strong and was stressed to absorb a sink rate of 17 feet per minute. The soft, low-pressure tyres were ideal for the unprepared terrain the Mohawk was expected to operate from.

So successful was the test programme that the Army ordered a further 35 production models under a $22 million contract. The first of these was delivered to the US Army Aviation School at Fort Rucker, Alabama, in 1960. There were a number of problems at first, not with the aircraft, but experienced by the pilots. Because the Army, up to this point in time, had only been flying slow piston-engined aircraft, the arrival of the Mohawks was like going from a sedate family car to a hotted-up sports model. The end result was that there were a few fatal crashes, due mainly to inexperienced pilots showing off the aircraft's power and sensitive control response. The Army overcame the acute shortage of experienced pilots by recruiting a number of ex-Marine Corps pilots who were in the reserves, thereby gaining a tremendous amount of experience and talent at minimum cost.

Because the propellers were so close to the cockpit, conventional bail-out procedures were out of the question, so Grumman had Martin Baker ejection seats installed. The crew had the choice of ejecting through the canopy or ejecting, after the canopy had been released; it appears that the former method was the most widely chosen, proving to be a lifesaver on a number of occasions.

The Mohawk was capable of monitoring enemy positions in daylight, darkness or inclement weather, using electronic and photographic sensors. It could operate from the most rugged of airfields in forward battle areas, and was at its best when used in guerrilla-type operations. As the guerilla uses darkness as his cover, so did the Mohawk, the difference being that the surveillance equipment carried by the Mohawk denied the guerrilla the protection of darkness. After some exhaustive evaluation tests in the Arctic, it was decided to test the aircraft under battle conditions. In July 1962, the 23rd Special Warfare Aviation Detachment (Surveillance) was formed and sent to Vietnam, together with six OV-1As. Their job was to provide reconnaissance information for the South Vietnamese Army: the pilots were Amercian but the observers were South Vietnamese. As armed surveillance aircraft, their

armament consisted of .50 calibre gunpods and 2.75 rocket pods, and pilots were instructed not to fire unless fired upon. As American involvement in Southeast Asia increased, the Mohawk's presence became invaluable to both the South Vietnamese and the Americans. Shortly after the OV-1's introduction, the 'defensive fire only' restriction was rescinded, and it operated in a close air-support role on both day and night missions. One OV-1 would be equipped with parachute flares to light the attack zone, to be followed by Mohawks delivering 2.75 rockets and .50 calibre machine gun fire.

It was realized that the Mohawk could play a far greater role against Vietcong jungle forces, and could give much-needed support to troop-carrying helicopters. In 1963, twenty-four specially-equipped JOV-1Cs of the 11th Air Assault Division were used as escort gunships for the helicopters, but they were later removed when the 11th AAD was converted to the 1st Cavalry Division (Airmobile), late in 1965. This action was part of an Army/Air Force agreement that turned over all fixed-wing, armed aircraft to the control of the Air Force; in return, the Army was permitted to arm its helicopters as, necessary. The Vietcong grew to hate the Mohawk, calling it the 'Whispering Death', and even offered a $1,000 reward to any of their soldiers who shot one down.

As with all Grumman-built aircraft, ruggedness was of primary importance. Because of its relatively slow speed and low-flying capabilities, the Mohawk was more vulnerable than most other aircraft, excepting helicopters. There were many instances of Mohawks coming back to base badly shot up, but still flying. One such aircraft returned with over ninety holes in one wing and numerous others in the fuselage, a veritable sieve! Another, nicknamed 'Old Yeller' because of the zinchromate painted over its battle scars, finally gave up the ghost after flying nearly 1,000 hours of combat. The crew members ejected over a field after pointing the aircraft out to sea. However, the aircraft turned round and actually crashed in an area designated for scrap.

Throughout the Vietnam conflict, the Mohawk provided continuous intelligence information. It was so useful for counter-insurgency that, in 1974, two were loaned, under great secrecy, to the Israelis for surveillance operations. They were returned to the United States in 1980, after the Israelis had purchased 4 Grumman E-2Cs of their own.

There were four types of OV-1 Mohawk, the OV-1A (visual and photographic system), the OV-1B (visual, photographic system and SLAR (sideways-looking airborne radar)), the OV-1C (visual, two photographic systems and an infra-red system) and the OV-1D (visual, three photographic stystems, SLAR or IT and a radiac meter).

The OV-1A, the first of the Mohawks, carried one independent, vertical-looking, five-position frame, photographic system with automatic exposure control, which could be operated by either the pilot or the observer.

The OV-1B was the same as the -1A in appearance, except for an SLAR antenna pod, fitted under the fuselage, which enabled the Mohawk to sweep large land and coastal areas for moving targets any time of the day and even during inclement weather. Any fixed or moving objects on either side of the OV-1B's flight path were recorded on film and transmitted to the observer and also to a ground station, on a real-time display. An autopilot was also installed to help the pilot fly uniform radar-mapping patterns. The wings of the -1B had to be extended by six feet because of the additional weight and, in the early stages of production, the speed brakes were removed because the mission flight profiles did not require them. They were later reinstated and only a very few of the aircraft do not have them today.

The OV-1C was physically the same as the -1A and -1B, and had two photographic systems and one infra-red system.

An OV-1A shows its excellent handling characteristics at low level.

Above right: Loading a ·50 calibre machine gun pod on to the outboard wing pylon of a Mohawk.

Below right: A Mohawk fires its rockets over the Vietnamese jungle.

Looking down at an OV-1C flying over the US Army's test range at Fort Benning, Georgia. The SLAR antenna can be seen projecting out in front of the nose of the aircraft.

The photographic system consisted of two KA-60C, 180-degree, panoramic cameras, for use at altitudes below 5,000 feet. One was mounted in the nose, as on the -1B, and aimed at an angle of 20 degrees below the horizon. The other was mounted in the aft of the fuselage and was rotated laterally to any of five positions (15 and 30 degrees below the horizon, left, right and vertical). Operating at a height of 2,000 feet, the cameras were capable of photographing flight lines of 120 miles and 220 miles in length respectively (nose and aft cameras), with a 60 per cent overlap. The AN/AAS-14, or infra-red surveillance system, recorded a continuous real-time image of the terrain beneath the aircraft, electronically detecting and reproducing the thermal differences in terrestrial objects. The signals received were converted on to video and transmitted simultaneously to the console in the cockpit and to a film recorder. A continuous pictorial image was imprinted on a five-image freeze mode, enabling the moving scene to be stopped for close inspection. It also had a built-in test feature, which enabled faulty assemblies to be replaced quickly.

To look at, the OV-1D, is deceptively similar to the -1A, -1B and -1C versions; not only can the OV-1D perform the same functions, but it has additional features incorporated into it. It has a third independent photographic system, with automatic exposure control, mounted in a fuselage blister, just aft of the KA-76 camera system, and this has an optic axis 90 degrees below the horizontal. The AN/AAS-14 infra-red surveillance system was updated to the AN/AAS-24, giving improved resolution, a larger monitor display image freeze mode to stop the moving scene for detailed examination; automatic marking of hot targets on film and an in-flight selection of video transfer functions and filters. It is built and installed in modules, which enables the system to be changed quickly, as with the other SLAR equipment. The SLAR AN/APS-94D, was an improved version of the one used in the OV-1B. Although it carried out the same functions as its predecessor, it had an increased range and superior target-detection capability; a reduced susceptibility to jamming; a display that moved toward the observer, simulating actual flight; a reduced processing time; and a yaw-stabilizing antenna.

In short, the Mohawk provided aerial surveillance once the battle lines had been defined, enabling the aircraft to monitor enemy aircraft well inside the enemy's own territory, without violating any other country's air space. It was the original 'spy in the sky' and not the aircraft the enemy would like to have around if subversive activities.

Although it was intended primarily for military use, in 1971 one OV-1B was loaned to the US Geological Survey Department to enable them to carry out geological and hydrological studies. The OV-1B was chosen because of its longer wing, which apparently gave the aircraft more stability. The first survey mission was flown over the jungles of Panama in search of surface water. In 1974, the OV-1B surveyed the Alaskan Oil pipeline and the pack ice in the Beaufort Sea. Because of the hostile weather environment, special emergency equipment had to be carried, and this, coupled with the maintenance problems, made the project a potential nightmare. Fortunately, all went reasonably well and the survey was completed without any serious problems.

A modern OV-1D demonstrates its versatility.

In 1975, the Geological Survey Department returned the Mohawk to the Army, who immediately handed it over to the Naval Air Test Centre at Patuxent River, Maryland.

Among other non-military users of the Mohawk are the US Custom Service, in their never-ending hunt for drug smugglers. The four OV-1Cs that are used carry a non-standard, nose-mounted, infra-red system to assist them in their search. After more than nine years, and countless hours in the air, the aircraft are still flying as well and making a considerable impact on the number of arrests and convictions of drug smugglers.

The Mohawk has set its own share of flying records. In June 1966, Col. Edward Nielson, US Army, flew an OV-1A on a 100-kilometre closed circuit, at an average speed of 292 miles per hour, to set a new turboprop speed record. In the same year, Grumman test pilot Jim Peters broke the world's altitude record for a turboprop aircraft when he flew an OV-1 to a height of 32,000 feet sustained altitude. This record was broken five years later by Capt. Richard Steinbock and CW2 Thomas Yaha, who flew their unpressurized OV-1C to a peak altitude of 39,880 feet and a sustained altitude of 36,352 feet.

Interest in the Mohawk was not confined to the USA; both France and Germany expressed an interest in the aircraft. France even went as far as signing a licence production agreement with Grumman, in exchange for the American manufacturing rights of the Breguet Atlantic Maritime Patrol aircraft, though neither agreement came to fruition. Two OV-1Bs were sent to West Germany in 1963 for evaluation purposes, to be carried out by *Heersflieger*, the German Army Aviation Corps. After some 386 hours of flight demonstration, the German markings were removed and replaced by French roundels for further tests by the French, but no sales were forthcoming from either country.

The US Army plans to use the Mohawk well into the 1990s, and although satellites have replaced some of the Mohawk's tasks, it still remains a valuable asset, and with a planned improvement programme that includes a service life extension of from 7,000 hours to 12,000 hours, upgraded Lycoming T53-704 engines, and a new communciations/navigation system, it will remain so for a long time to come.

OV-1 Mohawk technical details

Model	Surveillance, but some used as strike aircraft.	*Dimensions*	Wing span 48 ft., wing area 360 sq. ft., length 43 ft. 11 in., height 12 ft. 8 in.
Crew	Two: pilot and observer.	*Weight*	11,607 lb. empty, 19,230 lb. loaded.
Engine	Two Lycoming T-53-L-15 for all versions except the AO-1D, which had the T-53-L-701.	*Performance*	Max. speed 250 knots, cruising speed 180 knots. Initial climb rate 2,800 ft. per min., range 1,450 miles, stalling speed 55 knots.
Propellers	Two Hamilton-Standard three-bladed, ten-feet diameter Hydromatics, with constant speed, full feathering, full reversing, and electronic synchronization.	*Armament*	None fixed, but capable of taking rockets, bombs and guns, mounted in pods under the wings.
		Ceiling	30,000 ft.

139

A-6 Intruder

Called, amongst other things, Double Ugly, Q-Bird, Queer Bird, the Gliding Electric Show, and Tadpole, the Grumman EA-6B is one of the most sophisticated aircraft ever built anywhere in the world.

One of a family of aircraft, the Prowler, like all other variants, is based on the basic A-6A Intruder airframe. Twenty-five years after the first A-6 flew, the A-6F and the EA-6B are probably the world's most advanced avionics-equipped aircraft.

During the Korean War, the US Navy and Marine Corps realized that there was a need for an all-weather, close air-support, long-range, night attack, fighter-bomber, that could serve both the Navy on long range interdiction missions and the Marines on close air support. The intention was to replace both the Douglas AD and the A-4 but, due to the lack of technology at the time, it was not until late 1957 that the US Navy invited proposals for such an aircraft. Out of the eight companies which submitted a total of twelve designs, Grumman put forward only one proposal. TS-149, as the proposal specification was called, required a small, two-seat aircraft, with a minimum top speed of 500 knots, a 300 nautical mile radius for close air-support, and a 1,000 nautical mile radius for long-range, interdiction missions. The Navy wanted the new aircraft to be able to fly long distances at a low altitude by night, find and attack moving or stationary targets, then return to either a carrier or land base, all

without the aid of navigational references.

On 30 December 1957, Grumman were told that they had been selected as prime contractor for the project, including the entire weapons system. It was the first time that the Navy had called for an integrated system, rather than an assemblage of off-the-shelf electronic components. Electronic warfare had its roots back in the dark days of World War II, when radar was introduced. Although its initial use was on ground stations, radar had been installed in aircraft towards the end of the war and was being used to tremendous effect. The use of radar against the enemy, consequently prompted the need to counteract enemy radar, thus ECM (electronic countermeasures) was devised.

The end of World War II did not halt the development of ECM, but the United States forces were unable to test it under battle conditions until the Korean War. Although, initially, the North Korean equipment initially was very primitive compared to that of the western world, the introduction of sophisticated Russian enemy fire-control radar and other types of radar caused the research and development of ECM aircraft in the United States to be speeded up considerably. By the end of the Korean conflict, some progress has been made, but it had involved modifying aircraft that had been designed for other purposes. The need

Above: An A-6E on a pre-delivery flight.

140

for a purpose-built ECM aircraft was now quite clear, but an ECM capability did not form part of the original A-6 requirement.

The winning Grumman design was the only one submitted which had both crewmen seated side-by-side. The two seats were slightly staggered, with the pilot higher and more forward than the bombardier/navigator so that the pilot could have adequate visibility.

Two Pratt and Whitney J52 jet engines were built into the fuselage, although one of the initial designs had them in engine nacelles on the wings. The length of Grumman's aircraft was constrained by the carrier's elevator. The rear fuselage was clean and slim, whilst the nose of the aircraft gave the appearance of being squat and fat and, when viewed from above, gave the aircraft the unmistakeable shape of a tadpole.

As well as being an all-weather, electronic systems aircraft, the A-6 was also a versatile weapons carrier. In five stores stations under the wings the A-6 could carry a variety of weapons, ranging from rockets to bombs. This caused problems for the designers, because they had to fit the five stores stations, two engines and the main landing gear, within the 25 ft. 4 in. width limit of the folding wings. The width limit was set to allow two aircraft to pass each other through the fire doors of the lower deck on smaller carriers. Solving this problem also required an ingenious landing-gear arrangement, which housed the wheels in the leading edge glove; this gave the aircraft a very wide stance for ground stability.

Because carrier landings require a relatively low approach speed, the wings need an efficient high-lift system. On the A-6 this consisted of leading edge slats, double-slotted flaps (these were later changed to single-slotted, modified Fowler flaps), and wing spoilers for lateral control. The tail surfaces consisted of power-operated, horizontal stabilizers, with a quarter-chord sweepback of thirty degrees, and standard fin/ rudder vertical stabilizers, with a quarter-chord sweepback of twenty eight degrees. This tail arrangment had been used with great success on the F11F Tiger. Five major sub-assemblies made up the wing, consisting of a centre section, and port and starboard inner and outer sections. The centre section was a continuous box beam that passed through the fuselage, to which the inner panels were joined. The inner and outer wing panels had machined skins and were of multi-beam construction, whilst the wing-folded joints used four steel hinges with hydraulically-operated locking pins.

The first twenty-five A-6As were equipped with air brakes on either side of the fuselage, but subsequent aircraft and their variants had wing-tip air brakes. A-6As continued to use the side brakes in conjunction with the wing-tip brakes until aircraft No. 300. After that, A-6As and Es had only wing-tip brakes, because they produced sufficient drag by themselves. These airbrakes, when activated, opened above and below the wing-tips to an angle of 120 degrees, and covered an area of twenty-four square feet.

The A-6A prototype (A2F-1) had jet exhaust pipes that could be hydraulically tilted through twenty-three degrees. By vectoring the tailpipes downwards, the take-off speed of an A-6 with a close air-support mission load was reduced from eighty-six to seventy-eight knots. To ensure that there was adequate low-speed pitch control when the pipes were in the down position, geared elevators, which came up as the leading edge of the stabilizers, were provided.

The Navy decided that the tilt pipes were only effective at light 'Marine Corps' mission weights in reducing take-off distance or approach speed; they were not of the slightest use for carrier operations, so it was decided to eliminate the feature. Consequently, the geared elevators were not required, and they were replaced by a simple, power-operated slab, tail stabilizer. This saved weight, complexity and cost, and increased reliability and availability.

Fitting a catapult tow-link to the nosewheel strut added some weight to the conventional tricycle undercarriage, but revolutionized catapult operations. Previously, wire strops had been used, which were attached to hooks beneath the fuselage. The anti-skid braking system and the large tyres helped to make the A-6 a stable landing platform.

The A-6A Intruder airframe was of conventional assembly. The fuselage was of mainly semi-monocoque construction, the lower half being a mixture of steel and titanium between the engines and the non-structural doors that enclosed the engine compartment. Aluminium, honeycomb panels covered the fuselage fuel-cells, and the tailplane was of a multi-beam construction with machined aluminium skins. All the trailing edges were of aluminium honeycomb construction.

The A-6 made its first appearance early in April 1960 at Bethpage, where it carried out taxying trials. It was later put on a truck and taken to the Grumman facility at Calverton, where it made its first flight on 19 April, with test pilot Bob Smyth at the controls. The only avionics in the first aircraft were essential communications and navigational ones, plus, of course, the usual flight-testing instrumentation package. The first aircraft went through its flight testing without incident, not so the second, whose first flight was very nearly its last! On the ferry flight between Bethpage and Calverton a fuel shut-off valve between the two main tanks in the fuselage, which had been added for flight test purposes to control the centre of gravity position, was inadvertently left in the closed position. Consequently, the rear of the two tanks, which was feeding the engines, ran dry, with the result that both engines flamed out, right at the moment when the aircraft entered the downward leg into Calverton. The pilot, Ernie von der Hayden, showed great skill by easing the aircraft down very carefully into a dead-stick landing. Not only did it give an impressive display of the pilot's capabilities, but it also showed what great flying qualities the A-6A had.

At the end of December 1960 the first A-6 to be fitted out with avionics was flown. The flight, to test the avionics, was not a great success — in fact it was disastrous. as the avionics, never really worked. The reason given was that the system had not been put together and integrated in the laboratory first, before being fitted in the aircraft. It took quite a few weeks of hard work before the system was ready to test again and this time it worked well. By the end of February 1961 the terrain clearance mode display was working, but the first NPE trials in November 1961 revealed some major deficiencies in the pilot's and bombardier/navigator's displays. The problems concerned the brightness and resolution of the displays and the reliability of the basic system. These problems were too important to be ignored, so the whole system had to be upgraded. The bombardier/navigator's display was changed from a five-inch TV monitor display to a seven-inch cathode-ray tube; and the pilot's horizontal display, from a five-inch tube, to a direct storage tube. This caused the NPE trials to be delayed for nearly a year, but the end result made the delay worthwhile. With the NPEs completed, the A-6A was taken aboard the aircraft carrier *USS Enterprise* for delivery and acceptance trials off the Virginia Capes. The trials were near perfect and the A-6A established itself as an ideal carrier aircraft. In fact, it was to carry out over 10,000 carrier landings before it was involved in a major accident.

Because of the problems the A-6A was experiencing with some of its avionics, further NPE trials were instigated before the aircraft could be accepted for Fleet use. At one point, Grumman had between eight and ten aircraft at Patuxent River, carrying out either service, avionics or weapons tests. Pressure was starting to build up on the test crews as they struggled to get the avionics systems right – they were still having problems with reliability. Finally, on 10 October 1963, the Navy accepted the aircraft and it was delivered to the fleet and assigned to VA-42.

With VA-42 well into their training programme, a second squadron, VA-75, was formed. VA-75 was the first A-6A squadron to be assigned to a carrier as part of Carrier Air

Wing CVW-7, aboard the *USS Independence*. It sailed to the Gulf of Tonkin, Vietnam, from where it attacked successfully the bridges at Bac Bang, 125 miles from Hanoi. On one night raid over Haiphong, the target was bombed so heavily and so accurately, that the North Vietnamese thought that they were being bombed by B-52 Stratofortresses.

The carrier assignment was being used as a 'shakedown' deployment for the aircraft. The initial reaction was slightly disappointing, even though the A-6A's first combat experience was a success. The avionics system's reliability was only thirty-five per cent, although it did improve considerably by the end of the deployment. One problem that did cause a great deal of consternation was the premature detonation of bomb loads on release. This resulted in the loss of a number of A-6As. The problem came about because the multiple bomb racks were being used in conjunction with surplus World War II ordnance. The standard practice was to release the bombs whilst in a diving attitude; this frequently resulted in the bombs striking each other, causing detonation. The problem was cured by refitting the racks as multiple and triple ejection racks, and adding a small detonating charge causing separation on release.

The A-6A Intruder was equipped with DIANE (digital integrated attack navigation equipment) which was based on state-of-the-art, first-generation electronics of the 1950s. The system consisted of a digital ballistics computer, the Litton AN/ASQ-61, which produced data that assisted in the selection of weapons delivery, navigation commands and flight pattern data. The Sperry AN/ASW-16 AFCS (automatic flight control system) provided automatic flight path control and three-axis attitude control. A Norden AN/APQ-92 search radar provided information which enabled the A-6A to navigate to and from the target area, whilst searching and detecting moving or stationary targets. Additionally, a Litton AN/ASN-31 inertial navigation system which provided flight attitude information by means of accelerometers, mounted on a gyrostabilized platform; a Navan Avionics Facility AN/APQ-112 track radar, which tracked moving and stationary targets during weapons delivery; a Kaiser AN/AVA-1 vertical display, which was a television monitor that gave the pilot terrain clearance and elevation scan; a General Precision AN/APN-141 electronic altimeter set, which provided pulsed range tracking on a radar altimeter that measured the terrain clearance below the aircraft; and an AN/APN-153 radar navigation set (Doppler), which supplied the ballistics computer with drift angles and ground speed. All this equipment was mounted in the avionics bay, situated in the fuselage of the aircraft. Two bays in the forward section housed all the DIANE equipment, whilst the aft section housed the Air Data Computer and the Doppler radar and radar recorder. The entire nose section was hinged, enabling it to be raised for easy access for maintenance and replacement of the two radars housed within it.

VA-85 on board *USS Kittyhawk* was the next squadron to be equipped with the A-6A, followed closely by VA-35 of the *USS Enterprise*. Both squadrons went into action in Vietnam during 1966, and from the seventy to seventy-five per cent level of reliability achieved, it was clear that the problems experienced by VA-75 had been overcome. The A-6A proved its effectiveness as an all-weather fighter-bomber, carrying out missions when other squadrons not equipped with the A-6 Intruder, were grounded because of bad weather. There were still some problems to overcome, not least the difficulties that were experienced with the shipboard semi-automatic checkout equipment due mainly to the cramped conditions under which the maintenance crews had to work. This was overcome during later deployments, but it took quite some time.

The A-6A Intruder was also in service with the US Marine Corps. In November 1965 they deployed two squadrons VMA(AW)-242 and VMJC-1 to Da Nang, in South Vietnam. VMA(AW)-242 was equipped with the A-6A, whilst VMJC-1,

a reconnaissance squadron, was equipped with the new ES-6A variant. Twenty-one ES-6As were built and used primarily for ECM (electronic countermeasures), and secondarily as ELINT (electronic intelligence) gatherers for the high-speed, low-level A-6As during night interdiction missions over North Vietnam. To reduce the chances of detection, missions were flown singly or in pairs, and 12,000 to 13,000 lb. bomb loads were carried, depending on whether or not they were Marine or Naval aircraft. An additional role of the A-6A, was that of a pathfinder for the A-4s and A-7s, which did not have the sophisticated intrumentation of the Intruder.

The third Intruder squadron, VA-65, joined the *USS Constellation* in June 1966. The squadron was equipped with the advanced version of the Intruder and led the attacks on oil processing and storage plants thirty-five miles north-east of Vinh. Post-strike reconnaissance revealed smoke columns 5,000 feet above the city, which could be seen from 150 miles away. At the end of June, A-6A Intruders from the *USS Constallation* led a large-scale onslaught together with the USAF against oil tank farms at Haiphong. The result was complete devastation of the principal target areas. Both these major raids were carried out by A-6As using radar-directed approaches.

Although the A-6A was proving to be just the aircraft the US Navy and the Marine Corps had been looking for, it was realised that it still had a lot more to offer. In 1968, it was decided to modify the aircraft to carry the General Dynamics AGM-78 standard anti-radiation missile (ARM). This missile was designed to home in on the radiation emissions from ground radars that controlled the surface-to-air missiles (SAM) used by the North Vietnamese. Ten A-6As were converted by stripping out their existing armament and installing only attack navigation equipment. Known as 'Partial Systems Aircraft', they were designated A-6Bs. Three more were taken straight off the A-6 production line and modified to take the passive angle tracking/anti-radiation missile system (PAT/ARM). A few A-6As were modified later to take the target identification acquisition system (TIAS), but they were selected from existing fleet aircraft. All three variations of the A-6B were capable of carrying and firing the AGM-78 missile.

On 11 June 1969, the first A-6C took to the air. In reality, this was an updated A-6A, which was additionally equipped with a trails, roads interdiction multi-sensor (TRIM), which incorporated electro-optical sensors for use against targets that were invisible to the naked eye and radar. Twelve A-6As were taken from the production line and fitted with forward-looking, infra-red (FLIR) cameras, together with low-light television (LLTV) cameras, mounted on a limited coverage, gimballed platform, all within a fairing beneath the fuselage. They were then redesignated A-6Cs. Although they have now been phased out of service, they could be reactivated at any time because of their unique capabilities.

So versatile was the A-6A's airframe that it was decided to create a tanker version, called the KA-6D. Although a demonstration model flew in May 1966, it was to be four years before the first conversion of early production aircraft took to the air. This version retained the vertical display indicator and the navigation and communication equipment, which was relocated to the nose in place of the search and track radar. The DIANE computer and Doppler radar were removed and a hose reel, hose and drogue were located in the after fuselage in place of the communication equipment which was relocated. The A-6As to be converted were long endurance aircraft which were limited to 4 g stress because of the wing fatigue damage brought about by hard long use.

The KA-6S was an A-6A with refuelling capabilities. It carried no more fuel than the standard A-6, although the external tanks were later uprated to hold 400 gallons. The KA-6D carried a total of 3,844 gallons, 3,000 of which could be transferred to another aircraft at a rate of 350 gallons per minute. Still in service today, the KA-6D performs a necessary and important role, as was highlighted in the attack on Libya.

Of all the variants, the A-6E was probably the most versatile and, even though the first flight was back in 1970, the aircraft is still being uprated today. Initially, it was used to evaluate the IBM AN/ASQ-133 solid-state, digital computer, already in service with the LTA A-7 Corsair II and the General Dynamics F-111, but in November of 1970 the Norden AN/APQ-148 multi-mode, search and track radar was installed, replacing the separate search and track radars of the A-6As. This system improved, by more than ninety per cent, the probability of trouble-free operation of the attack/navigation system during the average mission. Built-in test equipment (BITE) and dynamic calibration significantly reduced the direct maintenance hours per flight hour to 28.9, with 2.3 hours mean flight time between maintenance. The BITE also simplified the ground support for the aircraft, erradicating all the line test equipment for the attack navigation system. It also enabled the number of technicians to be reduced by more than twenty.

To enhance the all-weather attack capability of the A-6E, several new systems were scheduled to be installed in the aircraft. Among them was the Rockwell AGM-53A Condor air-to-surface missile, giving the Intruder a stand-off strike capability of seventy miles. Immediately the missile had been launched, the bombardier/navigator monitored the missile, right to the point of impact.

The installation of ACLS (automatic carrier landing system), which, under operational conditions, gave a one-way data control link proved a great asset to crews, as did the CNI (communication, navigation and identification) package, complete with AN/ARN-84 TACAN and dual UHF receivers, which provided increased reliability and ease of maintenance. One of the most advanced and remarkable of all the avionic packages was TRAM (target recognition attack multi-sensor). The installation of TRAM has improved the all-weather attack capabilities of the A-6E, more than quadrupling the

An A-6E of VA-65 aboard the USS Enterprise *readying for launch.*

aircraft's ability and making it one of the most lethal fighting machines in the world. Not only can the A-6E detect, identify and attack a target, it can also assess the damage on video, record it and replay it to the bombardier/navigator. Grumman have referred to the A-6E TRAM-installed as the world's most advanced electro-optical, attack aircraft.

Integrated into TRAM is FLIR, as are laser sensors. These, together with the multi-mode radar, provide the ability to: identify a target under any lighting or weather conditions; find its range and track it with greater accuracy than ever before. The information is put on to real-time, television-type imagery, making it possible to view terrain features, such as road patterns and wooded areas, as well as radar targets, and to allow the delivery of laser-guided weapons. Instantaneous video recording replays are available for damage assessment and intelligence reports. The nerve centre of this system is a twenty-inch turret under the fuselage, just forward of the nose wheel. For take-offs and landings, the turret is stored facing aft to prevent foreign object damage to the sensor windows. It is capable of rotating a full 360 degrees, thus giving continuous, infra-red imagery

Two A-6Es of VA-196 on the side elevator of the USS Enterprise.

Grumman A-6E (TRAM) Intruder cutaway drawing key

1. Radome
2. Radome open position
3. Norden AN/APQ-148 multi-mode radar scanner
4. Scanner tracking mechanism
5. Intermediate frequency unit
6. ILS aerials
7. TRAM rotating turrent mounting
8. Target Recognition and Attack Multi-sensor turret (TRAM)
9. Taxying lamp
10. Deck approach lights
11. Nosewheel leg door
12. Hydraulic nosewheel steering unit
13. Catapult launch strop
14. Twin nosewheels (aft retracting
15. Retraction/breaker strut
16. Shock absorber leg strut
17. Torque scissor links
18. Radome latch
19. Hinged avionics equipment pallet (port and starboard)
20. Radar scanner mounting
21. Radome hydraulic jack
22. Flight refuelling probe
23. ALQ-165 ECM system forward spiral antenna
24. Refuelling probe spotlight
25. Windscreen rain repellant air duct
26. Front pressure bulkhead
27. Nosewheel bay-mounted pressure refuelling connection
28. Boundary layer splitter plate
29. Port engine air intake
30. Nosewheel bay electronic equipment racks
31. VHF aerial
32. UHF aerial
33. Intake duct framing
34. Temperature probe
35. Canopy emergency release handle
36. TACAN aerial
37. Folding boarding ladder
38. Integral boarding steps

39. Angle-of-attack transmitter
40. Boundary layer spill duct
41. Cockpit floor level

42. Rudder pedals
43. Engine throttle levers
44. Control column
45. Instrument panel shroud
46. Pilot's optical sighting unit/head-up display
47. Windscreen panels
48. Aft sliding cockpit canopy cover

49. Forward-Looking Infra-Red (FLIR) viewing scope
50. Navigator/bombardier's Martin-Baker GRU-7 ejection seat
51. Ejection seat headrests
52. Seat reclining mechanism
53. Centre console
54. Pilot's GRU-7 ejection seat
55. Safety/parachute harness
56. Port side console panel
57. Electrical system equipment
58. Destruct initiator
59. Leading-edge stall warning buffet strip

60. Engine intake compressor face
61. Engine bay venting air scoop
62. Accessory equipment gearbox
63. Pratt & Whitney J52-P-8B non-afterburning turbofan
64. Mainwheel door
65. Leading-edge antenna fairing (port and starboard)
66. ALQ-165 high, mid and low band ECM aerials
67. Mainwheel well
68. Hydraulic system reservoir
69. Cockpit rear pressure bulkhead
70. Cooling air spill louvres
71. Electrical equipment bay
72. Electronics and avionics equipment bay
73. Forward fuselage bag-type fuel tank
74. Weapons monitoring module
75. Sliding canopy rail
76. Canopy hydraulic jack
77. Canopy aft fairing

78. Starboard wing inboard integral fuel tank: total fuel capacity 1,951 Imp gal (2,344 US gal/8 873 l)
79. Fuel system piping
80. Inboard wing fence
81. Leading-edge slat drive shaft
82. Slat guide rails
83. Slat screw jacks
84. AGM-65 Maverick air-to-surface missiles
85. Triple missile carrier/launcher
86. Starboard wing stores pylons
87. AIM-9P Sidewinder "self-defence" air-to-air missile
88. Wing fold twin hydraulic jacks
89. Spar hydraulic latch pins
90. Wing fold hinge joint
91. Outer wing panel integral fuel tank
92. Outboard wing fence
93. Starboard leading-edge slat (open)

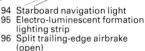

94. Starboard navigation light
95. Electro-luminescent formation lighting strip
96. Split trailing-edge airbrake (open)
97. Fuel jettison
98. Single-slotted Fowler-type flap (down position)

99. Roll control spoiler/lift dumper
100. Flap guide rails
101. Flap screw jacks
102. Spoiler hydraulic jack
103. Flap drive shaft

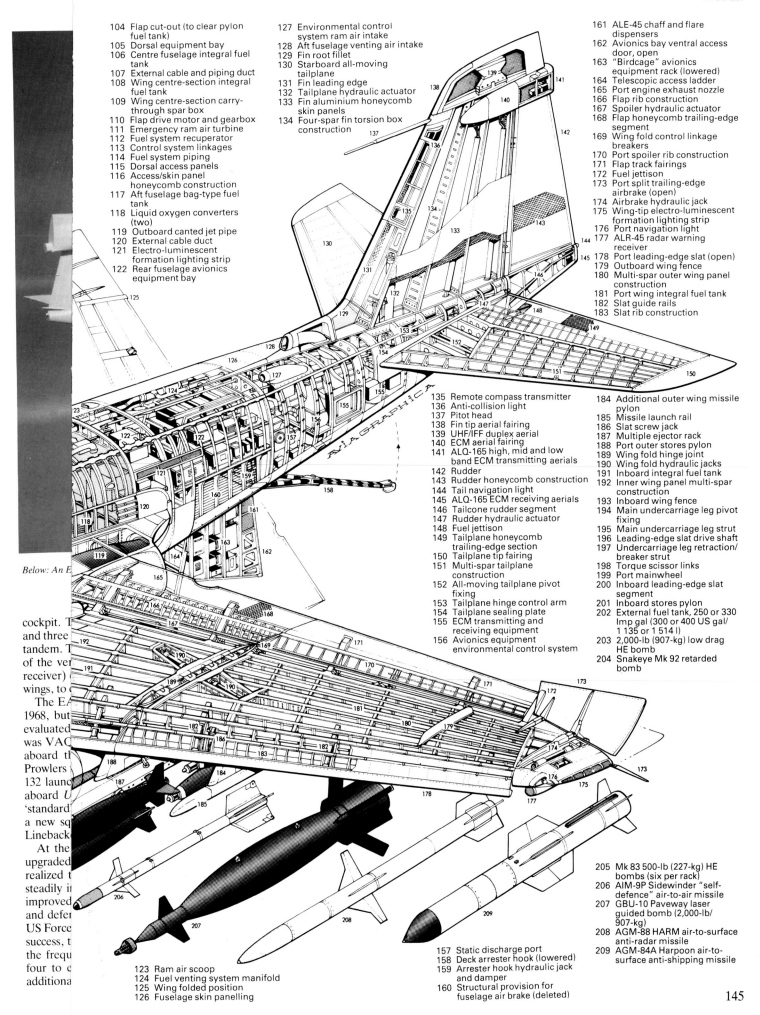

104 Flap cut-out (to clear pylon fuel tank)
105 Dorsal equipment bay
106 Centre fuselage integral fuel tank
107 External cable and piping duct
108 Wing centre-section integral fuel tank
109 Wing centre-section carry-through spar box
110 Flap drive motor and gearbox
111 Emergency ram air turbine
112 Fuel system recuperator
113 Control system linkages
114 Fuel system piping
115 Dorsal access panels
116 Access/skin panel honeycomb construction
117 Aft fuselage bag-type fuel tank
118 Liquid oxygen converters (two)
119 Outboard canted jet pipe
120 External cable duct
121 Electro-luminescent formation lighting strip
122 Rear fuselage avionics equipment bay

127 Environmental control system ram air intake
128 Aft fuselage venting air intake
129 Fin root fillet
130 Starboard all-moving tailplane
131 Fin leading edge
132 Tailplane hydraulic actuator
133 Fin aluminium honeycomb skin panels
134 Four-spar fin torsion box construction

135 Remote compass transmitter
136 Anti-collision light
137 Pitot head
138 Fin tip aerial fairing
139 UHF/IFF duplex aerial
140 ECM aerial fairing
141 ALQ-165 high, mid and low band ECM transmitting aerials
142 Rudder
143 Rudder honeycomb construction
144 Tail navigation light
145 ALQ-165 ECM receiving aerials
146 Tailcone rudder segment
147 Rudder hydraulic actuator
148 Fuel jettison
149 Tailplane honeycomb trailing-edge section
150 Tailplane tip fairing
151 Multi-spar tailplane construction
152 All-moving tailplane pivot fixing
153 Tailplane hinge control arm
154 Tailplane sealing plate
155 ECM transmitting and receiving equipment
156 Avionics equipment environmental control system

161 ALE-45 chaff and flare dispensers
162 Avionics bay ventral access door, open
163 "Birdcage" avionics equipment rack (lowered)
164 Telescopic access ladder
165 Port engine exhaust nozzle
166 Flap rib construction
167 Spoiler hydraulic actuator
168 Flap honeycomb trailing-edge segment
169 Wing fold control linkage breakers
170 Port spoiler rib construction
171 Flap track fairings
172 Fuel jettison
173 Port split trailing-edge airbrake (open)
174 Airbrake hydraulic jack
175 Wing-tip electro-luminescent formation lighting strip
176 Port navigation light
177 ALR-45 radar warning receiver
178 Port leading-edge slat (open)
179 Outboard wing fence
180 Multi-spar outer wing panel construction
181 Port wing integral fuel tank
182 Slat guide rails
183 Slat rib construction

184 Additional outer wing missile pylon
185 Missile launch rail
186 Slat screw jack
187 Multiple ejector rack
188 Port outer stores pylon
189 Wing fold hinge joint
190 Wing fold hydraulic jacks
191 Inboard integral fuel tank
192 Inner wing panel multi-spar construction
193 Inboard wing fence
194 Main undercarriage leg pivot fixing
195 Main undercarriage leg strut
196 Leading-edge slat drive shaft
197 Undercarriage leg retraction/breaker strut
198 Torque scissor links
199 Port mainwheel
200 Inboard leading-edge slat segment
201 Inboard stores pylon
202 External fuel tank, 250 or 330 Imp gal (300 or 400 US gal/1 135 or 1 514 l)
203 2,000-lb (907-kg) low drag HE bomb
204 Snakeye Mk 92 retarded bomb

205 Mk 83 500-lb (227-kg) HE bombs (six per rack)
206 AIM-9P Sidewinder "self-defence" air-to-air missile
207 GBU-10 Paveway laser guided bomb (2,000-lb/907-kg)
208 AGM-88 HARM air-to-surface anti-radar missile
209 AGM-84A Harpoon air-to-surface anti-shipping missile

123 Ram air scoop
124 Fuel venting system manifold
125 Wing folded position
126 Fuselage skin panelling

157 Static discharge port
158 Deck arrester hook (lowered)
159 Arrester hook hydraulic jack and damper
160 Structural provision for fuselage air brake (deleted)

Below: An E...

cockpit. T...
and three...
tandem. T...
of the ve...
receiver) ...
wings, to ...
The EA...
1968, but...
evaluated...
was VAQ...
aboard th...
Prowlers...
132 launc...
aboard U...
'standard...
a new sq...
Lineback...
At the...
upgraded...
realized t...
steadily i...
improved...
and defer...
US Force...
success, t...
the frequ...
four to e...
additiona...

conve
for th
fact t
impro
much
actua
play a
for, b
signif
No
has, v
has u
systei
year
Desig
Intru
pit di
been
forwa
After
mode
which
progi
three
rema
engir
Elect
Th
ance,
The
with
head
Navy
curre
the s
mode
it is
extre
displ
ISAI
of th
adde
In
the v
pane
the
(AM
orde
cepto
esco
som
extre
capa
on a
so is
A-6l
AM
Intr
Spai
allov
the j
T
impi
equi
as n
engi
requ
perf
incr
Elec
and
Altl

squadron VAW-123 at NAS Norfolk, Virginia. Further evaluation was carried out before the E-2C was assigned to fleet duty aboard the *USS Saratoga* in September 1974. In June 1975, VAW-125 Squadron took delivery of the E-2C and was deployed on the aircraft carrier *USS John F. Kennedy.*

Externally, there was no great difference between the E-2C and the -2A and -2B, except for the enlarged air scoop on top of the fuselage on the E-2C, and a 21-inch longer nose that accommodated the passive detection system antenna. Internally, certain structural members were strengthened when it was discovered that stress/corrosion cracking had appeared on the earlier models. The engines were changed from the Allison T56-A-8 to the more powerful Detroit Diesel Allison T56-A-422s that produced 4,502 shp and turned two four-bladed propellers of 13 ft. 6 in. diameter. The propellers fitted to the earlier E-2Cs were of the Aeroproducts hollow-steel blade type with square tips, but these were replaced with a unique propeller blade made of glassfibre/foam with rounded tips, manufactured by Hamilton-Standard. They were chosen because they were quieter, induced less vibration and had a longer fatigue life; they were later fitted to the C-2A Greyhound COD.

Because of the E-2C's increased amount of electronic equipment, and the complete redesigning of the vapour-cycle equipment cooling subsystem, the air scoop on the top of the fuselage had to be enlarged.

The avionics carried by the E-2C Hawkeye were some of the most sophisticated known at the time. Rotating at six rpm, the 24 ft. diameter radome scanned the horizon for targets. The information picked up by the Antenna Group AN/APS-171, housed in the rotodome, was transmitted to the IFF interrogator, RT-988/A, for identification. The IFF (identi-

An E-2C Hawkeye of VAW-117 parked on its wings-folded configuration aboard the carrier USS Enterprise.

fication friend or foe) transmitter sent out a challenge signal to the unidentified object; if the reply was friendly, the information was fed to an IFF Detector Processor, the OL-76/AF, and to a control indicator, AN/APA-172, for processing, display and identification. In the event of the Hawkeye itself being interrogated, the IFF transponder, AN/APX-72, was used to send reply signals.

Grumman and Litton-Amecon got together and developed the Litton AN/ALP-59 Passive Detection System, and it provided the early warning system for the Hawkeye. It operated on microwave frequencies, capturing short duration signals in real time. The heart of the avionics system was the OL-77ASQ computer programmer, which performed tracking, navigation and interception vectoring, data exchange (via Data Link), and generated data for display purposes. The

An E-2C Hawkeye of VAW-110.

processor, in fact, comprised two L-304 computers; ten, 8,192, word memory units; a recorder producer; a system test module; a passive-detection converter module for display; radar; navigation and communications; a 4,096-word refresher memory for the displays; input and output buffers for each of the functions; and a power supply.

To enable the computer programmer to perform target tracking, reports from the OK-93/AP and OL-76/AP radar detector processor group were produced, and threat and non-threat targets displayed, giving position, height and speed. Navigation was no longer by the stars and sextant, but by on-board computers, processing information from a Doppler navigation set, AN/APN-153(V); air data computer, A/A; carrier aircraft inertial navigation system (CAINS) AN/ASW-92(V) and other systems. The main computer processed all the information generated and displayed it to the pilot and co-pilot, giving the aircraft's position; time heading; magnetic heading ground track; drift angle; wind direction and speed; bearing and range-to-carrier centre; bearing and range-to-destination and barrier pattern.

Communication was by an AN/ARC-51A UHF two-way, double-sideband, voice transceiver, capable of transmitting and receiving on any one of 3,500 channel frequencies. When operated in conjunction with the AN/ARA-50 direction finder, the radio was capable of being used as an automatic direction finder. The data link communication, using data radio set AN/ARQ-158 UHF for voice and AN/ARQ-34 HF for data, enabled the Hawkeye to maintain contact with Navy and Marine tactical data systems. One rather unique system in the E-2C Hawkeye was the in-flight performance monitor, which enabled the operator to isolate faults in the avionics system.

During the Vietnam War, E2-A Hawkeyes were stationed around the perimeter of the task force whenever there was a possibility of attack by either surface ships or by air. One of the major roles of the E-2C was that of an airborne controller for the various combat air patrols that flew air cover for the task force. The presence of the Hawkeye also enabled task force commanders to reduce the number of interceptors required in the air, or on 'condition one' standby, during the hours of darkness. The E-2A Hawkeye played a major part in the destruction of many MiG-17s and MiG-21s. The Russian-built aircraft were detected by the Hawkeye as they swept in to attack, and, by diverting F-4s from their bomber escort duties, the fighters were able to intercept and destroy them using Sparrow or Sidewinder air-to-air missiles. Because of the large number of aircraft in the vicinity of the task force during this period, it became necessary to be able to identify them, and as many of the search and rescue aircraft did not respond to radio challenge, they had to be challenged electronically by the IFF system.

The modern-day E-2C Hawkeye will have at least one, if not two, squadrons of F-14A Tomcats assigned to it. Despite the obvious difference between the two aircraft, they are a perfect team. The E-2C can direct up to thirty-six fighters at any one time, and the AWG-9 Phoenix Missile System, carried by the F-14s, can engage up to six targets simultaneously, which gives a whole new meaning to the concept of tactical warfare.

After bad experiences with the reliability and maintainability of the E-2A and E-2B, the US Navy insisted that Grumman guarantee that of the E-2C; it passed even the Navy's expectations. During a six-month Mediterranean tour with the US Navy, four E-2Cs carried out 288 scheduled sorties, missing only eight, and all during the aircraft's first deployment with the fleet. This lethal team of fighter and AEW aircraft is capable of linking together with the task force commander, so that he can decide whether or not the targets being tracked and reported warrant strike or retaliation commands. The Tomcat has a unique system that enables the crew to use a two-way voice and data link-up into its own integrated weapons system. In a combat air patrol, the

Hawkeye would be in the centre of a circle of fighters and, by using the radar from the fighters on the edge of the circle, it would be able to extend its range by up to 115 miles into the sector scanned by the fighters' radar. The full circle of the Hawkeye's range, or surveillance-radar-envelope, is some three million cubic miles, but, by using the fighters' own radar as an extension, it is able to obtain real-time information from well beyond this range.

The complexity of the Hawkeye's avionics enables it to track more than 500 separate targets, by using data and information from F-14s, ground stations, aircraft carriers and other E-2Cs. At one point, the Hawkeye was even considered as a replacement for the Royal Air Force's Shackleton AEW Mk. 2, but the RAF opted for the Nimrod, which unfortunately was never the success it was hoped it would be. Britain has now decided to order E-3s from Boeing.

To date the only countries to have bought the E-2C Hawkeye are Japan, Egypt, Singapore and Israel. It was an Israeli E-2C Hawkeye that controlled the Israeli F-15s which attacked and destroyed five Syrian MiG-21s over Lebanon in June 1979.

In 1981, the Hawkeye took on a new role as a drug tracker. Operation Thunderbolt, as it was known, was a joint operation involving the US Navy, the US Coast Guard, US Custom Service and the Drug Enforcement Administration. The E-2C Hawkeyes were to be used to track low-flying aircraft coming from the coast of South America towards Florida. As the Hawkeye was designed as an all-weather, carrier based, airborne early warning/command and control aircraft, the operation did not differ much from a normal combat mission. Once detected, targets were kept under radar observation whilst Coast Guard aircraft were vectored in to intercept. So successful was the operation that, during one seventy-seven day period, forty-five aircraft were seized, ninety-seven arrests were made, 1,000 pounds of cocaine, 26,000 pounds of marijuana and 250 pounds of hashish oil were confiscated. Without question, the E-2C Hawkeye has made a tremendous difference in the fight against the drug menace.

In October 1985, Commander Ralph Zia, of VAW-125, and his crew, were ordered to launch their E-2C Hawkeye from the carrier USS Saratoga. They were not told their mission until they were airborne, which was to intercept an Egyptian Air Boeing 737, carrying four hijackers from the liner, Achille Lauro. Zia's job was to find the 737 and vector F-14s of VF-75 and VF-103 in to intercept. After finding the aircraft, Zia co-ordinated the interception and contacted the pilot on the E-2C's VHF radio. He persuaded the pilot that discretion was the better part of valour, and then watched as the F-14s escorted the 737 to Sigonella, Italy.

Although the twin-propellered aircraft might look out of place in today's fast-jet Navy, its achievements and ability have ensured it a place in naval aviation for many years to come.

With the success of the E-2C Hawkeye, Grumman realized that there was another role for that type of aircraft, carrier-on-board delivery. As it happened, the Navy were looking for a replacement for the Grumman C-1A Trader, so when Grumman proposed the new design to them, they ordered three. Designated the C-2A Greyhound, one was a static model for test purposes and the others for test flying and evaluation. Essentially, only the fuselage, nose landing gear and the stabilizers were new. The E-2C and the C-2A both used the same turboprop engines, had a fully pressurized fuselage, an all-weather capability and could be nose-tow launched. The Greyhound's fuselage incorporated an aft-loading cargo door, which enabled loading from deck level and, when not in use, formed part of the upswept rear fuselage. It could also accommodate thirty-nine troops, or twenty stretchers and four nursing staff, it had air-drop facilities and could even be used as a tanker for air-to-air refuelling. The configurations were virtually limitless, a veritable flying jeep.

The C-2A prototype on a test flight at the Naval Air Test Center.

A C-2A Greyhound on a test flight.

The C-2A had a 10,000 lb. payload, which could be carried nearly 2,000 miles. It could carry higher payloads still, but over a limited range. The first flight of the C-2A Greyhound took place on 18 November 1964, and within one month it was accepted by the Navy. Initially, only twenty were built and assigned to the Navy, but in 1982, Grumman received an order for a further thirty-nine to be delivered over seven years. The first was delivered in January 1985 and the last in 1989.

The E-2C and the C-2A are the largest transport aircraft designed specifically for carrier operations, although, in October 1963, a Hercules had made an experimental landing on the aircraft carrier *USS Forrestal*, to investigate the possibilities of using the C-130 for logistic support for the US fleet. The C-2A could operate from all the super-class carriers that were equipped with the appropriate catapult launchers and arrester gear. In addition, it was also capable of free deck take-offs, and able to use the deck elevators. The latter was made possible by automatic wing latches that hooked the folding wings to the outboard tail fins. The twin Allison T56-A-8/8A turboprop engines that powered the C-2A Greyhound, were almost identical to the ones that powered the E-2A, the only difference being that the prop shafts on the C-2A were enlarged. The fuselage was of a conventional semi-monocoque

A C-2A about to land aboard the carrier USS John F. Kennedy.

design, and was capable of carrying three 500 gallon fuel tanks internally for ferry flights. The landing gear was a conventional tricycle arrangement, the main gear being fitted with an extender system on each main strut, for catapulting. The steering nose gear was a strengthened version of the E-2A's, basically because of the higher gross weight of the C-2A and to give the aircraft the additional capability of being able to land on an unprepared field.

The aircraft was used extensively during the Vietnam War by Fleet Tactical Support Squadron 50 for daily delivery of mail, cargo and personnel from land bases to the fleet.

Fifteen C-2A Greyhounds and five C-1A Traders were used for this operation and their reliability proved to be an incredible ninety per cent throughout the conflict.

Today, the Hawkeye and the Greyhound still feature prominently in the US Fleet and will, it is certain, for many years to come. The E-2C is now scheduled to be equipped with an improved engine, the T56-A-427, giving more power to cope with the increased weight brought about by aircraft and systems improvements. An aircraft's ability relies a great deal on its reliability, and the Hawkeye and Greyhound are more reliable than most.

Grumman E-2C Hawkeye technical details

Model	Airborne early warning.
Crew	Pilots (2), radar operator (1), air control operator (1), combat information centre operator (1).
Engines	Two Detroit Diesel Allison T56-A-425 turboprops.
Dimensions	Wing span 80 ft. 7 in., folded span 29 ft. 4 in. Height 18 ft. 4 in., (radome high), 16 ft. 6 in. (radome lowered). Length 57 ft. 7 in., wing area 700 sq. ft., diameter of radome 24 ft.
Weight	38,009 lb. empty, 59,880 lb. gross.
Performance	Max. speed 348 mph, cruising speed 310 mph. Initial climb rate 2,515 ft. per min.

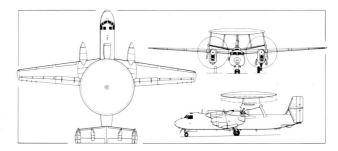

Fuel capacity	1,824 gallons, 912 gallons in self-sealing tanks in each in-board wing.

Grumman C-2A Greyhound technical details

Model	Carrier on-board delivery.
Crew	Two pilots.
Engines	Two Allison T56-A-8A turboprops.
Dimensions	Wing span 80 ft. 7 in., folded span 29 ft. 4 in. Height 15 ft. 11 in., length 56 ft. 8 in., wing area 700 sq. ft.

Weight	31,154 lb. empty, 54,286 lb gross.
Performance	Max. speed 328 mph, cruising speed 288 mph. Initial climb rate 2,330 ft. per min.

E-2 Hawkeye model variations

E-2A
Production model called the 'Hawkeye' for obvious reasons, but sometimes called the 'Hummer', because of the humming sound given out by the two Allison T56-A-8 turboprops. It carried a crew of five, two pilots and three radar operators, who operated the APS-96 radar which was optimized for overwater operations.

E-2B
All the E-2As were converted to E-2Bs by a number of modifications and the installation of a Litton L-304 general purpose computer. This computer enhanced the Hawkeye's whole operational flexibility.

E-2C
This became the most sophisticated AEW aircraft in the world. The APS-120 radar was upgraded to the APS-125, giving it overland target detection which was coupled to the ARPS (advanced radar processing system) which targeted the overland targets. Because of the increased avionics, the cooling system had to be revised. This meant enlarging the radiator over the front fuselage and, together with the extended nose used to incorporate the ESM (electronic support measures), the length of the fuselage was extended to 57 ft. 7 in. The engines were uprated to the T56-A-422, and later, when the plastic-bladed propellers were fitted, to T56-A-425s.

TE-2C
This was a trainer version and, externally, indistinguishable from the E-2C.

F-14 Tomcat

In 1942, Dr Alexander Lippisch, an aerodynamicist for the German aircraft manufacturer Messerschmitt, patented a design for a swept-wing aircraft. Across the English Channel, Barnes Wallis, designer of the Wellington bomber and the 'Bouncing Bomb', was carrying out experiments with similar models. Some years later, during the 1950s, he designed a supersonic airliner with variable swept wings that swung back against the fuselage — it was called the Swallow. The Vickers Swallow had its engines towards the wing-tips, the idea being that it would keep the longitudinal stability reasonably constant. A design model underwent extensive wind tunnel tests which revealed that the concept of wing-tip mounted engines was impractical. The design progressed no farther and was scrapped.

Also in the 1950s, across the Atlantic the Bell Aircraft Company successfully built and flew their swing-wing aircraft, the X-5. The X-5 was a captured German design – the Messerschmitt P.1101, – which was given to Bell for examination after the war. The German Me. P.1101 had ground adjustable, variable-sweep wings, whilst the Bell X-5 had an in-flight variable-sweep wing capability. Late in 1952, Grumman designed and built a swing-wing fighter, called the XF10F-1 Jaguar, which flew in May 1953. The Navy saw great potential in Grumman's swept-wing fighter and ordered ten; only one aircraft was ever built, however, and the orders for the other nine were cancelled, much to the relief of some of

the Grumman engineers. A replacement was urgently required for the ageing F-3H Demon and the F-4D, later to become the F-4D Skyray, which were the US Navy's principal fighter aircraft.

Interest in a new fighter began in the late 1950s, following reports on the latest Russian fighters, the TU-58 Fiddler and the MiG-21D Fishbed. The US Navy decided that they required a subsonic fighter, capable of delivering multiple missiles to a large number of targets. The aircraft they chose was a 'paper' aeroplane called the Douglas F6D Missileer. The F6D was designed to carry the Grumman two-stage XAAM-10 Eagle missile; a track-while-scan missile control system; an active homing radar guidance system, and a high-powered pulse Doppler system. It had a straight wing, on which six Eagle missiles could be externally mounted. Two newly-designed Pratt and Whitney TF30-P-2 engines were chosen for the F6D, and Grumman were in charge of designing and developing the missile. The project never got past the design stage, however, before it was cancelled by the then Secretary of Defence, Robert McNamara. He had decided that the cost was too high considering that the aircraft could only perform one role; a multi-role, combat aircraft was

Above: An F-111B showing a partial-swept wing configuration. It is interesting to note that the pilot appears to be wearing a full 'space type' helmet, denoting high altitude tests.

158

what was really required. The Navy continued to look, after the cancellation of the Douglas Missileer, so McNamara suggested that the US Navy and the USAF combine their requirements and select one aircraft. The aircraft chosen was the General Dynamics F-111A, a variable swing-wing aircraft, designed primarily for the USAF as a low-level interceptor. This was just the type of aircraft that General F. F. Everest, Tactical Air Command's new commander, wanted: he wanted an aircraft to replace the F-105, one that could fly non-stop to Europe without refuelling, fly low level at 1,000 miles per hour for 400 miles, and high level at 1,700 miles per hour. From the outset it was obvious that the requirements of both services were poles apart. The pressure on them to combine their needs continued, so the US Navy asked Grumman to join with General Dynamics and make a naval version of the F-111A, with longer wings and an armament of six Hughes AIM-54A Phoenix missiles with the AWG-9 weapon system. It was called the F-111B (TFX).

Although the F-111B was built for the Navy, the programme as a whole was run by the USAF. The F-111B's initial flight was on 18 May 1966 and, almost immediately, there were problems – the major one being weight. The Navy had estimated the F-111B's desired weight to be around the 60,000 pound mark; the weight of the F-111B was in excess of 70,000 pounds. Although this was acceptable to the Air Force, it was not to the Navy, and essentially killed any chance of the aircraft being accepted as a naval carrier aircraft. It was obvious that this weight would probably increase during development, and this was totally unacceptable to the Navy. McNamara insisted that the engine be upgraded to handle the increased weight, and out of this engine modification came the TF30-P-412, which is the basic engine in current F-14s. Problems were being experienced in certain areas of the flying envelope, amongst other things the engine inlets were causing compressor stalls. Pilots were complaining about the lack of visibility on approach to carriers due to the angle of attack, and serious reflection problems were caused by the angle of the windshield.

The Secretary of Defense, McNamara, who by this time was at the point of despairing over the project, called together all the top executives of the companies involved for twice monthly meetings. McNamara had even hired his own civilian project engineer, Bob Laidlaw, from North American/Rockwell, to supervise the meetings and be his own personal consultant. These meetings were held in Washington on Saturday mornings and included the Secretaries of the Navy and the Air Force. They tried unsuccessfully to solve their differences and the problems that were dogging the project. Among the Navy contingent at the meetings were Admiral Moorer and Vice-Admiral Connolly, and although they and the Navy realized that as far as they were concerned the project was a 'no-go', the Secretary of Defense did not, and pushed on with the project.

The swing-wing was one of the innovations developed for the F-111B, but during the wind tunnel tests the pivot points were discovered to be causing problems. They reduced the cross-sectional area and the fuel flow in low altitude supersonic flight; nothing seemed to be going right for the project. The aircraft was required to fly at supersonic speed at low altitude, utilizing the latest terrain-following radar, and to carry, the extremely heavy Phoenix missile system, with its multi-shot capability, at high altitudes. To enable the aircraft to do this, its drag had to be reduced drastically, so the wing pivots were located inboard and the engines pulled into the fuselage at the wing roots, instead of being outboard under each wing. This created problems with the airflow and cut engine efficiency tremendously. To put the whole project into its correct perspective, as a land-based bomber it would be adequate, but as a fighter or interceptor, it would be no good at all.

Admiral Connolly decided to go down to Fort Worth, Texas, where the F-111B was being tested, to see for himself what the aircraft was like. He flew the aircraft accompanied by an Air Force pilot and agreed that for Air Force use it had great potential, but for use by the Navy and to fly off carriers, it had none! Up to this point, there had been six variations, and a decision on which was to be the prime aircraft still had to be made. The R & D costs were climbing all the time. In 1966, $250 million was injected into the budget, and it was obvious to all concerned that this was to be the year of decision, as all previous assesments had only been in the region of $30 and $40 million.

Admiral Moorer, as Chief of Naval Operations, was in charge of requirements for the Navy at this time, and it was his job to decide what the Navy should or should not have. It was also his decision that the Navy did not want the F-111B. In the meantime, he was getting feedback information from the test pilots carrying out the trials at Patuxent River Naval Air Test Centre, that in no way could the F-111B successfully operate off an aircraft-carrier. It was unstable to the point of being dangerous, and this was totally unacceptable, especially when being flown in adverse weather conditions.

But still the civilian hierachy insisted that the F-111B be accepted by the Navy. It was around this time that Grumman made an unsolicited approach to the Navy with their concept of a new fighter, the F-14. Grumman was already involved with the F-111B as sub-contractor, building the aircraft's aft section for General Dynamics, but they realized that it was not suitable as a carrier aircraft, so had come up with a proposal of their own. The Navy looked at the proposal very carefully and realized that it could be the answer to all their problems. The design took the best features of the F-111B and placed them in a brand new airframe; what was more important, the R & D had already been done on the engine and weapon systems. All that had to be tested was the new airframe and that was the cheapest part of all. It also have the Navy an alternative proposal when they pushed for the cancellation of the F-111B programme. A comparison study was made between the F-14, the F-111 and a couple of other aircraft. The result was that the F-14 was a far better aircraft that any of the others, but still Secretary of Defence McNamara pushed for the F-111B.

Admiral Moorer was summoned to the Secretary of the Navy's office and asked if he would back the F-111B project and again the Admiral said 'No!' The Navy realized that they were getting nowhere with their objections and so decided to take advantage of the Senate Preparedness Sub-Committee offer of help. A hearing was held, chaired by Senator Stennis, who was also the Chairman of the Senate Armed Services Committee, and he wanted a good reason why his committee should disapprove the $200 million for the project.

The Department of Defense was represented by the new Secretary of the Navy, Paul Ignatius, Assistant Secretary of the Navy for R & D, Bob Frosch, Chief of Naval Operations, Admiral Tom Moorer, Deputy Chief of Naval Operation (Air), Vice-Admiral Tom Connolly and Rear-Admiral Gerry Miller. For over six hours Stennis asked questions and Paul Ignatius answered them, and it was quite obvious that nothing concrete was going to be said regarding the future of the F-111B project.

It was at this point that Rear-Admiral Miller, who had been working closely with Stennis's right-hand man, left the room. Five minutes later one of Stennis's aides entered the room and placed a note in front of Stennis. Stennis barely glanced at it, asked a couple of innocuous questions, then said, 'This question is for Admiral Connolly; he is the Air Boss for the Navy and this is his area of responsibility. Admiral, would you support this additional money for the F-111B?

Admiral Connolly looked at Stennis and replied, 'No Sir, I would not.'

The Secretary of the Navy, Paul Ignatius, immediately said, 'Well, we are going to put better engines in the aircraft and make a better airplane out of it.'

Stennis turned back to Admiral Connolly and said,

159

'Admiral, with the new engines would you change your mind?'

Admiral Tom Connolly took a deep breath and said, 'Senator, there isn't enough thrust in all Christendom to make a fighter out of that airplane.'

That, to all intents and purposes, was the end of the F-111B, and also the end of Tom Connolly's hopes of promotion to four-star Admiral!

Although the F-111B project was dead as far as the Navy was concerned, problems regarding the funding for the F-14 project began to raise their heads. Admiral Zumwalt was still head of the study group of the F-111B and he decided to push for $96 million of the budget to be channelled into the F-111B project, in case the F-14 project folded. The 'Hedge' as it was known, was approved by Admiral Moorer and was the point of discussion when the House Armed Services Committee met. Again, the person in the 'hot seat' at the meeting was Vice-Admiral Connolly, and when asked by the chairman, Mendel Rivers if he had anything good to say about the F-111B Admiral Connolly replied, 'Mr Chairman, I don't know of any aviator, reserve or regular, anywhere in the world, who has anything good to say about that airplane!'

Grumman sensed that a cancellation of the F-111B project was likely, and so began a series of project studies of alternative fighters, still using the Pratt and Whitney TF30 engines and AWG-9 avionics system. In October 1967, Grumman proposed a design called the 303-60 to the US Navy, and in May the following year the F-111B project was officially cancelled. Two months later, the US Navy invited proposals for a new fighter to be submitted, designating it the VFX. Of all the designs and proposals sumitted, only one had a fixed wing, all the others having variable swing wings. It was made known that the aircraft would be purchased in two stages, the VFX-1 with the TF30 engines and later the VFX-2 with the Advanced Technology Engine (ATE), then currently under joint development by the US Navy and the USAF. Two companies were chosen to resubmit designs to the Naval Air Systems Command, Grumman and McDonnell-Douglas. One month later, in October 1968, it was announced that Grumman had been selected as the prime contractor for the Navy's new fighter aircraft. Certain conditions were laid down by the Navy regarding the design of the aircraft, however, such as the two-man crew being carried in tandem and not side-by-side as in the F-111B, and it also had to be powered by two Pratt and Whitney TF3C-P-412 engines. Its armament was to be six Phoenix missiles, or six AIM-7 Sparrow missiles with two AIM-9 Sidewinders and an internally mounted M-61 rotary cannon. All in all, the aircraft was to be the most sophisticated and lethal fighter in the world.

The contract for the F-14A RDT&E (Research, Development, Test and Evaluation) was signed on 3 February 1969, and less than two years later this remarkable aircraft took off on its maiden flight. The F-14A was the most complicated project ever undertaken by Grumman, although the Lunar Module came close. The aircraft was to be the product of six thousand configurations, culminating in eight different designs. Starting with 303-60, this design had podded engines and a variable sweep wing. This being the first of the designs, it did not contain the sophisticated blend of electronics and airframe subsystems that subsequent models did. Grumman carried out extensive tests in the wind tunnel, with the result that some slight modifications were made, enough to change the design number to 303A. Modification of the nacelles resulted in the design number being changed yet again, to 303B. Design number 303C was to produce the twin vertical tails that were to be in the final design, and had the engines built into the fuselage, rather than in separate pods. The variable geometric wings were set high on the fuselage, unlike the design 303D, which, although retaining the engines built into the fuselage and, the twin vertical tails, had a low variable geometric wing. The 303E was a variation

of the 303B, but with a reduction of 4,920 pounds in overall weight. The 303F was similar to the 303D, the only difference, but an important one, being that it had a fixed wing. The next design, the 303G, had the podded engines and the high-set variable geometric wing, but this design had a fighter-only capability, the weaponry consisting of the AWG-10 fire control system and four Sparrow missiles, but no provision for the Phoenix missile. This was one of the main reasons why the design was dropped. Poor subsonic drag, reduced maximum afterburner supersonic thrust and poor subsonic longitudinal stability, were among the reasons why design number 303D was dropped. This left only 303E, B, C, and F. Both B and C had the high geometric wing, but C had the engines built into the fuselage and B had the podded engines. C was discarded because of poor subsonic combat performance, inferior fuel flow and afterburner thrust, because it had no potential for ATE engines, and because its take-off weight would have been 4,920 pounds heavier for the Sparrow fighter mission than the 303E. B was discarded because of the high wing, and F because of the fixed wing. The only design left was the 303E, ultimately chosen to become the F-14 Tomcat.

The construction of the F-14 was a revolution in aircraft manufacture. Approximately twenty-five per cent of the aircraft was made of titanium, the majority in the box beam to which the wings were attached. The box beam had a dual role: not only did it absorb all the transmitted wing loads, but it was also used as a fuel tank. A new technique was used to weld the beam – electron-beam welding, when two pieces of titanium were welded into their molecular components, resulting in a strength loss of only three per cent. This was well within the acceptable safety margins. The strength of the titanium and the electron-beam welding was proven when the first pre-production F-14A crashed on 30 December 1970 and the wing-box was found six feet underground, virtually undamaged.

Grumman realized that they were taking a chance by using titanium, because although it is stronger and lighter than steel, it is difficult to work with. Even the usually simple task of drilling holes takes on a completely new perspective. The area to be drilled has to be completely submerged in freon gas to chill the metal, otherwise the drill bit heats the area to a point where the titanium becomes brittle and loses its strength. Holes have to be drilled precisely and a computerized drill is used to ensure that they are. The rivets are made slightly larger than the holes and are pushed in with such force and accuracy, that it causes the two metals to fuse together, thus eliminating the need for a sealant.

The F-14A first flew was on 21 December 1970, without incident, but on the second, there was a complete loss of the hydraulics, and both pilots had to eject to safety. The cause was pinpointed to a failure in the titanium hydraulic piping due to fatigue. The second F-14 flew five months later, with the titanium piping replaced by stainless steel.

The F-14 Tomcat had a number of unique features that set it apart from any other aircraft in the world. It had a variable swing-wing, an integrated computer and AWG-9 weapons system, and carried the Phoenix missile; all in all, possibly the most lethal fighting machine of all time. The F-14 does not have any ailerons, but uses differential tail movements, assisted by wing spoilers, for roll control. Because the F-14 was virtually spin-resistant under natural conditions, Grumman decided to use this to produce an aircraft with no angle-of-attack restrictions and one that would not depart from controlled flight. The leading edge of the F-14's wing consists of one full span slat, whilst the trailing edge is divided into three slotted flaps. The inboard trailing flap is used solely for landings and take-offs. The Tomcat has a number of unique features, none more so than the swing-wing. Also, designed to operate with the swing-wing, there are a pair of 'glove vanes' that come out of the fixed wing glove, situated inboard of the movable portion. As the wings sweep back, the vanes go forward at programmed speeds, to prevent the centre of the pressure of lift from moving aft, thus reducing drag. The wing automatically adjusts to the best variable sweep position at any point in the flight envelope by means of an on-board computer. Under combat conditions, the pilot selects the MSP (Mach sweep programmer) and the variable sweep wing is under constant automatic control. This feature enables the F-14 to take three different roles: Air Superiority, fleet air defence and air-to-ground attack.

With the AWG-9 weapon system installed, the Navy virtually has the perfect fighter. The AWG-9 is a Hughes development, and consists of a radar, a computer, cockpit displays and weapon interface. The radar can operate in both pulse and Doppler modes, giving the F-14 four times the range and approximately fifteen times the area coverage of the F4J Phantom which uses the Westinghouse AWG-10. The

AWG-9 radar can detect fighter targets at a range of over 100 miles, and the TCS (television camera system) has been added so that visual identification of targets can be made at long range. The AWG-9 also has the ability to monitor twenty-four targets, classifying them into priorities, whilst deciding which six to attack simultaneously. It even performs some navigation problems, if required; however there is one function unique to the F-14, called Data Link. This is a voiceless, two-way communication system that enables the air warfare commander on aircraft carrier to place an additional eight targets on the NFO's display.

The Tomcat's four main weapons are the AIM-54 Phoenix missile, the Sidewinder AIM-9N missile, the Sparrow III

A US Navy F-14 Tomcat from the Naval Air Test Centre, launching an AIM-54 Phoenix long-range, air-to-air missile.

Grumman American

In 1972, Grumman acquired the American Aviation Company, which manufactured light aircraft. This was the second time Grumman had been involved in light aircraft manufacture, the first being with the G-63 Kitten and G-72 Tadpole back in the 1940s.

American Aviation had produced four types of aircraft, prior to the take-over, the Bede BD-1, AA-1 Yankee, AA-1A and the AA-5. Grumman updated the AA-1A to the -1B, later updating it again to the -1C by converting it to a dual-purpose training and touring aircraft, aimed at the private and flying school markets. Both the -1B and -1C were later redesignated Tr-2 and T-Cat, and a de luxe version of the T-Cat was later produced, the Lynx. The AA-5 was updated by enlarging the tailplane, extending the rear cabin windows and enlarging the baggage compartment, and was redesigned the AA-5A. Later, a de luxe version was built and called the Cheetah. The AA-5A and the Cheetah were powered by an Avco Lycoming O-320-E2G engine, but with the installation of the more powerful Avco Lycoming O-360-A4K engine, the designation and name were changed to AA-5B and Tiger.

Grumman, at this time, was developing a four-seat, twin-engined model, powered by two Avco Lycoming 0-320-D1D engines. It was aimed at the flying school market, for multi-engined conversion courses. Later, in 1977, a de luxe version was built called the Cougar, which had full blind-flying instrumentation, dual controls and the latest navigation and communication avionics.

The journey into the light aircraft manufacturing world was short-lived, the Grumman American Corporation, as it was called, being purchased by American Jet Industries in 1978, who renamed it the Gulfstream American Corporation.

Grumman American Aircraft technical details

AA-1/T-Cat/Lynx

Type	Two-seat tourer and trainer.
Engine	One Avco Lycoming 0-235-C2C flat-four piston engine.
Dimensions	Wing span 24 ft. 5 in., wing area 98.11 sq. ft., length 19 ft. 2¾ in., height 6 ft. 5¾ in.
Performance	Max. speed 144 mph, crusing speed 135 mph, service ceiling 11,200 ft., range 512 miles.
Weight	Empty 940 lb., loaded 1,500 lb.

AA-5A/Cheetah and AA-5B/Tiger

Type	Four-seat monoplane.
Engine	One Avco Lycoming 0-320-E2G flat-four piston engine.
Dimensions	Wing span 31 ft. 6 in., wing area 139.70 sq. ft., length 22 ft., height 7 ft. 6 in.
Performance	Max. speed 157 mph, cruising speed 136 mph, service ceiling 12,560 ft., range 647 miles.
Weight	Empty 1,303 lb., loaded 2,200 lb.

GA-7/Cougar

Type	Four-seat monoplane.
Engine	Two Avco Lycoming 0-320-D1D flat-four piston engines
Dimensions	Wing span 36 ft. 10¼ in., wing area 184 sq. ft., length 29 ft. 10 in., height 10 ft. 4¼ in.
Performance	Max. speed 193 mph, cruising speed 131 mph, service ceiling 18,300 ft., range 1,336 miles.
Weight	Empty 2,515 lb., loaded 3,800 lb.

The X-29

When the X-29 was first rolled out from its hangar at Calverton, the first impression it gave was that it was coming out backwards. This was because the FSW (forward-swept wing) was mounted far back along the fuselage, and the horizontal stabilizers, or canards as they are known, were mounted on the fuselage in front of them, just aft of the cockpit. To all intents and purposes, it appeared as if someone had reversed the wings and tail.

Unique as it may have appeared, the forward-swept wing had its origins back in the 1940s: the Junkers Ju-287 used a similar idea to enable its bomb bay to be enlarged to carry an extra-large bomb. This was achieved by moving the forward-swept wings' wing roots further aft than conventional wing roots. It also gave an added bonus, as far as bomb release was concerned, because it minimized considerably the trim change that was normally necessary. The Ju-287's forward-swept wing was not conducive to high-speed flight, however, as the wings had a tendency to twist and, ultimately, to come away from the fuselage. The aircraft made a total of seventeen flights before it was seized by the allies.

After the war, the HFB-320 Hansa business jet reintroduced the forward-sweeping wing, with the same fifteen-degree forward sweep as the Ju-287's. The main idea at the time, was to overcome the problem of wing-tip stall, although the problem seemed to transfer itself to the wing roots, but this was considered less dangerous. The problem of wing twist did

not occur on the HFB-320, as it was not a high-performance aircraft.

In 1976, Grumman, General Dynamics and Rockwell International held a series of wind tunnel tests and feasibility studies, spread over a four-year period. At the end, in September 1981, Grumman were selected to design and build the aircraft. Designated the X-29, it was the first X-series experimental aircraft for over a decade.

The X-29 is a hybrid: the forward section of the fuselage, including the cockpit, being that of a Northrop F-5A; the landing gear of an F-16, as is the flight control actuator and the accessory gearbox. The only new part is the fuselage, aft of the cockpit, and the wings. The flight control system is of the 'fly-by-wire' type and consists of a three-channel digital system with analogue computer back-up. This makes the system triple redundant, miminizing the failure risk during flight. The unconventional flight controls operate three control surfaces: the all-moving, close-coupled canards, the wing trailing edges, and flaps, fitted to the rear of the strakes, that extend along the edge of the fuselage, alongside the engine exhaust.

Close-coupled canards, in front of a forward-facing wing, channel the air flow over the inside the wing surface, which in

Above: The first Grumman/DARPA revolutionary FSW (Forward Sweeping Wings) X-29A on a test flight.

171

Above left: The X-29 lifts off on its first test flight.

Below left: The nose section of the X-29 (F-1S) at Calverton prior to assembly of the aircraft.

carried out at Grumman's Calverton Facility, on 14 December 1984, then, on 12 March 1985, the aircraft were taken to NASA's Ames Dryden Flight Research Facility, at Edwards Air Force Base, California, with NASA having overall responsibility for the tests.

There are no plans at present to use the X-29 for any other purpose than that of a demonstrator for the advanced technology features already incorporated in the design. There was a suggestion that the X-29 could be used by the USAF as an advanced tactical fighter, and this could be a possibility. The weight of a typical fighter aircraft, armed to carry out a USAF mission, would be approximately 42,000 pounds, but a fighter similar to the X-29 would weigh 30,000 pounds only.

There are already a number of features on the drawing boards that will be installed in the X-29 for testing. Among them is a two-dimensional engine nozzle called ADEN (asymetric deflecting exhaust nozzle), that will be able not only to deflect the thrust up and down, but also reverse the thrust for braking. This would give the aircraft a STOL capability. Grumman has three programme objectives; the first, to prove that the forward-swept wing is a viable prospect; the second is to show that the aircraft is airworthy and capable of flying an extended flight envelope; and the third to channel all the results of the tests back to the government and industry for future benefit. When all the tests are completed, it is hoped that the end result will be a light, cost-effective fighter that will have a greatly enhanced manoeuvrability, much lower stall speeds and very much improved low-speed handling. The overall cost is bound to exceed $100 million, but future generations of aircraft will prove that the money was well spent.

X-29 technical details

Type	Experimental, single-seat fighter.
Engine	General Electric F404-GE-400 turbofan
Dimensions	Wing span 27 ft., length 48 ft., height 14 ft. Max. fuel capacity 4,000 lb. Weight empty 13,600 lb. Weight gross 17,600 lb.
Performance	Data not available at present.

Grumman into Space

Some 2,400 Grumman engineers were assigned to the Lunar Module Project and its landing on the moon was the ultimate triumph for the Grumman engineers, and was equalled only by the safe return home of the Apollo 17 crew, in December 1972, which meant that the success rate of the Lunar Module Project had been one hundred per cent.

The relationship between Grumman and NASA had begun back in the 1950s, when Grumman had formalized a Space Steering Group, headed by preliminary design engineer Al Munier. The group made a bid for the NASA contract to build the Mercury capsule, and won. The development contract, however, was awarded to McDonnell Douglas, because the US Navy thought that Grumman had too heavy a commitment to its naval aircraft development at the time, to undertake development of the Mercury spacecraft. These doubts were probably unfounded, because it is unlikely that Grumman would have made a bid for the contract if they had been unable fulfill it.

In 1960, against extremely stiff opposition, Grumman was awarded a contract to build and test four orbiting astronomical observatories (OAOs), and it was this contract that was to put Grumman in the forefront of space engineering technology. It has to be remembered, that when a vehicle operates outside the earth's atmosphere, the laws of aerodynamics no longer apply, so a completely new set of rules had to be written, and it was only the brave and far-sighted that could afford to venture into this world and hope to survive. The OAO contract was won competing against some of the top companies in the aerospace field, and represented the largest, most expensive and advanced of the unmanned satellite projects of the 1960s. When solving its problems, Grumman's aerospace engineers made dramatic inroads into many branches of space technology, and the experience gained on OAO was to prove invaluable in later years when they were developing the lunar exursion module.

But what was the orbiting astronomical observatory? It was a telescope that orbited 500 miles above the earth at an inclination of 32 degrees from the equator, and was used to observe binary stars, comets, planets, ovae and supernovaen. The satellite was an octagonal-shaped structure, eighty inches in diameter, ten feet in length, and had a gross weight of 3,900 pounds. A hollow tube ran the length of the OAO, holding the experimental equipment. The tube could also carry telescopic mirrors up to thirty six inches in diameter. Later on similar missions later, the satellite was to carry X-ray, gamma-ray and optical telescopes. A solar cell measuring 111 square feet and generating one thousand watts, supplied electric power to the systems on board.

The man who led the OAO project was Walter Scott, a preliminary design engineer. He reported to Joe Gavin, who was later to head the Lunar Module Project and eventually become Chairman of the Board and President of Grumman Aerospace.

Goddard Space Flight Centre, under whose aegis the project was controlled, requested that the spacecraft have an operational of one year. This proved to be difficult, because what was required was a telescope with the ability to point at a certain star and hold the position for a given length of time. To enable the OAO to hold or move from a position it required a method of propulsion. A system of gas jets seemed the most appropriate, but if the spacecraft was to be moved or adjusted any number of times, the gas would soon run out. So after many experiments, it was decided to use a combination of dry gas jets and two inertia wheels; one for coarse adjustment and one for fine. The fine adjustment was so fine, in fact, that it took thousands of turns of the inertia wheel to manoeuvre the spacecraft through a very small angle. The third form of propulsion devised by the Grumman engineers was a scientific breakthrough in the propulsion field.

Basically the Earth's magnetic field was used to produce a torque on the spacecraft. Using magnetometers to sense the direction of the Earth's magnetic field, by placing three electro-magnets at the correct angle with the aid of a small computer, it was possible, by activating the right magnet, to make the spacecraft move in any direction required. The use of the magnetometer was the result work carried out in the field of anti-submarine detection, another of Grumman's interests.

When anybody or anything has to work or operate in space, there are two major problems – extremes of both cold and heat. With satellites and manned orbital spacecraft, it is possible to alleviate these by slowly rotating the spacecraft so that one side is never permanently exposed to either extreme. However, because the telescope had to remain in a constant position, ways of dispersing the heat and preventing the reverse side of the OAO from freezing had to be devised. Once again, the knowledge gained on this thermal control project was to be invaluable later in the manufacture of the lunar module.

In all, four OAOs were launched, but only two were successful. The first failed after three days in orbit, because of an electric arcing problem in the power supply. This created problems with the recharging of batteries from the solar cells, resulting in malfunctions in the telemetry and command systems. Although the mission was a failure, the information it managed to send back showed that the investigation of distant stars and planets from space was indeed feasible. The experience gained also led to improvements in subsequent OAOs.

The OAO was controlled by three ground stations in North and South America. Since the spacecraft was out of reach of the controlling stations for long periods of time, its onboard computers had impressive storage capabilities, and cut in when communications were lost, but reverted back to ground-to-satellite communications when back within range. Of the OAO's four transmission systems one had the ability to send back pictures in analog form.

The second OAO was launched on 7 December 1968, and was an unqualified success. For more than four years and some 22,000 orbits of the earth, the spacecraft's eleven telescopes of the spacecraft examined the stars and were fortunate enough to be able to observe a supernova (an exploding star some million times brighter than our sun) in a galaxy over twenty million light years away. The mission wasn't without its incidents, however. On a number of occasions, ground control lost contact with the spacecraft and had to regain control by reprogramming the onboard computers. It took a team of over twenty technicians, maintaining a twenty-four hour watch from three ground stations, to keep the spacecraft operational. So efficient was the OAO that it transmitted more information back to earth than the scientists could cope with. The spacecraft was finally switched off on economic grounds.

The third OAO had a booster rocket problem and never left the earth's atmosphere; it burned up somewhere over Africa. The last of the OAO spacecraft, the OAO-3, named Copernicus, was launched by an Atlas Centaur rocket from Cape Canaveral on 21 August 1972. On board was an 80 cm ultra-violet telescope with a mirror made from thin silica ribs. During its eight-year operational life, the OAO also studied the black hole in Scorpius, and it showed that a giant star was losing matter to its invisible companion. One of the most important projects carried out by Copernicus was to measure the deterioration of the earth's ozone layer. Scientists carried out the measurements by studying a bright star – first from outside the earth's atmosphere, when the star was high in the sky, then through the earth's atmosphere as the star sank below the horizon. The measurements are still being carried out and the results, say the scientists, are not encouraging.

There were three X-ray telescopes on board Copernicus, whose task was to search and map X-ray sources from distant stars. Amongst the information sent back were details of the nuclei of comets, and this was to prove useful for the visit of Halley's Comet in 1985/6. Copernicus was shut down on economic grounds, but operated considerably beyond its planned one-year designed operational life.

While the OAO spacecraft were being built, tested and launched, Grumman received another contract from NASA: to design and manufacture nine canisters and adaptors for the Echo series of high-altitude balloons. These were two giant plastic balloons, each of 135 feet in diameter, that were to be used as reflector communication satellites, enabling broadcasts to be beamed across continents. The project was to provide a canister for the Echo balloon that would be attached to the nose of the launch rocket and which, when at the correct altitude, would be fired into orbit. The magnesium canister was ellipsoid in shape and made in two sections. The adaptor was fixed to the nose of the rocket followed by the canister. At a given altitude, explosive bolts were fired and the canister separated from the adaptor. When the canister reached its pre-arranged height, another set of explosive bolts fired and separated the two halves. This released the balloon inside, which then inflated, allowing it to go into orbit. Launched in 1964, Echo was a resounding success, everything working first time and going to plan.

Grumman then decided to leave the field of orbital spacecraft, to concentrate on a development study of a lunar exploration system. This was to be carried out by a new group called the Advanced Space Systems Department. This led to Grumman's involvement with the Apollo Space Programme, and began with bids for the Command and Service Modules. They had entered the competition for the contract as a subcontractor to General Electric, but were unsuccessful – North American being the winner.

NASA scientists and engineers were, at this point, confident that they could send men to the moon and back, but what they did not know was how to land them on the surface and bring them back. Three options were under consideration:

1. A large rocket would take the astronauts to orbit round the moon, then part of the rocket would separate and land. After exploration and with part of the propulsion system still intact, they would take off and return to Earth.

2. After launch, the rocket would go into orbit around the earth and rendezvous with other previously-launched spacecraft. After all the sections had been assembled, a smaller rocket would then be boosted to the moon.

3. The three sections of the spacecraft, the Command Module, the Service Module and the Lunar Module would be put into a lunar orbit, when the Lunar Module would separate from the other two and descend to the moon's surface. After leaving the moon, the Lunar Module would rendezvous with the other two in lunar orbit, the astronauts would then transfer to the Command Module, then discard the Lunar Module and return to earth.

The last option, which came to be known as the lunar orbit rendezvous (LOR) plan, was accepted, although with a few alterations.

In 1962, NASA invited contractors to carry out feasibility studies of the LOR. Grumman bid for the contract, and once more they were beaten, this time by Ling-Temco-Vought. NASA asked Grumman to continue its own independent study of the project, however, and in April 1962 Grumman joined forces with RCA and presented a Lunar Excursion Module study to NASA. RCA's sole interest in the LEM was the electronics and communications they left the rest to Grumman. This time Grumman decided to bid for the

contract as a prime contractor not, as in the past, as a subcontractor.

In August 1962, after a great deal of discussion, NASA decided in August 1962, to invite tenders for proposals for a Lunar Excursion Module. It was certain that NASA was looking for an LOR proposal, which was the one favoured by Grumman. Later that year, Grumman put forward its proposals, including its reasons for supporting the LOR proposal. One month later, Grumman chairman and President, Clint Towl, headed a team of engineers who had been invited to NASA in Houston, Texas, to present fully the company's proposals. The presentation lasted for four hours and when it finished Grumman was committed to possibly one of the most bizarre ideas of the century, to make a machine that would take a man to the surface of the moon and bring him back. Grumman's bid for the Lunar Excursion Module was $386 million. In 1969, Neil Armstrong and Buzz Aldrin stepped on the surface of the moon – Grumman had helped towards making that possible.

The man behind the development of the Lunar Module (the word 'Excursion' was dropped – it was thought flippant), was a former scholar and Grumman employee by the name of Tom Kelly. Kelly was born on Long Island and went to Cornell University to study engineering; during the summer vacations he worked at the Bethpage plant. After graduating, in 1951, he returned to Grumman as a full-time engineer. In 1956, Kelly was conscripted into the US Air Force for two years and, on leaving, spent one year at Lockheed before returning to Grumman. His return coincided with the first space discussions and Kelly was assigned, with another engineer, to explore all the possibilities of Grumman's involvement.

The first Lunar Module was an engineering mock-up called the M-1, and it was built in 1964. It gave NASA a general idea of what the spacecraft would finally look like. Grumman had their own Lunar Module Test Article (LTA-1) which they used for testing electrical and electronic systems. On 17 September 1967, Grumman delivered a thermal vacuum test article called the LTA-8 to the NASA Manned Spacecraft Centre, Houston. It was to complete a series of tests in the Space Simulation Laboratory, undergoing temperature and vacuum extremes, simulating a typical moon environment.

But what did this spacecraft, looking more like a giant spider from another planet, consist of? It was a two-stage spacecraft having both a descent stage and ascent stage. It was constructed from over one million parts, and was the only manned spacecraft ever designed to operate purely in space, in fact it was the only real manned spacecraft ever designed. The lower stage, or descent stage, was the unmanned section, and contained the landing gear, a descent engine which had a throttle and four compartments that carried all the lunar experiments. The upper section, or ascent stage, was the manned portion, and contained a pressurized crew compartment, equipment stowage areas and an ascent rocket engine. The crew area was equipped with all the systems necessary to support the lives of two astronauts. Separation from the Command and Service Module (CSM) was controlled from the Lunar Module, as was the lunar landing, lunar launch, and rendezvous and docking with the CSM. Only the cabin area of the Lunar Module was pressurized, although the inter-connecting tunnel between the CSM and the Lunar Module could be pressurized for of crew transfer. The ascent stage also contained the aft equipment bay, tank sections, engine supports, windows and hatches. The temperature and air pressure for the crew compartment and mid-section was controlled by the Environmental Control Subsystem (ECS). Directly behind the cabin was a smaller compartment called the mid-section. This housed the ascent engine assembly, lunar sample containers, communications and life support umbilicals. It also contained the waste management system, oxygen purge system, food stowage, lunar boots and components of the Electrical Power Subsystem (EPS) and Guidance

Navigation and Control Subsystems (GN and CS). The ascent engine was aligned with the centre of gravity in the mid-section, which also housed the docking hatch.

An unpressurized area containing the Electrical Replacement Assemblies (ERAs) was situated aft of the mid-section pressure-tight bulkhead. It also housed two oxygen tanks for the ECS (these were the tanks that provided oxygen for breathing), two helium tanks for the ascent stage propellant,

and pressurization and batteries for the electrical power subsystem (EPS). The aluminium alloy structural skin of the Lunar Module was surrounded by a complete layer of insulation, and a thin aluminium skin provided thermal and micrometeoroid protection for the astronauts and their

The Lunar Excursion Module under construction, showing the insulation being installed.

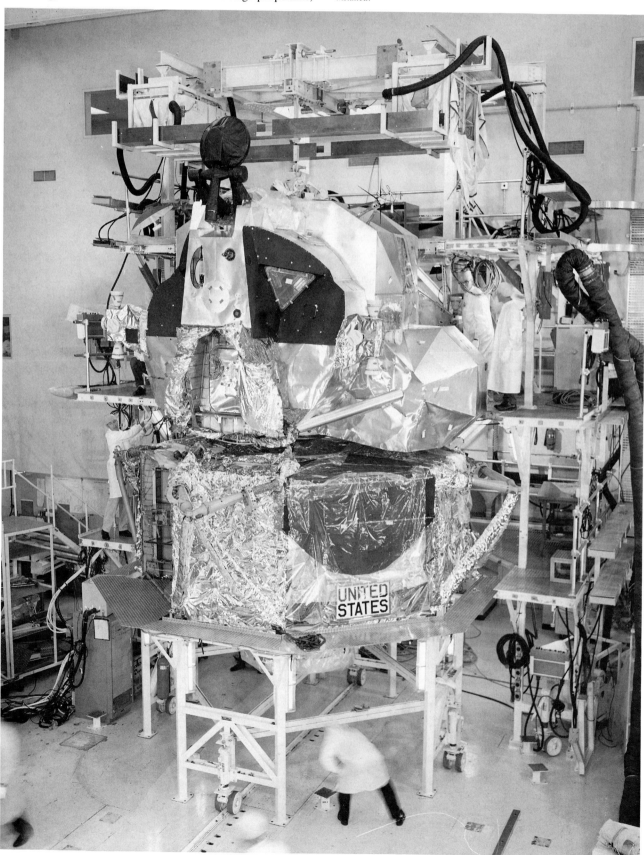

equipment. There was a gap of approximately three inches between the inner and outer skins.

The cabin was basically ninety-two inches in diameter and was stiffened by two-inch circular frames, ten inches apart and fixed between the structural skin and the outer shield. There were two triangular-shaped windows either side of the display and instrument console, which allowed the astronauts forward and downward vision. Above the left-hand window, in the top part of the bulkhead, was the docking window. To aid in the docking with the CSM, a sighting reticule was built into the glass, which enabled the commander, by leaning slightly backwards, to dock the two spacecraft. All three windows in the Lunar Module had approximately two square feet of viewing area and were made up of two separate pieces of glass. The outer pane provided radiation and thermal protection and was made of Vycor glass, whilst the inner pane was made of a strong Chemcor glass.

The descent stage was the unmanned portion of the Lunar Module, and, in addition to the descent engine, contained the tanks for the water and oxygen used by the ECS. Six spare batteries for the Portable Life Support Systems (PLSS) and four batteries for the EPC were also kept in the lower stage. The lower stage was constructed of aluminium alloy (as was the ascent stage), although some chem-milling had been done to reduce weight. Dr Sidney Schwartz of Grumman's Advance Development Systems Analysis, put forward the idea of making some internal parts of the Lunar Module edible. As bizarre as this may appear, it did have some merit. The idea was that, in the event of the Lunar Module having to make an unscheduled extended stay on the moon's surface – due to a malfunction or some other problem – food would be available. Parts, such as handles, knobs, clipboards, panels, and even partitioning, when soaked in water for between eight and ten hours, produced a banana-flavoured breakfast cereal type of food. The edible material consisted of powdered milk, corn starch, wheat flour, hominy grits (a cereal-like cream of wheat) and banana flakes, all of which were baked in a press at 300 degrees F, under 3,000 pounds of pressure. ESM (edible structural material), as it was called when in its preformed shape, was harder than Masonite, capable of being machined or drilled, and had only 300 calories per gram.

Although the idea was considered, it never got beyond the discussion stage, basically because it was not practical, but it gave a whole new meaning to the expression 'eating oneself out of house and home'.

One of the major problems that designers and engineers faced was the dissipation of heat from the side of the spacecraft which faced the sun. Even though the spacecraft was rotated regularly, there was still a problem. It was solved by circulating a water-glycol solution through the channels built into the side panels of the spacecraft. The Heat Transport Section (HTS), as it was known, consisted of two cooling circuits, one primary and one secondary. The secondary was purely a back-up in the event of the primary malfunctioning. The waste heat collected during the flight was vented through valves overboard, whilst HTS coolant pumps circulated the coolant liquid.

After the two spacecraft had arrived in orbit around the moon, the transfer from the CSM to the Lunar Module was carried out by using the docking tunnel, situated at the top centreline of the ascent stage. The lower portion of the forward cabin section housed the ingress/egress hatch, which was used for leaving and entering the Module whilst it was on the moon's surface. It was also used for EVA transfer for crew and equipment whilst on the moon. The pressurized, plug-type hatches in each tunnel were manually controlled and were sealed with a pre-loaded silicone seal. The tunnels were a very snug fit for the astronauts when they were using them whilst wearing their space suits. Buzz Aldrin had to be pulled through the tunnel by Neil Armstrong, prior to placing his foot on the moon's surface.

The Lunar Module's landing gear was of a cantilever design and consisted of four sets of legs connected to outriggers that extended from the ends of the descent stages structural beams. Each leg consisted of a primary strut and footpad, a drive-out mechanism, two secondary struts and two lock-down mechanisms. The primary struts absorbed the compression loads, whilst the secondary struts absorbed both compression and tension loads. The boarding ladder was fixed to a primary strut on the forward landing gear.

On launch, the landing gear was stowed in a retracted position, and remained that way until the spacecraft reached lunar orbit. Prior to descending to the moon's surface, explosive bolts released the landing gear, and springs in the drive-out mechanism extended the legs. Once extended, the landing gear was locked mechanically into place.

The first Lunar Module Test Article (LTA-1OR), was carried aboard the unmanned Apollo 4 flight on 9 November 1967. It carried instruments that would measure the vibration, accoustic and structural integrity of the spacecraft during the first twelve minutes of launch. On launch, the Lunar Module was in a folded configuration within the spacecraft's Lunar Module Adaptor (LMA), situated between the Command and Service Module and the S-V1B booster. To keep the Lunar Module rigid inside the adaptor during launch, the outriggers were attached to the LMA at their apex. Just prior to removal, explosive bolts were fired and the upper segment of the LMA divided into four parts. The segments, which were hinged to the lower section, folded back allowing the Lunar Module to be withdrawn from the CSM.

Apollo 5, Lunar Module 1

At 5.48 pm on 22 January 1968, a Saturn IB rocket blasted off from Launch Complex 37B at the Kennedy Space Centre. Apollo 5's mission was to verify the operation of the Lunar Module structure itself and its two primary populsion systems. It was also to evaluate the Lunar Module staging and the orbital performance of the S-1VB stage and instrument unit. Soon after achieving orbit, the nose cone, which replaced the CSM, was jettisoned and the Lunar Module separated. The first firing of the descent engine went virtually as planned, except that the Lunar Module's guidance system shut down after only four seconds of operation. This was because the engine's velocity did not build up as quickly as predicted. Houston pinpointed the problem in the guidance system itself and not in the hardware design. This enabled the engineers and scientists at Mission Control to pursue an alternative mission which achieved the same objective. After the mission had been completed at 2.45 am the following day, the Lunar Module stages were left in a decaying orbit to burn up on re-entry at a later date. A second unmanned flight was scheduled, but due to the success of the first, Lunar Module 2 was cancelled. The LM-2 now stands in the National Air and Space Museum in Washington DC.

Apollo 6, LTA 2R

This provided flight test data on the Saturn V launch load, and on the thermal integrity and compatability of the launch vehicle and spacecraft.

Apollo 7

This was a manned space flight, with no Lunar Module.

Apollo 8, LTA-B

Lunar Test Article B was placed aboard Apollo 8, and was designed to simulate the weight and mass of a Lunar Module. It consisted of two concentric rings, arranged to form a cylinder, with four internal water ballast tanks.

Apollo 9, Lunar Module 3 (Spider)

Apollo 9 was launched by a Saturn V launch vehicle on 3 March 1969. After establishing an earth orbit, the CSM separated from the S-IVB, and was transposed and docked

thoughts, the full realization of what had happened struck home. There they were, the three of them, in a broken-down spacecraft, two hundred thousand miles from home. Coupled with this, was the fact that they were going to have to swing around the moon before they could start to head home. As the spacecraft swung around the moon and headed back to earth, the crew knew that there was one more crucial barrier left and that was a mid-course correction. As there was a great deal of debris surrounding the spacecraft, the alignment had to be made using the sun as a reference, not a star as was normally used. The alignment made and the mid-course correction completed, the strange combination of a dead Service Module, a Command Module with no power and a Lunar Module, headed for home. Four hours before re-entry, the crew entered the Command Module, and by powering from the Lunar Module, achieved separation from the Service Module. It was only then that they were able to see the extent of the damage that had been caused by the explosion. Three hours later, they parted company, with their faithful Lunar Module, Aquarius, somewhat sadly, and returned to earth. It was over, perhaps the greatest rescue mission of all time. The reason why the Lunar Module had towed the Service Module for three hundred thousand miles, was to protect the ablative heat-shield on the Command Module from the extreme cold of space. Without the heat-shield, the Command Module would not have survived the extremely high temperatures of re-entry. Later, Grumman jokingly sent North American/Rockwell, a bill for more than $400,000, for towing the Command and Service Modules for 300,000 miles.

Apollo 14, Lunar Module 8 (Antares)
After the Apollo 13 experience, the preparations for Apollo 14 were carried out with even more thoroughness, if that was at all possible. At 4.03 pm on 31 January 1971, astronauts Alan Shepard, Stuart Roosa and Edgar Mitchell blasted off the pad at the Kennedy Space Centre. Earth orbit and the trans-lunar injection were carried out with no problems, but the transposition of the CSM and the Lunar Module, took six attempts. An inspection of the docking mechanism was carried out, but nothing untoward was discovered, and it was decided, that as there was no indication that the docking mechanism would not work again, to forget it. The spacecraft entered lunar orbit on 4 February and descended to the moon's surface the following day. As Alan Shepard stepped on to the moon's surface, it seemed fitting that the first American in space should be one of those to walk on the moon. Shepard and Mitchell completed two EVAs, including the first use of the Mobile Equipment Transporters (MET). On the second EVA, just before entering the Lunar Module for the last time, Shepard dropped a golf ball on to the surface, and with a makeshift club, drove it some 350 metres, probably setting a new course record at the most exclusive golf club in the universe.

After transferring all their equipment to the Lunar Module, the spacecraft took off to rendezvous with the CSM. Docking and transferring completed, the Lunar Module was again dispatched to the moon's surface, for the benefit of the seismologists. The spacecraft was placed on an earth trajectory, after its thirty-fourth orbit of the moon, and more experiments were carried out on the way back to earth.

Apollo 15, Lunar Module 10 (Falcon)
Apollo 15 was the first spacecraft to carry the Lunar Roving Vehicle (LVR), which was carried in the lower descent stage of the Lunar Module. Launched on 28 July 1971, with astronauts Dave Scott, Alfred Worden and Jim Irwin aboard, the spacecraft made its earth orbit and its trans-lunar insertion without incident. On 30 July, with Scott and Irwin aboard, the Lunar Module separated from the CSM and headed for the moon's surface. After landing in the Hadley Apennine region, Scott carried out a thirty-three-minute

EVA from the upper hatch of the Lunar Module. He described and photographed in great detail the landing site and the surrounding area.

The actual exploration of the Hadley Apennine region began on the morning of 31 July. The Lunar Rover was unfolded from the side of the Lunar Module and prepared for operation. The first EVA lasted for six hours and thirty-three minutes, during which a number of experiments were carried out and a large amount of lunar rock collected. The Lunar Rover was one of the greatest assets the astronauts had for exploration. It had enough battery-power to take the two astronauts fifty-five miles, at a maximum speed of seven miles per hour, but the distance travelled on the first EVA was only twenty-two miles.

The third EVA lasted seven hours and twelve minutes, in which Scott and Irwin collected core samples and started to stow away some of their gear in the Lunar Module. Their last EVA lasted only four hours and fifty minutes, and was to check that all the experiments that had been left behind were still working. Just prior to leaving the surface, Scott and Irwin placed a tiny aluminium sculpture, called the 'Fallen Astronaut', in a small crater. With it, they placed a plaque that listed the names of the fourteen astronauts and cosmonauts who had died. NASA had approved the memorial on the understanding that there was to be no commercial exploitation. Al Worden had supplied the statue, whilst Jim Irwin had ensured that all the Russian names had been correctly spelt.

The lift-off from the moon's surface was the first to be televised. The camera was mounted on the Lunar Rover, and television audiences all over the world saw the upper stage separate from the lower, in a shower of sparks and debris. Two hours after leaving the surface, the Lunar Module rendezvoused with the CSM. Just prior to sending the Lunar Module crashing back on to the moon's surface, the crew launched a small satellite that would measure interplanetary and earth magnetic fields near the moon.

Just after their trans-earth insertion, Al Worden undertook a thirty-eight minute EVA and became the first man to make a deep-space walk. On 7 August Apollo 15 entered the earth's atmosphere and descended. The only thing to mar a near perfect flight was that one of the main parachutes failed to deploy, giving the spacecraft a rather hard, but nevertheless safe, landing.

Apollo 16, Lunar Module 11 (Orion)
The penultimate Apollo mission to the moon was launched on 16 April 1972. On board, the three astronauts, John Young (who had previously orbited the moon in Apollo 10), Thomas K. Mattingly and Charles Duke, placed their spacecraft into an earth orbit. After checking that all the systems were functioning properly, they carried out the Lunar Module transposition with the CSM. During the transposition a number of minor anomalies were noticed. One of them, on the S-IVB stage, caused unpredicted engine thrust to occur when it separated from the CSM, preventing a final targeting of the stage. During the flight to the moon, unexplained light-coloured particles from the Lunar Module were noticed floating about, and it was discovered later that some of thermal paint was peeling off.

After going into lunar orbit, the two spacecraft separated, and the Lunar Module descended to the moon's surface. The first EVA was carried out on 21 April, but television coverage of the surface activity was delayed due to the sterrabie antenna on the Lunar Rover becoming inoperable. After fixing the antenna on the Lunar Rover, the vehicle was made ready for exploration. The EVA lasted for seven hours and eleven minutes, although the distance travelled by the astronauts in the Lunar Rover was only four kilometres. The second EVA, which began at 11.35 am on the following day, was to explore an area some five kilometres away at a place called Stone Mountain. The exploration lasted seven hours and twenty three minutes, and covered a distance of eleven kilometres. At 8.03 pm the same evening, after all the samples of lunar rock had been stored aboard the Lunar Module, the two astronauts climbed aboard and prepared for lift-off. The television camera aboard the Lunar Rover was activated, and millions of viewers back on earth watched as Apollo 16 blasted from the moon's surface. After rendez-vousing with the CSM and transferring all the equipment and samples, the Lunar Module was prepared for jettisoning the next day. A problem arose whilst the Lunar Module was being jettisoned: attitude control was lost, causing a malfunction in the de-orbit manoeuvre, which in turn caused the Lunar Module to be placed in a decaying orbit instead of crashing back on to the moon's surface. A particle and magnetic fields satellite was launched from the CSM, but this too had a problem and went into the wrong orbit, resulting in a much shorter operational life. The spacecraft headed back to earth, during which time Mattingly carried out a one hour and twenty four minute space-walk to retrieve some film cassettes. On 27 April, the spacecraft splashed down safely in the Pacific Ocean.

Apollo 17, Lunar Module 12 (Challenger)

The final manned Apollo lunar explorer, Apollo 17, was launched on 7 December 1972. The crew, Eugene Cernan, Ronald Evans and Harrison Schmitt, had to spend an additional three hours in the CSM, because of a countdown sequence failure. This was the only hardware failure during the entire Apollo programme to cause a launch delay. Earth orbit was achieved, and the insertion into a lunar trajectory carried out without problem. The transposition of the CSM with the Lunar Module was completed during the trans-lunar part of the flight, and again was incident free. A number of scientific experiments were carried out during the flight to the moon on all the Apollo missions, and Apollo 17 was no exception. Apollo 17 entered lunar orbit on 11 December, and after completing the separation of the Lunar Module from the CSM, Cernan and Schmitt made a powered descent to the surface. The first EVA began four hours later, and after off-loading the Lunar Rover and experimental packages, the two astronauts decided to go ahead with some of their tasks, rather than wait until the following day.

The area in which the Lunar Module had landed was known as *Taurus-Littrow*, and was near the coast of the great frozen sea of basalt, the *Mare Serenitatis*. The unique visual beauty of this valley was the epitome of an ethereal vision. Of all the landing sites chosen, it would have been hard to find one that ended the exploration of the moon in such a memorable way. The second EVA lasted seven hours and thirty-seven minutes, and it was during this period that the now-famous orange soil was discovered. It was to be the subject of geological discussion for many years to come.

The third and final EVA was on 13 December, during which a great variety of geological samples were taken. Just prior to entering the Lunar Module for the last time, a plaque was unveiled on the landing gear. It said, quite simply:

> Here man completed his first
> exploration of the Moon
> December 1972 A.D.
> May the spirit of peace in which we came
> be reflected in the lives of all mankind.

It was signed by the crew of Apollo 17 and by the then President of the United States of America, Richard Nixon.

The Lunar Module, Challenger lifted off the moon at 5.55 pm on 14 December, and joined Ronald Evans in the orbiting CSM. After docking and transferring the equipment and samples, the Lunar Module was sent crashing back on to the moon's surface. The CSM then set course for earth, where on 19 December the spacecraft splashed down safely in the Pacific Ocean.

With the end of the Apollo space programme, Grumman's

President, Lew Evans, directed that Grumman concentrate its efforts on the development of a Space Shuttle-type vehicle. In 1972 President Nixon had announced that the United States were going to build a Space Shuttle Transportation System, a combination of spacecraft and aircraft, capable of operating in an earth orbit. The launch costs would be drastically reduced from those of the Apollo programme. The Shuttle would fit the needs of many types of missions, and would reduce the cost of payloads, through the elimination of current size, weight and the reliability constraints of the one-shot launches. It would not only be able to deliver civilian and military satellites into space, but would also provide the means by which they could be maintained, or even returned to earth for repair. In addition to normal astronaut crews, it would also carry non-astronaut passengers, interested in conducting scientific and other investigations. Moreover, it could be used as a rescue vehicle in the event of an accident in space involving another manned spacecraft.

Back in the 1950s, atmosphere glide tests at hypersonic speeds were carried out by reliable, non-ablative, lifting bodies. Lifting-bodies, or to give them their correct name, lifting-body research vehicles, were the brainchild of Dr Alfred J. Eggers Jnr. The whole idea of the aircraft/spacecraft concept was that the craft could attain aerodynamic stability and lift, without the use of wings, from a specially-shaped body. The craft would also be capable of landing on a runway at normal landing speeds. The results from these experimental craft confirmed the feasibility of controlling lifting-bodies during critical landing phases. The idea of a Space Shuttle grew from these tests, together with the mounting pressure to reduce the cost of placing payloads into earth orbit by means of disposable rockets.

The M2-F2 lifting-body research vehicle.

In 1969, even before Neil Armstrong had set foot on the moon, NASA had invited bids from aerospace companies for a Phase A study of a low-cost, manned spacecraft, called Integral Launch and Re-entry Vehicle (ILRV). There were four proposals from various aircraft companies, all of which were partially discarded. The best ideas taken from each were incorporated into a proposal for a fully reusable, two-stage, vertical take-off and horizontal landing system, carrying payloads in the area of 50,000 pounds and with a gross lift-off weight of 3.5 million pounds.

Grumman had not involved itself in the Phase A study, but concentrated on a variety of studies that it was already conducting, and submitted a proposal for the Phase B. The Phase B proposal was for a detailed design definition study, based on the results of Phase A. Eastern Airlines, the Northrop Corporation, General Electric and a number of smaller companies also submitted proposals.

In February 1970, Grumman submitted two proposals to NASA, 518 and 532. Design 518 had a fully reusable, two-stage configuration, with a gross lift-off weight of 3.5 million pounds. The Orbiter was of a lifting-body design, coupled to a delta-winged booster. Grumman were warned at this stage that the Office of Management and Budget, because of funding problems, could jeopardize full development of this design, so Grumman proposed a second, the 532. This design was smaller and simpler. It had a modified S-IC booster, enabling the spacecraft to have an early flight. It also meant that the concept grew step-by-step in technical capability, and most important, the cost could be controlled.

NASA, for reasons of their own, decided to award the initial $8 million study contract to the North American and McDonnell-Douglas consortium, but gave Grumman a $4 million study contract to look into the lower-cost options in the fully-reusable system. Boeing had also been unsuccessful in their bid for part of the initial contract, so joined Grumman in an alternative study. Whilst Grumman concentrated on the Orbiter, Boeing became involved in the Booster vehicle. Between them, they developed three different concepts:

Stage-and-one-half

This was a spacecraft with an on-board, cryogenic propulsion system, and drop tanks, containing supplementary propellants. Various thrust augmentation designs, such as strap-on solid rocket motors and cryogenic or hypergolic strap-on propulsion units, were also considered.

Reusable Orbiter and expendable first stage

This design consisted of a single reusable Orbiter to be used on an interim basis, with the S-IC or other expendable boosters.

Reusable Orbiter and Booster

This design included a fully reusable, two-stage vehicle, as well as a phased development vehicle. The latter employed J-2S engines initially in both Orbiter and Booster, with solid rocket motor thrust, if required on the Booster.

Although there were only three concepts, there were twenty-nine configurations, and after six weeks of deliberation, NASA reduced this to nine. A further six weeks of deliberation probed more deeply into the configurations and finally one was chosen: a reusable Orbiter with a high-pressure cryogenic engine, two expendable drop tanks and a 120-inch solid rocket motor. One should remember that this was an alternative study, and after five months of intensive research, Grumman and Boeing concluded that, in the long term the fully reusable system was the best. However, Grumman believed that it was necessary to explore further the minimum risk: fully reusable systems, including a reusable Orbiter with an expendable S-IC stage, which would eventually be phased into a reusable booster. If this was not acceptable, an alternative was to treat the Orbiter and Booster as two separate developments in order to achieve a reduced peak in annual funding.

Grumman and Boeing produced another concept some months later: a fully reusable, two-stage configuration, with hydrogen tanks externally-mounted on the Orbiter, and a heat-sink Booster. It was called the H33 and offered many advantages over the more conventional fully reusable system, placing hydrogen tanks on the outside of the Orbiter, shortening the fuselage by fifteen feet and reducing the dry weight by 30,000 pounds. This permitted the Orbiter to carry more propellant, as it was considerably lighter, reduced the size of the mated configuration by sixty-three feet, the gross lift-off weight by 1.3 million pounds, and the dry weight by 286,000 pounds. This configuration reduced the cost of the total programme by a massive $1.2 billion. Grumman and Boeing recommended the H33 concept to NASA because it was lighter, simpler and cheaper, and such was the delight of

the NASA officials that they awarded them an additional $1.5 million contract, to conduct a design definition of the concept and compare it with the more conventional full reusable system with an internal tank. At the end of the twelve-month contract, Grumman and Boeing confirmed and substantiated the advantages of the external hydrogen tank on the Orbiter and heat-sink Boosters.

In 1971, as a result of these findings, Dr James Fletcher, NASA Administrator, requested that all Space Shuttle studies include a cost-effective programme and investigate the development of a fully reusable Orbiter with external hydrogen tanks. It was believed also that if the oxygen was placed on the outside of the Orbiter, along with the hydrogen, the Orbiter's weight, length and complexity would be reduced even further. With these new concepts in mind, NASA decided to offer a four-month, $2.8 million extension to the three major companies involved Grumman/Boeing, North American, and McDonnell Douglas. It was stipulated that a flight-date in the 1970s was to be the target, and the primary goals of the study were to:

1. Select Orbiter and main engine development approaches.
2. Select external tank (hydrogen or hydrogen/oxygen).
3. Select interim and final booster.
4. Define the recommended programme.
5. Investigate alterations to the Orbiter design in an attempt to further reduce the cost.

Using the H33 concept as a guideline, Grumman presented its evaluation of three alternative programmes at the mid-term review of the four-month extension. Following the review, NASA announced some major changes in the ground rules for Space Shuttle programmes, primarily due to cost. It was proposed to take advantage of current technology and adapt it to the then prevailing requirements.

The Grumman team showed that the J-2S engine, favoured by most, could be eliminated from further consideration, because it required a great deal of alteration if it was to be compatible with the Shuttle. The Grumman Orbiter used in the cost analysis was derived from the MSC 040A designs. The moderately cambered and twisted wing was sized and positioned for a 150 knot landing speed. The tail fin and rudder were sized for positive, directional stability and control, throughout hypersonic, transition, transonic and subsonic regimes. The flight deck had a low profile, so that the aft observation windows were exposed when the cargo bay doors were opened. The RCS nose module was completely buried, and only a small portion of the wing modules protruded above the upper surfaces, which were well clear of the sensitive leading edge and tip regions. The two OMS Modules, each with an Apollo Lunar Module ascent engine, were partially buried in the sides of the rear fuselage. The Orbiter cabin was located between the payload bay and the docking mechanism. The total habitable cabin volume of approximately 2,500 cubic feet, included a flight deck (680 cubic feet), an airlock (407 cubic feet), an airlock/payload interconnecting tunnel (100 cubic feet), avionics and environmental control and life support systems (EC/LSS) hardware (290 cubic feet), and living quarters (800 cubic feet). The flight deck contained a two-man flight station for controlling the vehicle. On the lower deck, an airlock gave access to both the docking port and, via an interconnecting tunnel, the payload bay. The remainder of the lower deck contained the required avionics, a waste and food management system and a separate area for rest, sleeping and eating.

The spacecraft's structure consisted of an aluminium skin, stringers and frames, covered initially with an ablative TPS, providing heat protection to 3,000 degrees on the wing, leading edge and nose cap. The wing had a continuous carry-through, consisting of an aluminium truss beam and rib structures, with stiffened aluminium covers. The pressurized cabin was an integral structure: housing the crew, closing the front end of the payload bay, retracting nose gear loads and providing the external HO tank's front mounting. Apart from the cargo bay and main engine cut-outs, all other structural interruptions, such as RCS and OMS modules, nose and main landing and docking gear, were positioned to avoid major load paths. Grumman recommended that NASA proceed with the Orbiter that contained an external hydrogen/oxygen tank.

The contract to build the Space Shuttle Orbiter was later awarded to Rockwell, which was a bitter blow to everyone at Grumman, who, quite realistically, had thought that of all the aerospace companies that were being considered they stood the best chance.

Although Rockwell had been awarded the prime contract for the Orbiter, Grumman's experience and expertise was not wasted. Rockwell awarded them a contract to design, develop and construct the Orbiter's wings.

The Orbiter's wings are of a double-delta configuration, with a leading edge that initially sweeps 81 degrees from the fuselage, transitioning to a 45 degree sweep to the tip. The wings were constructed with corrugated web spars and chordwise truss-type ribs. A great deal of consideration was given to the minimization of weight, and the secondary stresses induced by the very high temperatures that the wings would experience during re-entry. Both wings were built simultaneously on a calibrated jig, so that they were identical in every way. When completed, they were taken to Rockwell in California, to be attached to the Orbiter. Each wing covered a total area of 1,690 sq. ft., measured 30 feet from wing-tip to fuselage, and was 60 feet long at its longest point, where it joined the fuselage.

Another aspect of the Shuttle was the need for an aircraft to help train the pilots who would fly in it, so NASA chose Grumman to adapt the Gulfstream II business jet. A standard Gulfstream II, with a modified flight deck, had a pair of vertical vanes fitted under the wings which were controlled by an onboard simulator systems computer, making the aircraft

The shuttle orbiter's training cockpit in a Gulfstream III.

The Gulfstream III shuttle training aircraft.

handle just like the Shuttle Orbiter. The vanes pivoted to produce the lateral acceleration that the astronaut-pilots would experience on the Orbiter's flight deck during the landing sequence. The pilot's controls were also modified to match the Orbiter's, the trim wheel, which controlled the trim and pitch, and the standard control column being replaced by a rotating, manually-operated controller. A modified version of an Attitude Directional Indicator, used on the Lunar Module, displayed roll, pitch and yaw information commands. The ground and glide paths were displayed on a monitor in front of the pilot.

It should be remembered that the Shuttle Orbiter is basically a glider. As the engineless Orbiter enters the earth's atmosphere, at a speed of 18,000 mph and a height of 400,000 feet, it has to be able to slow to a mere 200 mph for landing. At 70,000 feet the Orbiter adopts a nose-up attitude, called flaring, and by using its split tail rudder, will brake from a supersonic 900 mph to a subsonic 464 mph at 26,000 feet. The approach has to be perfect, because in the event of a miscalculation the Orbiter has no power to go round again for a second attempt.

The right-hand seat on the Shuttle Training Aircraft (STA) was· occupied by the instructor-pilot, where he used an onboard computer to simulate the desired landing co-ordinates. The computer was capable of flying the aircraft to touchdown, or it could allow the astronaut-pilot, in the left-hand seat to experience the Orbiter's handling qualities through manual control. In reality, the automatic pilot would be used to land the Orbiter, the pilot following the spacecraft down with one hand on the speed brake and the other on the manual controller. In the event of any mid-course corrections being necessary, the pilot could override the computer. The Orbiter had a descent-rate of about 15,000 feet per minute, which is eight times steeper than that of the average airliner.

On the flight deck, the flight simulation engineer handles all the air-to-ground communications and assists the instructor pilot to monitor all the simulation systems. While this is going on, the astronaut is flying the STA and has turned the aircraft into one of two 18,000 feet wide heading-alignment circles, about six miles from touchdown. As the aircraft reaches the heading alignment phase, a ground-based Microwave Scanning Beam Landing System commands the computer on the STA to fly the aircraft partially around the alignment circle, until at a 45 degree angle to the runway heading. The aircraft's speed will now be about 460 mph, it will be 13 miles and two minutes from touchdown and at a height of 25,000 feet. Thirty degrees from the final approach, the speed is slowed to about 390 mph. Five degrees from the final heading, and at a true air speed of 400 mph the glide slope is 24 degrees. The first flare takes place at 1,700 feet and is held until the aircraft is less than two miles from the end of the runway. The aircraft then follows the standard instrument approach, with speed decreasing and at an attitude of three degrees. At 500 feet, the astronaut-pilot calls for the landing gear to be lowered and to simulate this, only the nose gear is lowered on the Gulfstream. A second flare, at an altitude of 100 feet and 900 feet, the end of the runway, reduces the descent rate to 180 feet per minute, at a speed of 200 mph. At 50 feet above the runway, a green light is illuminated on the instrument panel, showing the astronaut-pilot that he is at the point where the Orbiter should touch down. At this point, the instructor-pilot, pushes a 'SIM EXIT' button, and the autopilot, autothrottle and thrust reversers close down. The STA has simulated a safe landing. The advantage the Gulfstream has over the Orbiter is, that at the point of touchdown, the pilot can apply power, raise the gear and fly around again. Astronauts who have flown the Orbiter and the Gulfstream say that the landing of both is remarkably the same.

Although Grumman's contribution to the space programme is at present only small, it is, nevertheless, very important, and I am certain that in years to come, when flights to distant planets become a reality, Grumman will be in the forefront.

Glossary of abbreviations

A&AEE	Aeroplane and Armament Experimental Establishment
AEC	Automatic Engine Control
AEW	Airborne Early Warning
ACLS	Automatic Carrier Landing System
ACM	Air Control Manoeuvring
ADEN	Asymetric Deflecting Exhaust Nozzle
APU	Auxiliary Power Unit
AMRAAM	Advanced Medium Range Air-to-Air Missile
AMRARM	Advanced Medium Range Anti-Radiation Missile
ARM	Anti-Radiation Missile
ASPJS	Airborne Self-Protection Jamming System
ASW	Anti-Submarine Warfare
ATDS	Airborne Tactical Data System
ATE	Advanced Technology Engine
BIS	Board of Inspection and Survey
BLC	Boundary Layer Control
CAINS	Carrier Inertial Nagivation System
CAP	Combat Air Patrol
COD	Carrier On-Board Delivery
COIN	Counter Insurgency
CNI	Communication, Navigation and Identification
CSM	Command and Service Module
DARPA	Defence Advanced Research Agency
DFI	Derivative Fighter Engine
DIANE	Digital Integrated Attack Navigation Equipment
ECLSS	Environmental Control and Life Support Systems
ECM	Electronic Countermeasures
ECMS	Engine Condition Monitoring System
ECS	Environmental Control Subsystem
EPS	Electrical Power Subsystem
ERA	Electric Replacement Assemblies
ETPS	Empire Test Pilot School
EVA	Extra Vehicular Activity
FAA	Federal Aviation Authority
FAA	Fleet Air Arm
FLIR	Forward Looking Infra-Red
FSW	Forward-Sweeping Wing
GCA	Ground Control Approach
GNCS	Guidance Navigation and Control Subsystem
GPS	Global Positioning System
HARM	High Speed Anti-Radiation Missile
HOTAS	Hand On Throttle And Stick
HTS	Heat Transportation Section
HUD	Head-Up Display
HVAR	High Velocity Aircraft Rockets
IFF	Identify Friend or Foe
ILRV	Integral Launch and Re-entry Vehicle
ILS	Instrument Landing System
INA	Inspector of Naval Aircraft
IRAN	Inspect, Repair As Necessary
IRSTS	Infra-Red Search and Track System
ISAR	Inverse Synthetic Aperture Radar

JATO	Jet Assisted Take-Off
JTIDS	Joint Tactical Information Distribution System
LEM	Lunar Excursion Module
LIM	Linear Induction Motor
LLTV	Low Light Television
LMA	Lunar Module Adaptor
LMTA	Lunar Module Test Article
LOR	Lunar Orbit Rendezvous
MAD	Magnetic Anomaly Detector
MET	Mobile Equipment Transporter
MIT	Massachusetts Institute of Technology
MSC	Manned Space Centre
MSP	Mach Sweep Programme
NACA	National Advisory Committee for Aeronautics
NAF	Naval Air Factory
NAF	Naval Air Facility
NART	Naval Air Reserve Training
NAS	Naval Air Station
NASA	National Air and Space Administration
NASM	National Air and Space Museum
NATC	Naval Air Test Centre
NPE	Navy Preliminary Examination
NPO	Nozzle Pump Operator
OAO	Orbiting Astronomical Observatory
OMS	Orbiting Manoeuvring System
OMV	Orbiting Manoeuvring Vehicle
PLSS	Portable Life Support System
RAE	Royal Aircraft Establishment
RADAR	Radio Detecting And Ranging
RCM	Radar Countermeasures
RCS	Reaction Control System
R&D	Research and Development
RDT&E	Research Development Test and Evaluation
SAM	Surface-to-Air Missile
SAR	Synthetic Aperture Radar
SEAM	Sidewinder Expanded Acquisition Mode
SDI	Strategic Defence Initiative
SIR	System Integrated Receiver
SLAR	Sideways-Looking Airborne Radar
STA	Shuttle Training Aircraft
STARS	Surveillance Target Attack Radar System
STOL	Short Take-Off and Landing
TAC	Tactical Air Co-ordinator
TACAN	Tactical Air and Navigation
TCS	Television Camera System
TIAS	Target Identification Acquisition System
TJS	Tactical Jamming System
TLRV	Tracked Levitated Research Vehicle
TPS	Thermal Protection System
TRAM	Tactical Recognition Attack Multi-sensor
TRIM	Tactical Roads Interdiction Multi-sensor
VSTOL	Vertical Short Take-Off and Landing

Bibliography

The Grumman Story Richard Thruelsen
Wings of the Navy Eric Brown
The American Fighter Enzo Angelucci and Peter Bowers
United States Naval Aircraft Gordon Swanborough and Peter Bowers
US Naval Fighters of W.W.II Timothy O'Leary
The American Flying Board Richard C. Knott
Hellcat Barrat Tillman
Carrier Air Power Norman Friedman
Fly Navy Brian Johnson
The Naval Air War in Vietnam Peter Merskey and Norman Polmar

F-14 Tomcat James Perry Stevenson
EA-6B Prowler and EA-6A Intruder James Wogstad and Philip Fridell
F9F Panther and Cougar Jim Sullivan
Grumman F8F Bearcat Edward T. Maloney
Grumman TBF/TBM Avenger B. R. Jackson and T. E. Doll

Numerous magazines from all over the world were referred to and it would be an almost impossible task to name all of them. Suffice it to say, that their contribution to this book was of the most enormous help.

Index